Theodorus S. Drage

The Great Probability of a North West Passage

Deduced from observations on the letter of Admiral de Fonte, who sailed from the Callao of Lima on the discovery of a communication between the South Sea and the Atlantic Ocean. Proving the authenticity

Theodorus S. Drage

The Great Probability of a North West Passage
Deduced from observations on the letter of Admiral de Fonte, who sailed from the Callao of Lima on the discovery of a communication between the South Sea and the Atlantic Ocean. Proving the authenticity

ISBN/EAN: 9783337319205

Printed in Europe, USA, Canada, Australia, Japan

Cover: Foto ©Andreas Hilbeck / pixelio.de

More available books at **www.hansebooks.com**

THE
GREAT PROBABILITY
OF A
NORTH WEST PASSAGE:
DEDUCED FROM
OBSERVATIONS
ON THE

Letter of Admiral DE FONTE,

Who failed from the *Callao* of *Lima* on the Difcovery of a Communication

BETWEEN THE

SOUTH SEA and the ATLANTIC OCEAN;

And to intercept fome Navigators from *Bofton* in *New England*, whom he met with, Then in Search of a NORTH WEST PASSAGE.

PROVING THE

AUTHENTICITY of the Admiral's LETTER.

With Three Explanatory MAPS.

1ft. A Copy of an authentic *Spanifh* Map of *America*, publifhed in 1608.
2d. The Difcoveries made in *Hudfon*'s Bay, by Capt. *Smith*, in 1746 and 1747.
3d. A General Map of the Difcoveries of Admiral *de Fonte*.

By THOMAS JEFFERYS, Geographer to the King.

WITH

AN APPENDIX.

Containing the Account of a Difcovery of Part of the Coaft and Inland Country of LABRADOR, made in 1753.

The Whole intended for

The Advancement of TRADE and COMMERCE.

LONDON:
Printed for THOMAS JEFFERYS, at Charing-Crofs.
MDCCLXVIII.

TO THE RIGHT HONOURABLE

WILLS EARL OF HILLSBOROUGH,

&c. &c. &c.

ONE OF HIS MAJESTY'S PRINCIPAL SECRETARIES OF STATE,

FIRST LORD COMMISSIONER OF TRADE AND PLANTATIONS,

ONE OF HIS MAJESTY'S MOST HONOURABLE PRIVY COUNCIL, AND F.R.S.

THE Discovery of a North-west Passage having deserved the particular Attention of that great Minister of State Sir *Francis Walsingham*, with the Approbation of the greatest Princess of that Age, I presumed to ask the Permission to inscribe the following Sheets, on the same Subject, to your Lordship, wrote with no View of setting any further Expeditions on Foot, or with respect to any particular System, but as a candid and impartial Enquiry, to shew the great Probability there is of a North-west Passage. The Importance of the Subject, treated with the greatest Regard to Truth, are the only Pretensions I have to merit your Patronage.

Your Lordship will appear, to the latest Posterity, in the amiable Light of being zealous for the Glory of his Majesty, the Honour of the Nation, for promoting the commercial Interests, the Happiness of his Majesty's

a   Subjects

Subjects in general, and of those in *America* in particular. I therefore have the most grateful Sense of your Benevolence and Humanity in condescending to grant me this Favour, as it will be known for Part of that Time that I had the Honour to be

YOUR LORDSHIP'S

MOST HUMBLE AND

OBEDIENT SERVANT,

THE AUTHOR.

THE
PREFACE.

THE Opinion of there being a North-weſt Paſſage between the *Atlantic* and *Southern Ocean* hath continued for more than two Centuries; and though the Attempts made to diſcover this Paſſage have not been attended with the deſired Succeſs, yet in Conſequence of ſuch Attempts great Advantages have been received, not by the Merchant only but by the Men of Science. It muſt be a Satisfaction to the Adventurer, though diſappointed in his principal Deſign, that his Labours have contributed to the Improvement of Science, and the Advancement of Commerce.

There was a Generoſity with reſpect to the Diſcovery of a North-weſt Paſſage, or a Reſpect to the great Abilities of thoſe who promoted the various Undertakings for making ſuch Diſcovery, to the Crown which patronized them, and the Eſtates of the Kingdom who promiſed a moſt munificent Reward to ſuch who ſhould compleat ſuch Diſcovery, that thoſe who were of a contrary Opinion treated the Subject with a becoming Decency. But the Cenſures that have been of late made by our Countrymen, and more particularly by Foreigners, our Anceſtors have been treated as ſo many Fools, or infatuated Perſons, buſied to compleat an impracticable and a meerly chimerical Project, and are accuſed by a foreign Geographer to have proceeded ſo far as to forge a fictitious Account under the Title of a Letter of Admiral *de Fonte*. That the Iniquity of the *Engliſh* Writers is not ſuch (neither was ever known to be ſuch) nor, was it in their Inclination, could they ſo eaſily deceive the World; and the

Falſhood

(viii)

Falshood of this Assertion could be no otherway made apparent than by considering such Letter with a just Criticism, and examining the Circumstances relating thereto. Though the present Age may not pay much Regard to these Censures, yet if they are passed unnoticed, might hereafter be considered as Truths unanswerable at the Time those Censures were made. Therefore to do Justice to the Character of our Ancestors, to the present Age in which such great Encouragement hath been given to these Undertakings, and that Posterity might not be deceived, were Motives (had they been duly considered without a Regard to the Importance of the Subject) which might incite an abler Pen to have undertaken to vindicate the Authenticity of *de Fonte*'s Letter: As for a long Time nothing of this Kind appeared, nor could I hear that any Thing was undertaken of this Sort, by any Person to whom I could freely communicate my Sentiments, and the Informations which I had collected on this Subject, as the Discovery of a North-west Passage hath been the Object of my Attention for some Years, considered myself under the disagreeable Necessity of becoming an Author in an Age of such refined Sentiments, expressed in the greatest Purity of Language: But if I have succeeded in the greater Matters, I hope to be excused in the lesser.

I have inserted the Letter of *de Fonte*, as first published in the *Monthly Miscellany*, or *Memoirs of the Curious*, in *April* and *June* 1708, very scarce or in very few Hands; not only as I thought it consistent with my Work, but that the Curious would be glad to have a Copy of such Letter exactly in the same Manner in which it was first published, to keep in their Collections.

As to the Observations respecting the Circumstances of the Letter of *de Fonte*, the Manner by which it was attained, its being a Copy of such Letter which the Editors procured to be translated from the *Spanish*, and as to such Matters as are to be collected from the Title of such Letter, and from the Letter in Support

port

port of its Authenticity, I submit those Observations to superior Judgments: If confuted, and it appears I have misapprehended the Matter, am not tenacious of my Opinion, but shall receive the Conviction with Pleasure, being entirely consistent with my Design, which is, That the Truth may be discovered, whether this Account is authentick or not.

In my Remarks of the Letter I have endeavoured to distinguish what was genuine, from what hath been since added by other Hands; have made an exact Calculation of the Courses; have considered the Circumstances of such Letter, giving the Reasons of the Conduct that was used in the various Parts of the Voyage, and shewing the Regularity and Consistency there is through the Whole, and without Anachronisms or Contradictions as hath been objected, part of which I was the better enabled to do from some Experience which I have had in Affairs of this Sort. I must observe, the Calculations were made without any Regard had to the Situation of *Hudson*'s or *Baffin*'s Bay; but begun at the *Callao* of *Lima*, and pursued as the Account directs from the Westward: And it was an agreeable Surprize to find what an Agreement there was as to the Parts which, by such Courses, it appeared that the Admiral and his Captain were in, consistent with the Purpose they were sent on, and the Proximity of where they were to *Hudson*'s and *Baffin*'s Bay.

To state particularly all the Objections which have been made to this Account, I thought would have greatly increased the Bulk of the Work. There is no material Objection which I have any where met with, but is here considered. Also to have added all the Authorities which I have collected and made Use of, would have made it more prolix; so have contented myself with only giving such Quotations as appeared absolutely necessary to insert, and then to mention the Authors particularly. I think I have not perverted the Meaning, or forced the Sense, of any Author made Use of, to serve my Purpose.

To

To shew the Probability of a Passage, have traced the Opinions relating to it from the Time such Opinions were first received; and also determined where it was always supposed to be or in what Part such Passage was: Have considered the various Evidence that there is relating to such Passage; and proposed what appears to be the properest Method at present for prosecuting the Discovery.

There are three Maps, all of which appeared necessary for the better understanding this Account. The one contains Part of *Asia* and the *Russian* Discoveries on the Coast of *America*; the Expedition of *de Fonte*, and clears up that seeming Inconsistency of the *Tartarian* and *Southern Ocean* being contiguous in that Part of *America*, from the Authority of the *Japanese* Map of *Kempfer*, which must be of some Repute, as it is so agreeable to the *Russian* Discoveries: If true in that Part, there is no Reason to suppose but it is in like Manner true as to the other Part which is introduced into this Map. This Map exhibits the Streight that *de Fuca* went up, the Communication which there may be supposed agreeable to the Lights which the Accounts afford us between the Sea at the Back of *Hudson*'s Bay with that Bay, or with the *North Sea* by *Hudson*'s Streights, or through *Cumberland* Isles. There is also added a second Map, to shew what Expectations may be had of a Passage from *Hudson*'s Bay, according to the Discoveries made in the Year 1747. The third Map is an exact Copy from that published in the *Monarquia Indiana de Torquemada*, in which the Sea Coast of *America* is exhibited in a different Manner from what it usually was in the Maps of that Time, compleated by the Cosmographers of *Philip* the Third. The Work itself is in few Hands, and the Map, as far as appears, hath been only published in that Book, is now again published, as it illustrates this Work, and may be otherwise agreeable to the Curious; having a Desire not to omit any Thing which would render the Work compleat, or that would be acceptable to the Publick.

I have

I have used uncommon Pains to be informed as to what could be any way serviceable to render this Work more compleat; and must make this publick Acknowledgement, as to the Gentlemen of the *British Museum*, who, with great Politeness and Affability, gave me all the Assistances in their Power to find if the Copy from which the Translation was made was in their Possession; which after an accurate Search for some Weeks it did not appear to be, and also their Assistance as to any other Matters which I supposed would be of Service. I cannot pass by Mr. *Jeffery's* Care and Exactness in executing the Maps, whose Care and Fidelity to the Publick not to impose any Thing that is spurious, but what he hath an apparent and real Authority for, is perhaps not sufficiently known.

The Voyage, an Extract from which is added by Way of Appendix, was made from *Philadelphia*, in a Schooner of about sixty Tons, and fifteen Persons aboard, fitted out on a Subscription of the Merchants of *Maryland, Pennsylvania, New York*, and *Boston*, on a generous Plan, agreeable to Proposals made them, with no View of any Monopoly which they opposed, not to interfere with the *Hudson*'s Bay Trade, or to carry on a clandestine Trade with the Natives of *Greenland*, but to discover a North-west Passage, and explore the *Labrador* Coast, at that Time supposed to be locked up under a pretended Right, and not frequented by the Subjects of *England*, but a successful Trade carried on by the *French*; to open a Trade there, to improve the Fishery and the Whaling on these Coasts, cultivate a Friendship with the Natives, and make them serviceable in a political Way: Which Design of theirs of a publick Nature, open and generous, was in a great Measure defeated by private Persons interfering, whose Views were more contracted.

They did not succeed the first Year as to their Attempt in discovering a North-west Passage, as it was a great Year for Ice;

that

that it would be late in the Year before the Western Part of *Hud-son's* Bay could be attained to, and then impossible to explore the *Labrador* that Year, therefore the first Part of the Design was dropped, and the *Labrador* was explored. The next Year a second Attempt was made as to a Passage; but three of the People who went beyond the Place appointed by their Orders, and inadvertently to look for a Mine, Samples of which had been carried home the Year before, and this at the Instigation of a private Person before they set out from home, without the Privity of the Commander, were killed by the *Eskemaux*, and the Boat taken from them. After which Accident, with some disagreeable Circumstances consequent thereon amongst the Schooner's Company, and after an Experiment made of their Disinclination to proceed on any further Discovery, it was thought most prudent to return. This short Account is given by the Person who commanded in this Affair, to prevent any Misrepresentation hereafter of what was done on these Voyages.

CONTENTS.

	Page
LETTER of Admiral *de Fonte* as published in *April* 1708	1
———————————————— *June*	6
OBSERVATIONS *on the Title affixed*, &c.	11

The Reason of this Work.
The Translation made from a Copy of the Letter. Title and the Copy of the Letter wrote in the *Spanish* Language.

Copiest assured there was such an Expedition as this of Admiral *de Fonte*	12
An Account of this Expedition not published in *Spain*.	
The Consequence of such Expedition not being published	14
The Knowledge or Certainty of this Expedition from Journals only	15
Monf. *de Lisle* his Account of a Journal.	
This Account by Monf. *de Lisle* defended	17
This Translation of *de Fonte*'s Letter how considered when first published	
Don *Francisco Seyxas y Lovera* his Account of a Voyage of *Thomas Peche*	18
Observations on that Account	19
The Tradition of there being a Passage between the *Atlantic* and *Southern Ocean* credible	20
Accounts received from various Persons relating thereto not to be discredited	
Indians, their Account of the Situation of such Streight how to be considered	21
The Reasons why we cannot obtain a particular Information as to the original Letter of *de Fonte*	22
Evidence relating to this Account of *de Fonte*, which Distance of Time or other Accidents could not deface, yet remains	24
No authenticated Account of the Equipment of the Fleet to be expected from *New Spain*	25

(xiv)

	Page
This Account of *de Fonte* authentick, and no Forgery.	
The Editors published this Account as authentick	26
The Reflection that this Account is a Forgery of some *Englishman* obviated	27
The Design in publishing this Translation.	
The Purpose of *de Fonte*'s writing this Letter not understood by the Editors	28
The Editors unjustly reproached with a Want of Integrity.	
The Censures as to the Inauthenticity of this Account of *de Fonte* not founded on Facts.	
Invalidity of the Objection that no Original hath been produced.	
The Suspicion of the Account being a Deceit or Forgery from whence.	
The original Letter was in the *Spanish* Language	29
Observations as to the Name *Bartholomew de Fonte*	30
De Fonte was a Man of Family	31
The *Spanish* Marine not in so low a Condition as they were under a Necessity to apply to *Portugal* for Sea Officers to supply the principal Posts.	
What is to be understood of *de Fonte* being President of *Chili*	32

REMARKS on the Letter of Admiral de Fonte.

The Advice of the Attempt from *Boston*, in what Manner transmitted from *Old Spain* to the Viceroys.	
The Appellation of industrious Navigators conformable to the Characters of the Persons concerned.	
The Court of *Spain* knew that the Attempt was to be by *Hudson*'s Bay.	
This Attempt particularly commanded the Attention of the Court of *Spain*	34
As to the Computation by the Years of the Reign of King *Charles*.	
The Times mentioned in the Letter do not refer to the Times the Voyage was set out on	
There was sufficient Time to equip the four Ships	35
How the Design of this Attempt might come to the Knowledge of the Court of *Spain*.	
Reasons why both Viceroys should be informed	36

De

De Fonte received his Orders from *Old Spain*,
Wrote his Letter to the Court of *Spain*.
De Fonte and the Viceroys did not receive their Orders from the same Persons - - - - - - 37
What is the Purpose of the introductory Part of this Letter.
The Names of the Ships agreeable to the *Spanish* Manner.

From Callao to St. Helena.

Observations as to the Computation of Course and Distance in the Voyage of *de Fonte* - - - - - 38
From whence *de Fonte* takes his Departure.
As to the Distance between the *Callao* of *Lima* and *St. Helena*, no Fault in the Impression.
An Account of the Latitude and Longitude made Use of, which agrees with *de Fonte*'s Voyage.
Remarks as to the Expression, anchored in the Port of *St. Helena* within the Cape - - - - - - 39
An Interpolation of what is not in the original Letter.
Observations as to the taking the Betumen aboard.
An Error as to Latitude corrected - - - - 40
An Error as to the Course corrected.

From St. Helena to the River St. Jago.

Observations as to *de Fonte* taking fresh Provision aboard at the River *St. Jago* - - - - - - 41
A Comment or spurious Interpolation.
The Course *de Fonte* sailed from the River *St. Jago*.

From St. Jago to Realejo.

A Proof that Glosses and Comments have been added to the original Text - - - - - - - 42
The Latitude not mentioned in the original Letter of *de Fonte*.
The Times that *de Fonte* is sailing between the respective Ports from the *Callao* to *Realejo* no Objection to the Authenticity of this Account.
Boats provided for *de Fonte* before he arrived at *Realejo* - - 43

(xvi)
Page

From Realejo *to the Port of* Salagua.
Obfervations as to the Iflands of *Chiametla*.
————— ————— ————— Port of *Salagua*.
————— ————— ————— Mafter and Mariners -   -   - 44
An Interpolation or Comment added.
The Tranflator not exact as to his Tranflation.
Remark as to the Information *de Fonte* received as to the Tide at
    the Head of the Bay of *California* -   -   -   - 45
Pennelossa appointed to difcover whether *California* was an Ifland.
The Account given of *Pennelossa*, as to his Defcent, not in the ori-
    ginal Letter.

From the Port of Salagua *to the* Archipelagus *of* St. Laza-
rus *and* Rio Los Reyes.
De Fonte leaves *Pennelossa* within the Shoals of *Chiametla* - - 46
Courfe corrected.
Remark as to Cape *Abel*.
————— as to the Weather and the Time he was running eight Hun-
    dred and fixty Leagues - - - - - 47
A Neglect as to inferting a Courfe.
Computation of Longitude altered - - - - 48
The Courfe *de Fonte* fteered, he accounts as to the Land being in a
    Latitude and Longitude agreeable to the late *Ruffian* Difcoveries.
    Acts with great Judgment as a Seaman.
The Agreement of the Table of Latitude and Longitude with the
    Ruffian Difcoveries. And the *Suefta del Eftrech D'Anian* not laid
    down on a vague Calculation - - - - 49
Former Authorities for it.
So named by the *Spaniards*.
A fuperior Entrance to that of *Martin Aguilar* and of *de Fuca*.
The *Archipelago* of *St. Lazarus*, properly fo named by *de Fonte*.
A North-eaft Part of the *South Sea* that *de Fonte* paffed up - - 50
His Inftructions were to fall in with the Iflands which formed the
    Archipelago, and not the main Land.
Rio los Reyes, in what Longitude.
A further Proof that his Courfe was to the Eaftward - - 51

(xvii)

Page

Proceedings of Admiral de Fonte *after his Arrival at* Rio de los Reyes.

The Tranflation very inaccurate in this Part.
The Date of the 22d of *June* an Error.
De Fonte difpatches one of his Captains to *Bernarda* with Orders.
Jefuits had been in thofe Parts, from whofe Accounts the Inftructions were formed - - - - - - 52
Remarks as to the Orders fent *Bernarda*.

De Fonte *fails up* Rio de los Reyes.

De Fonte fets out on his Part of the Expedition - - 53
Was at the Entrance of *Los Reyes* the 14th of *June*.
Obferved the Tides in *Los Reyes* and *Haro*.
Precaution to be ufed in going up the River.
An additional Note as to the Jefuits.
Obfervations as to the Jefuits.
Knew not of a Streight - - - - - 54
Could not publifh their Miffion without Leave.

De Fonte *arrives at* Conoffet.

Receives a Letter from *Bernarda* dated 27th of *June* - - 55
The 22d of *June* was not the Time *Bernarda* received his Difpatches.
The Letter is an Anfwer to the Difpatches he received from *de Fonte*.
Remarks on the Letter.
Alters the Courfe directed by *de Fonte*.
Affures *de Fonte* he will do what was poffible, and is under no Apprehenfion as to a Want of Provifions - - - 56
The Name of *Haro*, and of the Lake *Velafco*, a particular Compliment.
This Letter of *de Fonte* wrote in *Spanifh*.

Defcription of Rio de los Reyes *and Lake* Belle.

De Fonte not inactive from the 14th to the 22d of *June* - - 57
Very particular in his Account.
Shews how far the Tides came to from Weftward.

	Page
De Fonte *leaves his Ships before the Town of* Conoffet.	
The Time *de Fonte* had ftaid at *Conoffet* - - -	58
Was before acquainted with the Practicability of *Bernarda* fending a Letter.	
How the Letter from *Bernarda* was fent.	
De Fonte waited to receive the Letter before he proceeded.	
Parmentiers, whom he was.	
Frenchmen were admitted into *Peru*.	
Reafons for the Jefuits coming into thefe Parts without paffing the intermediate Country - - - - -	59
Parmentiers had been before in thefe Parts.	
His Motive for going into thofe Parts, and furveying the River *Parmentiers* - - - - - - -	60
The People Captain *Tchinkow* met with, no Objection to the Character of the *Indians* in thefe Parts.	
Parmentiers not a general Interpreter - - -	61
Voyages had been made to thefe Parts.	
An Omiffion in the Tranflator.	

A Defcription of the River Parmentiers, *Lake* de Fonte, *and the adjacent Country.*

The Form of the Letter again obferved by the Tranflator -	62
Lake *de Fonte*, fo named in Compliment to the Family he was of.	
Lake *de Fonte* a Salt Water Lake.	
A Comparifon of the Country with other Parts.	
Why *de Fonte* ftopped at the Ifland South of the Lake -	63

De Fonte *fails out of the Eaft North-eaft End of the Lake* de Fonte, *and paffes the Streight of* Ronquillo.

An additional Comment.
De Fonte's Obfervation as to the Country altering for the worfe.
A purpofed Silence as to the Part come into after paffing the Streight of *Ronquillo*.

De Fonte *arrives at the* Indian *Town, and receives an Account of the Ship.*

A further Inftance of *Parmentiers* having been in thefe Parts -	64

(xix)

	Page
De Fonte had been on the Inquiry.	

The Proceedings of de Fonte *after meeting with the Ship.*

The Reason of the Ship's Company retiring to the Woods	65
De Fonte had particularly provided himself with some *Englishmen*.	
Shapley, the Navigator of the Ship, first waits on the Admiral.	
Particulars as to *Shapley*.	
A Disappointment of the Intelligence the Author hoped to attain	66
A Tradition amongst the antient People of there having been such a Voyage.	
Major Gibbons, an Account of him	67
Seimar Gibbons, a Mistake of the Translator	68
Massachusets, the largest Colony in *New England* at that Time.	
The Ship fitted out from *Boston*.	
Remarks on *de Fonte's* Address to *Major Gibbons*, and Conduct on this Occasion.	
De Fonte only mentions what is immediately necessary for the Court to know	70
The *Boston* Ship returned before *de Fonte* left those Parts.	
A remarkable Anecdote from the Ecclesiastical History of *New England*.	
The Circumstances of which Account agree with this Voyage	72
A further Tradition as to *Major Gibbons*.	
That the Persons met by *Groseliers* were not *Major Gibbons* and his Company.	

De Fonte *returns to* Conosset.

The various Courses, Distances, &c. from *Rio de los Reyes* to the Sea to the Eastward of *Ronquillo*	73
The prudent Conduct observed in the Absence of the Admiral	74

De Fonte *receives a Letter from* Bernarda.

The Latitude and Longitude of *Conibasset*, &c.	75
Observations as to the Messenger who carried the first Letter from *Bernarda*.	
Observations as to the Messenger with the second Letter	76
The various Courses, Distances, &c. that *Bernarda* went.	
The Probability of sending a Seaman over Land to *Baffin's* Bay.	

	Page
Remarks on the Report made by the Seaman	77
Bernarda going up the *Tartarian Sea* is agreeable to the *Japanese* Map.	
A Parallel drawn between *Conoffet* and Port *Nelson*.	
The physical Obstacles considered	78
Bernarda's Observations as to the Parts he had been in.	
Whether the Parts about *Baffin*'s Bay were inhabited	79
An Objection as to the Affability of the Inhabitants further considered.	
As to the Dispatch used by *Indians* in carrying Expresses.	
Bernarda directed by the Jesuits as to the Harbour where he meets *de Fonte*.	
De Fonte sent a Chart with his Letter	80
Miguel Venegas, a *Mexican* Jesuit, his Observation as to the Account of *de Fonte*'s Voyage, &c.	
The Design with which his Work was published.	
Arguments for putting into immediate Execution what he recommends	81
Don Cortez informs the King of *Spain* that there is a Streight on the Coast of the *Baccaloos*.	
Attempts made by *Cortez*	82
What is comprehended under the Name of *Florida*.	
King of *Portugal* sends *Gasper Corterealis* on Discovery.	
The Name *Labrador*, what it means.	
Promonterum Cortereale, what Part so named.	
Hudson's Streights named the River of *Three Brothers* or *Anian*.	
When the finding a Streight to Northward became a Matter of particular Attention of the *Spaniards*	83
Undertaken by the Emperor.	
By *Philip* the Second.	
By *Philip* the Third, and the Reasons	84
The Opinions of *Geographers* as to the North Part of *America*.	
How the Maps were constructed at that Time	85
Unacquainted with what *Cortez* knew of the Streight	86
Instanced by the Voyage of *Alarcon* that the Land was thought to extend farther to Northward than afterwards supposed by the Voyage of *Juan Rederique de Cabrillo*	87

Vizcaino,

(xxi)

	Page
Vizcaino, his Voyage, and the Discovery of *Aguilar*.	
Spaniards never meant by the Streights of *Anian*, *Beerings* Streight	88
Remarks on the Deficiency of the *Spanish* Records.	
Uncertainty of attaining any Evidence from such Records.	
Father *Kino*'s Map of *California* altered by Geographers	90
The Objection of *Venegas* as to the Authenticity of *de Fonte*'s Account considered	91
Misrepresents the Title of the Letter	92
Doth not deny but that there was such a Person as *de Fonte*.	
The *Jesuits* and *Parmentiers* having been before in these Parts not improbable	93
Master and Mariners mentioned by *de Fonte*, a probable Account.	
Whence the Tide came at the Head of the Gulph of *California*	94
De Fonte retires, Command taken by Admiral *Caſſanate*.	
Seyax y Lovera, the Authority of his Account defended	95
Venegas omits some Accounts for Want of necessary Authenticity.	
Most of the Discoveries are reported to be made by Ships from the *Moluccas*	96
What Ships from the *Moluccas* or *Philippines* were forced to do in case of bad Weather.	
The Probability of a Discovery made by a Ship from the *Philippines* or *Moluccas*.	
The People of the *Philippine* Islands those who most talked of a Passage.	
Salvatierra, his Account of a North-west Passage discovered	97
This Account gained Credit	98
Was the Foundation of *Frobisher*'s Expedition.	
Thomas Cowles, his Account defended	99
Juan de Fuca, his Account	100
Remarks on that Account	101
Expeditions which the Court of *Spain* order correspond in Time with the Attempts for Discovery from *England*	103
The Discovery of the Coast of *California* for a Harbour for the *Aquapulco* Ship not the Sole Design	104
Reasons that induced *Aguilar* to think the Opening where he was was the Streight of *Anian*	105
Observation on the preceding Accounts.	
Have no certain Account of what Expeditions were in those Parts	106

c   A a

	Page
An exact Survey of those Coasts not known to have been made until the Year 1745.	
The Streight of *Anian* at present acknowledged	107
The first Discoverers gave faithful Accounts.	
Reasons for *de Fonte*'s Account being true	108
Accounts of Voyages not being to be obtained no just Objection to their Authenticity.	
As to the Inference in *de Fonte*'s Letter of there being no North-west Passage	109
The Proximity of the *Western Ocean* supposed by all Discoverers	111
Observations on the Northern Parts of *America* being intermixed with Waters.	
The Objection as to the Distance between the *Ocean* and the *Sea* at the Back of *Hudson*'s Bay	112
Reasons why a Passage hath not been discovered.	
A great Channel to Westward by which the Ice and Land Waters are vented.	
Accounts of *de Fonte*, *de Fuca*, and *Chacke*, agree	113
Indians mentioned by *de Fonte* and those by *de Fuca* not the same.	
Why *de Fonte* did not pass up the North-east Part of the *South Sea*	114
The Persons who were in those Parts got no Information of a Streight	115
The Representation of the *Jesuits* the Foundation of *de Fonte*'s Instructions.	
The Court of *Spain* not of the same Opinion with *de Fonte* or the Jesuits on his Return	116
There is a Sea to Westward of *Hudson*'s Bay	117
Joseph le France, his Account considered	118
Agrees with the Account of *de Fonte* and *de Fuca*	119
Improbability of the *Tete Plat* inhabiting near the Ocean	120
Which Way the *Boston* Ship made the Passage, uncertain.	
Whether through *Hudson*'s Bay	122
Observations as to *Chesterfield*'s Inlet.	
As to *Pistol* Bay and *Cumberland* Isles	123
A Quotation from *Seyxas y Lovera*.	
Observations thereon	124

(xxiii)

	Page
Observations as to its having been the constant Opinion that there was a North-west Passage	125
The great Degree of Credibility there is from the Circumstances of *de Fonte*'s Voyage.	
What Foundation those who argue against a North-west Passage have for their Argument	126
Where the Passage is supposed, and an Explanation of the Map	127
Remarks as to Expeditions to be made purposely for the Discovery.	
The Inconveniencies which attended on former Expeditions.	
Prevented for the future by a Discovery of the Coast of *Labrador*.	
The advantageous Consequences of that Attempt	128
Method to be pursued in making the Discovery.	

APPENDIX.

	Page
Fall in with the Coast of *Labrador*	131
Stand more to Southward.	
Tokens of the Land	132
Meet with the *Eskemaux*.	
Enter a Harbour	133
The Country described.	
People sent to the Head of the Harbour report they had seen a House	134
A more particular Account.	
The Report of Persons sent to survey the Country.	
Proceed on a further Discovery	136
Enter up an Inlet.	
Prevented proceeding in the Schooner by Falls	137
Proceed in a Boat, meet with Falls.	
Description of the Country.	
Sail out of the Inlet and go to Northward	139
See Smokes and go in Pursuit of the Natives	140

Proceed

	Page
Proceed up a third Inlet.	
See Smokes again.	
Enter a fourth Inlet.	
Meet with a *Snow* from *England*	143
The Captain of the *Snow*, his Account and other Particulars.	
Observations as to the *Eskemaux*	145
Snow had joined Company with a *Sloop* from *Rhode Island*.	
An Account of where the *Eskemaux* trade	147
Eskemaux come along-side	147
Schooner leaves the *Snow*.	
Eskemaux come aboard the Schooner	148
Mate of *Snow* comes aboard the *Schooner*, and his Account	150
Why mentioned	151
The Trade in these Parts could only be established by the Regulations of the *Government*.	
Eskemaux coming to trade with the Schooner intercepted.	
The Inlet searched	152
Pass into three other Inlets.	
An Account of them and the Country.	
Reasons for leaving off the Discovery	153
Fishing Bank sought for and discovered.	
An Island of Ice of a surprising Magnitude and Depth.	

April 1708.

MEMOIRS for the CURIOUS.

A Letter from Admiral Bartholomew de Fonte, *then Admiral of* New Spain *and* Peru, *and now Prince of* Chili; *giving an Account of the most material Transactions in a Journal of his from the Calo of* Lima *in* Peru, *on his Discoveries, to find out if there was any North West Passage from the* Atlantick *Ocean into the South and Tartarian Sea.*

THE Viceroys of *New Spain* and *Peru*, having advice from the Court of *Spain*, that the several Attempts of the *English*, both in the Reigns of Queen *Elizabeth*, King *James*, and of Capt. *Hudson* and Capt. *James*, in the 2d, 3d and 4th Years of King *Charles*, was in the 14th Year of the said King *Charles*, A. D. 1639, undertaken from some Industrious Navigators from *Boston* in *New England*, upon which I Admiral *de Fonte* received Orders from *Spain* and the Viceroys to Equip four Ships of Force, and being ready we put to Sea the 3d of *April* 1640. from the Calo of *Lima*, I Admiral *Bartholomew de Fonte* in the Ship *St Spiritus*, the Vice-Admiral *Don Diego Pennelossa*, in the Ship *St Lucia*, *Pedro de Bernarda*, in the Ship *Rosaria*, *Philip de Ronquillo* in the *King Philip*. The 7th of *April* at 5 in the Afternoon, we had the length of *St Helen*, two hundred Leagues on the *North* side of the Bay of *Guajaquil*, in 2 Degrees of *South* Lat. and anchored in the Port *St Helena*, within the Cape, where each Ship's Company took in a quantity of *Betumen*, called vulgarly *Tar*, of a dark colour with a cast of Green, an excellent Remedy against the Scurvy and Dropsie, and is used as Tar for Shipping, but we took it in for Medicine; it Boils out of the Earth, and is there plenty. The 10*th* we pass'd the Equinoctial by Cape *del Passao*, the 11*th* Cape *St Francisco*, in

(2)

<small>April 1708.

Eighty Leagues N. N. W. and 25 Leagues E. and by S.</small>

one Degree and seven Minutes of Latitude North from the Equator, and anchor'd in the Mouth of the ‖ River *St Jago*, where with a Sea-Net we catch'd abundance of good Fish; and several of each Ship's Company went ashoar, and kill'd some Goats and Swine, which are there wild and in plenty; and others bought of some Natives, 20 dozen of *Turkey* Cocks and Hens, Ducks, and much excellent Fruit, at a Village two *Spanish* Leagues, six Mile and a half, up the River *St Jago*, on the Larbord side or the Left hand. The River is Navigable for small Vessels from the Sea, about 14 *Spanish* Leagues *South East*, about half way to the fair City of *Quita*, in 22 Minutes of *South* Latitude, a City that is very Rich. The 16th of *April* we sailed from the River *St Jago* to the Port and Town *Raleo*, 320 Leagues W. N. W. a little Westerly, in about 11 Degrees 14 Min. of N. Latitude, leaving Mount *St Miguel* on the Larboard side, and Point *Cazamina* on the Starboard side. The Port of *Raleo* is a safe Port, is covered from the Sea by the Islands *Ampallo* and *Mangreza*, both well inhabited with Native *Indians*, and 3 other small Islands. † *Raleo* is but 4 Miles over Land from the head of the Lake *Nigaragua*, that falls into the North Sea in 12 Degrees of North Latitude, near the Corn or Pearl Islands. Here at the Town of *Raleo*, where is abundance of excellent close grain'd Timber, a reddish Cedar, and all Materials for building Shipping; we bought 4 long well sail'd Shallops, built express for sailing and riding at Anchor and rowing, about 12 Tuns each, of 32 foot Keel. The 26th, we sailed from *Raleo* for the Port of *Saragua*, or rather of *Salagua*, within the Islands and Shoals of *Chamily*, and the Port is often call'd by the *Spaniards* after that Name; in 17 Degrees 31 Minutes of North Latitude, 480 Leagues North West and by West, a little Westerly from *Raleo*. From the Town of *Saragua*, a little East of *Chamily* at *Saragua*, and from *Compostila* in the Neighbourhood of this Port, we took in a Master and six Mariners accustomed to Trade with the Natives on the East side of *California* for Pearl; the Natives catch'd on a Bank in 19 Degrees of Latitude North from the *Baxos* St *Juan*, in 24 Degrees

<small>*The great Ships that are built in New Spain are built in Raleo.*</small>

of

of North Latitude 20 Leagues N. N. E. from Cape St *Lucas*, the
South East point of *California*. The Master Admiral *de Fonte* had
hir'd, with his Vessel and Mariners, who had informed the Admiral, that 200 Leagues North from Cape St *Lucas*, a Flood from
the North, met the South Flood, and that he was sure it must be
an Island, and *Don Diego Pennelossa* (Sisters Son of * *Don Lewis de
Haro*) a young Nobleman of great Knowledge and Address in Cosmography and Navigation, and undertook to discover whether *California* was an Island or not ; for before it was not known whether
it was an Island or a *Peninsula* ; with his Ship and the 4 Shallops
they brought at *Ralco*, and the Master and Mariners they hir'd at
Salagua, but Admiral *de Fonte* with the other 3 Ships sailed from
them within the Islands *Chamily* the 10th of May 1640. and having
the length of Cape *Abel*, on the W. S. W. side of *California* in 26
Degrees of N. Latitude, 160 Leagues N. W. and W. from the Isles
Chamily; the Wind sprung up at S. S. E. a steady Gale, that from
the 26th of *May* to the 14th of *June*, he had sail'd to the River
los Reyes in 53 Degrees of N. Latitude, not having occasion to lower
a Topsail, in sailing 866 Leagues N. N. W.' 410 Leagues from Port
Abel to Cape Blanco, 456 Leagues to *Riolos Reyes*, all the time most
pleasant Weather, and sailed about 260 Leagues in crooked Channels, amongst Islands named the ‖ *Archipelagus de St Lazarus* ;
where his Ships Boats sail'd a mile a head, sounding to see what
Water, Rocks and Sands there was. The 22d of *June*, Admiral
Fonte dispatched one of his Captains to *Pedro de Barnarda*, to sail
up a fair River, a gentle Stream and deep Water, went first N. and
N. E. N. and N. W. into a large Lake full of Islands, and one very
large *Peninsula* full of Inhabitants, a Friendly honest People in this
Lake ; he named Lake *Valasco*, where Captain *Barnarda* left his
Ship ; nor all up the River was less than 4, 5, 6, 7 and 8 Fathom
Water, both the Rivers and Lakes abounding with Salmon Trouts,
and very large white Pearch, some of two foot long ; and with 3
large *Indian* Boats, by them called *Periagos*, made of two large
Trees 50 and 60 foot long. Capt. *Barnarda* first sailed from his

April 1708.

Don Lewis de Haro *was great Minister of* Spain.

‖ *So named by* de Fonte*, he being the first that made that Discovery.*

April 1708. Ships in the Lake *Valafco*, one hundred and forty Leagues Weſt, and then 436 E. N. E. to 77 Degrees of Latitude. Admiral *de Fonte*, after he had difpatch'd Captain *Barnarda* on the Difcovery of the North and Eaſt part of the *Tartarian* Sea, the Admiral fail'd up a very Navigable River, which he named *Riolos Reyes*, that run neareſt North Eaſt, but on feveral Points of the Compaſs 60 Leagues at low Water, in a fair Navigable Channel, not leſs than 4 or 5 Fathom Water. It flow'd in both Rivers near the ſame Water, in the River *los Reyes*, 24 foot Full and Change of the Moon; a S. S. E. Moon made high Water. It flow'd in the River *de Haro* 22 foot and a half Full and Change. They had two † Jeſuits with them that had been on their Miſſion to the 66 Degrees of North Latitude, and had made curious Obſervations. The Admiral *de Fonte* received a Letter from Captain *Barnarda*, dated the 27th of *June*, 1640. that he had left his Ship in the Lake *Valafco*, betwixt the Iſland *Barnarda* and the Peninfula *Conibaffet*, a very ſafe Port; it went down a River from the Lake, 3 falls, 80 Leagues, and fell into the *Tartarian* Sea in 61 Degrees, with the Pater Jeſuits and 36 Natives in three of their Boats, and 20 of his *Spaniſh* Seamen; that the Land trended away North Eaſt; that they ſhould want no Proviſions, the Country abounding with Veniſon of 3 ſorts, and the Sea and Rivers with excellent Fiſh (Bread, Salt, Oyl and Brandy they carry'd with them) that he ſhould do what was poſſible. The Admiral, when he received the Letter from Captain *Barnarda*, was arrived at an *Indian* Town called *Conoffet*, on the South-ſide the Lake *Belle*, where the two Pater Jeſuits on their Miſſion had been two Years; a peaſant Place. The Admiral with his two Ships, enter'd the Lake the 22d of *June*, an Hour before high Water, and there was no Fall or Catract, and 4 or 5 Fathom Water, and 6 and 7 generally in the Lake *Belle*, there is a little fall of Water till half Flood, and an Hour and quarter before high Water the Flood begins to ſet gently into the Lake *Belle*; the River is freſh at 20 Leagues diſtance from the Mouth, or Entrance of the River *los Reyes*. The River and Lake abounds with Salmon,

† One of theſe that went with Capt. Barnarda on his Diſcovery.

Salmon-

Salmon-Trouts, Pikes, Perch and Mullets, and two other forts of Fish peculiar to that River, admirable good, and Lake *Belle*; also abounds with all those forts of Fish large and delicate: And Admiral *de Fonte* says, the Mullets catch'd in *Rios Reyes* and Lake *Belle*, are much delicater than are to be found, he believes, in any part of the World.

April 1708.

The rest shall be incerted in our next.

June 1708.

MEMOIRS for the CURIOUS.

The Remainder of Admiral Bartholomew de Fonte's *Letter; giving an Account of the most material Transactions in a Journal of his from the Calo of* Lima *in* Peru, *on his Discoveries to find out if there was any North West Passage from the* Atlantick *Ocean into the South and Tartarian Sea; which for want of Room we could not possibly avoid postponing.*

See the Memoirs for April 1708. and you'll find the beginning of this Curious Discovery.

WE concluded with giving an Account of a Letter from Capt. *Barnarda*, dated the 27th of *June*, 1640. on his Discovery in the Lake *Valasco*. The first of *July* 1640, Admiral *de Fonte* sailed from the rest of his Ships in the Lake *Belle*, in a good Port cover'd by a fine Island, before the Town *Conosset* from thence to a River I named *Parmentiers*, in honour of my Industrious Judicious Comrade, Mr *Parmentiers*, who had most exactly mark'd every thing in and about that River; we pass'd 8 Falls, in all 32 foot, perpendicular from its Sourse out of *Belle*; it falls into the large Lake I named Lake *de Fonte*, at which place we arrived the 6th of *July*. This Lake is 160 Leagues long and 60 broad, the length is E. N. E. and W. S. W. to 20 or 30, in some places 60 Fathom deep; the Lake abounds with excellent Cod and Ling, very large and well fed, there are several very large Islands and 10 small ones; they are covered with shrubby Woods, the Moss grows 6 or 7 foot long, with which the Moose, a very large sort of Deer, are fat with in the Winter, and other lesser Deer, as Fallow, &c. There are abundance of wild Cherries, Straw-berries, Hurtle-berries, and wild Currants, and also of wild Fowl, Heath Cocks and Hens, likewise Patridges and Turkeys, and Sea Fowl in great plenty on the South side: The Lake is a very large fruitful

fruitful Island, had a great many Inhabitants, and very excellent Timber, as Oaks, Ashes, Elm and Fur-Trees, very large and tall.

June 1703.

The 14th of *July* we sailed out of the E. N. E. end of the Lake *de Fonte*, and pass'd a Lake I named *Estricto de Ronquilio*, 34 Leagues long, 2 or 3 Leagues broad, 20, 26, and 28 Fathom of Water; we pass'd this strait in 10 hours, having a stout Gale of Wind and whole Ebb. As we sailed more Easterly, the Country grew very sensibly worse, as it is in the North and South parts of *America*, from 36 to the extream Parts North or South, the West differs not only in Fertility but in Temperature of Air, at least 10 Degrees, and it is warmer on the West side than on the East, as the best *Spanish* Discoverers found it, whose business it was in the time of the Emperor *Charles* the V. to *Philip* the III. as is noted by *Aloares* and a *Costa* and *Mariana*, &c.

The 17th we came to an *Indian* Town, and the *Indians* told our Interpreter Mr *Parmentiers*, that a little way from us lay a great Ship where there had never been one before; we sailed to them, and found only one Man advanced in years, and a Youth; the Man was the greatest Man in the Mechanical Parts of the Mathematicks I had ever met with; my second Mate was an *English* Man, an excellent Seaman, as was my Gunner, who had been taken Prisoners at *Campecky*, as well as the Master's Son; they told me the Ship was of *New England*, from a Town called *Boston*. The Owner and the whole Ships Company came on board the 30th, and the Navigator of the Ship, Capt. *Shapley*, told me, his Owner was a fine Gentleman, and Major General of the largest Colony in *New England*, called the *Maltechusets*; so I received him like a Gentleman, and told him, my Commission was to make Prize of any People seeking a North West or West Passage into the South Sea, but I would look upon them as Merchants trading with the Natives for Bevers, Otters, and other Furs and Skins, and so for a small Present of Provisions I had no need on, I gave him my Diamond

Ring,

June
1708.

Ring, which coſt me 1200 Pieces of Eight, (which the modeſt Gentleman received with difficulty) and having given the brave Navigator, Capt. *Shapley* for his fine Charts and Journals, 1000 Pieces of Eight, and the Owner of the Ship, *Scimer Gibbons* a quarter Caſk of good *Peruan* Wine, and the 10 Seamen each 20 Pieces of Eight, the 6th of *Auguſt*, with as much Wind as we could fly before, and a Currant, we arrived at the firſt Fall of the River *Parmentiers*, the 11th of *Auguſt*, 86 Leagues, and was on the South ſide of the Lake *Belle* on board our Ships the 16th of *Auguſt*, before the fine Town *Conoſſet*, where we found all things well; and the honeſt Natives of *Conoſſet* had in our abſence treated our People with great humanity, and Capt. *de Ronquillo* anſwer'd their Civility and Juſtice.

The 20th of *Auguſt* an *Indian* brought me a Letter to *Conoſſet* on the *Lake Belle*, from Capt. *Barnarda*, dated the 11th of *Auguſt*, where he ſent me word he was returned from his Cold Expedition, and did aſſure me there was no Communication out of the *Spaniſh* or *Atlantick* Sea, by *Davis* Srait; for the Natives had conducted one of his Seamen to the head of *Davis* Srait, which terminated in a freſh Lake of about 30 Mile in circumference, in the 80th Degree of North Latitude; and that there was prodigious Mountains North of it, beſides the North Weſt from that Lake, the Ice was ſo fix'd, that from the Shore to 100 Fathom Water, for ought he knew from the Creation; for Mankind knew little of the wonderful Works of God, eſpecially near the North and South Poles; he writ further, that he had ſailed from *Baſſet* Iſland North Eaſt, and Eaſt North Eaſt, and North Eaſt and by Eaſt, to the 79th Degree of Latitude, and then the Land trended North, and the Ice reſted on the Land. I received afterwards a ſecond Letter from Capt. *Barnada*, dated from *Minhanſet*, informing me, that he made the Port of *Arena*, 20 Leagues up the River *los Reyes* on the 29th of *Auguſt*, where he waited my Commands. I having ſtore of good Salt Provisions, of Veniſon and Fiſh, that Capt. *de Ranquillo* had ſalted

(by

(by my order) in my abfence, and 100 Hogſheads of *Indian* Wheat or Mais, failed the 2d of *September* 1640. accompanied with many of the honeſt Natives of *Conoſſet*, and the 5th of *September* in the Morning about 8, was at an Anchor betwixt *Arena* and *Mynhanſet*, in the River *los Reyes*, failing down that River to the North Eaſt part of the South Sea; after that returned home, having found that there was no Paſſage into the South Sea by that they call the North Weſt Paſſage. The Chart will make this much more demonſtrable.

Tho the Style of the foregoing Piece is not altogether ſo Polite, (being writ like a Man, whoſe livelihood depended on another way) but with abundance of Experience and a Traveller, yet there are ſo many Curious, and hitherto unknown Diſcoveries, that it was thought worthy a place in theſe Memoirs; *and 'tis humbly preſum'd it will not be unacceptable to thoſe who have either been in thoſe Parts, or will give themſelves the trouble of reviewing the Chart.*

OBSERVATIONS

ON

The Title affixed, and on other Circumstances relating to the Letter of Admiral de Fonte, *shewing the Authenticity of that Letter, and of the Account therein contained.*

OBSERVATIONS have been made by several Geographers of different Nations on the Letter of Admiral *de Fonte*, to shew that such Letter is not deserving of Credit, is to be thought of as a mere Fiction or Romance, and is a Forgery composed by some Person to serve a particular Purpose. But it will appear, as we proceed in a more particular Consideration of the Title and Circumstances relative to the Letter of Admiral *de Fonte* than hath been hitherto used, and from the following Remarks on the Subject of such Letter*, That those Observations made by the Geographers have many of them no just Foundation, the rest afford not a sufficient Evidence to invalidate the Authenticity of that Letter, and of the Account it contains.

It is only from a Copy of the Letter of *de Fonte* that the Translation hath been made, which is now published, as is plain from a Title being affixed, *A Letter from Admiral* Bartholomew de Fonte, *then Admiral of* New Spain *and* Peru, *and now Prince of* Chili. As *Prince* is never used in this Sense with us, it is apparently a literal Translation of the *Spanish* Word *Principe*, consequently this Title was wrote in the *Spanish* Language, and we cannot otherwise conclude but in the same Language with the Letter. From this and other Defects of the like Sort, which will be noticed as we proceed in our Observations, the

---

* Memoires et Observations Geographiques et Critiques sur la Situation de Pays Septentrionaux, &c. a Lausanne, 1765.—Pa. 115, &c.

Translator muſt be acquitted from all Suſpicion of being any way concerned in this pretended Forgery.

By the Copieſt affixing this Title, it is evident he was well aſſured that there had been ſuch an Expedition.

The Anecdotes, as to the Vice-admiral *Penneloſſa*, in the Body of the Letter, what is therein mentioned as to the Jeſuits, evidence that a minute and particular Inquiry was made by the Copieſt; that he had thoroughly informed himſelf of every Particular of this Affair; that he was aſſured that the Account by him copied contained the moſt material Tranſactions in a Journal of *de Fonte*'s, and that *de Fonte* was then, probably from his advanced Age, in the Service of the Government in another Station.

This Expedition not being ſolely to intercept the Navigators from *Boſton*, but alſo to diſcover whether there was a Paſſage in thoſe Parts thro' which the *Engliſh* expected to make a Paſſage, *viz.* by the back Part of *Virginia*, by *Hudſon*'s or by *Baffin*'s Bay; it was an Undertaking which required that the Perſon who had the conducting of it ſhould not only be a Man of good Underſtanding, but a judicious and experienced Seaman. The Time required to attain ſuch Qualifications implies, that *de Fonte* muſt have been of a mature Age when he went on this Command; and *de Fonte* being alive at the Time that the Copy was taken, it muſt have been taken within twenty Years, or in a leſs Time after ſuch Expedition, as the Copieſt ſpeaks of *Penneloſſa* as a young Nobleman. The Copieſt therefore could not be impoſed on, as his Inquiries were made in ſuch a Time, either with reſpect to the Perſons concerned, or with reſpect to the Letter not being a genuine Account of the Voyage.

A Perſon might be ſo circumſtanced as to attain the Favour of copying ſuch Letter, induced by ſome private Motive, without an Intention of making it publick, as Publications were not at that Time ſo frequent as of late Days; neither is it leſs probable that a Copy ſo taken may, in Proceſs of Time, come into other Hands and then be publiſhed.

Mr. *Gage* obſerves, in his Dedication to Lord *Fairfax*, ' The Reaſon
' of his publiſhing a New Survey of the *Weſt Indies* to be, becauſe that
' nothing had been written of theſe Parts for theſe hundred Years laſt
' paſt.

(13)

'paſt, which is almoſt ever ſince from the firſt Conqueſt thereof by the
'*Spaniards*, who are contented to loſe the Honour of that Wealth and
'Felicity, which they have ſince purchaſed by their great Endeavours,
'ſo that they may enjoy the Safety of retaining what they have for-
'merly gotten in Peace and Security.' And though *de Fonte* declares
that there was no North-weſt Paſſage, yet that there ſhould be no Publication of the Account of the Voyage is conſiſtent with this eſtabliſhed
Maxim.

The North-weſt Paſſage he mentions is not to be underſtood, in
an unlimited Senſe, for a Paſſage between the *Atlantick* and Weſtern
Ocean to the Northward, but the Meaning is confined to that Paſſage
expected by *Hudſon*'s Bay: For *de Fonte* ſays, that he was to make a
Prize of *any ſeeking a North-weſt or Weſt Paſſage* *; by the latter he
meant where *Penneloſſa* was ſent to ſearch; and *Bernarda* ſays, there was
no Communication out of the *Spaniſh* or *Atlantick* Sea, by *Davis* Streight;
and there was an Extent of Coaſt which *de Fonte* only ran along, and
had, but at Times, a diſtant View of; and as to the Jeſuits, by whatever Means they got into thoſe Parts, it is evident they had not ſeen
all the intermediate Country. Therefore tho' the Court of *Spain* was
ſatisfied that the Paſſage was not where *de Fonte* had ſearched; yet there
might be a Paſſage where he had not ſearched, and publiſhing this Account of the Voyage would be an Aſſiſtance to the Adventurers, as
it would confine them in their Searches to thoſe other Parts which
were curſorily paſſed by *de Fonte*, and where perhaps they might ſucceed: Or this Account particularly deſcribing the Northern and
Weſtern Part of *America*, not hitherto known, would be of great Service to Rovers, who had already found their Way into thoſe Seas, by
directing them to the Coaſt and Harbours, and giving them an Account
of a Country where they could retire to with tolerable Security from any
Interruption from the *Spaniards*, a good Climate, hoſpitable People, and
a Plenty of Proviſions to be had; Circumſtances which might enable
them to continue their cruizing in thoſe Seas much longer than without
ſuch Lights as they would receive from this Account they would be enabled to do.

* Vide Letter.

It

It is well known that the *Spaniards* claimed all to the Northward as their Dominion, which they intended in due Time to acquire the Poffeffion of, and the Publication might give an Infight to the *Englifh* Settlers in *America* to be beforehand with them in attaining a Settlement in thofe Parts.

Their Attempt to intercept the *Englifh* Subjects, when made Publick to the World, would have given Umbrage to the Court and People of *England*, which the *Spaniards* would not unneceffarily, and efpecially at a Time when they had their Hands full of a War with the *French*, who had alfo incited the *Catalonians* to rebel, and had joined them with their Troops. The *Spaniards* were, at the fame Time, endeavouring to recover the Dominions of *Portugal*. And *de Fonte* had refpect to the critical Situation their Affairs were in, even before he fet out on his Voyage, hence his political Behaviour when he met with the Navigators from *Bofton*, committed no Act of Hoftility, yet made Ufe of the moft effective Means to prevent their proceeding further.

As no Publication was permitted of this Expedition, this therefore could come but to the Knowledge only of a very few Perfons in *Old Spain*. Such a fingular Tranfaction being foon, from their Attention to other Matters, and their Miniftry foon after entirely changed, no more talked of, unlefs it fhould have been revived by fomething of the like Nature again happening on the Part of the *Englifh*. As no Attempt was made by the *Englifh* for almoft a Century, this Tranfaction, in that Time, fell into Oblivion. At the Time fuch Attempt was renewed, then the *Spaniards* were better acquainted with the Purpofe of our fettling in *America*, they had altered their Defigns of extending their own Poffeffions, there was alfo another Power who might pretend that fuch Paffage, if made, was Part in their Dominion, fo obftruct our free proceeding and interrupt our fettling; the *Spaniards* therefore having no immediate Occafion for any Refearches back to the Records to acquaint themfelves as to the Practicability or Impracticability of our Attempts, or to take Directions for their own Proceedings, the Remembrance of this Expedition continued dormant.

In

(15)

In *New Spain*, the fitting four Ships to go on Discovery, as such Undertakings had been very frequent, it would not engage any extraordinary Attention of the Publick there; it often happened that what was done on such Voyages was kept a Secret. The more curious and inquisitive Persons would attain but an imperfect Account, by Inquiry from the People on board the Ships, as the Ships were divided, and they would receive no satisfactory Information of what was most material, and the principal Object of their Inquiry by those who went in the Boats, as Seamen delighting in Stories often tell what they neither heard or saw. The Consequences of the Voyage not known, because not understood, a weak Tradition of this Expedition would remain to Posterity; and the only Knowledge or Certainty to be acquired, as to this Expedition, would be from Journals accidentally preserved, of some Persons who had gone the Voyage.

Monf. *de Lisle* gives us an Extract of a Letter from Monf. *Antonio de Ulloa*, wrote from *Aranguer* the 19th of *June* in the Year 1753*, to Monf. *Bouguer e le Mounier*, to answer the Queries they had made on the Subject of the Letter of Admiral *de Fuente*. That curious and able *Spanish* Officer sent them in Answer, That in the Year 1742 he commanded a Ship of War the *Rose*, in the South Sea; he had on board him a Lieutenant of the Vessel named *Don Manuel Morel*, an antient Seaman, who shewed him a Manuscript; *Monf. Ulloa* forgot the Author's Name, but believes it to be *Barthelemi de Fuentes*. The Author in that Manuscript reported, that in Consequence of an Order which he had received from the then Viceroy of *Peru*, that he had been to the Northward of *California*, to discover whether there was a Passage by which there was a Communication between the North and South Sea; but having reached a certain Northern Latitude, which *Monf. Ulloa* did not recollect, and having found nothing that indicated such Passage, he returned to the Port of *Callao*, &c. *Monf. Ulloa* adds, he had a Copy of such Relation, but he lost it when he was taken by the *English* on his return from *America*.

* Novelles Cartes des Decovertes de L'Amiral de Fonte, et autres Navigateurs, &c. Par de Lisle. Paris 1753.—P. 30.

It is evident, from this Account being seen in 1742, it is not the same from which the Translation is made which we now have, that being published in 1708. And as *Monf. de Lifle* afserts, that the Letter is conformable with what *Monf. Ulloa* said at *Paris* three Years before, with this Difference only, that he said positively at that Time, that the Relation which he had seen at *Peru*, and of which he had taken a Copy, was of Admiral *de Fonte*, this Manuscript, which contained the Account of the Voyage, may rather be supposed to be a Relation, or Journal kept by some Person, who was aboard Admiral *de Fonte's* Ship, a Friend or Ancestor of *Morel*, than a Copy the same with this Letter, as it only mentioned the Purport of the Voyage, seems not to have the particular Circumstances as to intercepting the *Boston* Men. This Account is an Evidence so far in Favour of this Letter, as it proves that this Letter is not the only Account that there is of this Voyage, and that another Account was seen and copied at *Peru* many Years after this Letter was published in *England*. But if it be supposed that it is one and the same Account, and that from the *English*, it would not have been accepted of and kept by *Morel*, and shewed as a Curiosity, unless he was satisfied that it was a true genuine Account of such Voyage, and as to which he would naturally inquire, being on the Spot, where he might probably be informed, and unless he was at a Certainty that what that Account contained was true, would he have produced the Manuscript, or permitted his Captain to take a Copy of it as genuine; yet we may with greater Probability suppose, that this Manuscript which *Morel* had was no Translation from the *English*, but in itself an Original. Monf. *Ulloa* speaking of *Morel* as an antient Seaman, cannot mean that he was in the Expedition of *de Fonte*, only implies his being acquainted with some one who was, with whom, from his Course of Years, he might have sailed, and attained this Journal.

What is said in the Letter of Monf. *Ulloa*, that he forgot the Name of the Author of the Manuscript, but believes it was *Bartelemi de Fuentes*, that the Author of that Manuscript gave an Account of. It must be considered, that when Monf. *Ulloa* wrote he was in *Old Spain*, many Years after he had seen the Account, and three Years after he was at *Paris*; and though he genteelly answers the Inquiries sent him, agreeable

able to his Conversation at *Paris*, yet does not express himself so positively as when at *Paris*, as in the Letter he only believes it to be *Bartelemi de Fonte*. *Monf. Ulloa* would sooner not have answered the Letter than deny what he had formerly said; and if Monf. *de Lisle* had advanced that for which he had no proper Authority, both as a Gentleman and an Officer he would not have submitted to such a Falshood: But from Monf. *Ulloa* being tender in the Account, being of a Matter which might not make any great Impression on him at the Time he received it, ten Years since, out of his Hands, and three Years after he was at *Paris*, this Account is more worthy of Credit, and he might be more cautious, now he was to give it under his Hand, to soften the Reproach of his Countrymen for his not acting like a true *Spaniard*, in being so communicative in this Matter. The Account which Monf. *de Lisle* hath given, was with a Permission of Monf. *Ulloa* to make Use of his Name, as the Letter Monf. *Ulloa* sent testifies. Where Monf. *de Lisle* hath not the Liberty to mention the Name of his Author, he only says, that there was a Person equally curious, and as well instructed in the Affair as Monf. *de Ulloa*, who assured him positively that there was such a Relation.

Though Monf. *de Lisle* had a particular System to support, yet, at the same Time, he had a great publick Character to preserve. Monf. *Bougier, Mounier*, and *Ulloa*, were living at the Time he gave this Account to the Publick; they would be asked as to what they knew of the Affair; and a more particular Inquiry would be made of Monf. *de Lisle*, as to the Information he received from the namelefs Person; and as there were several of his Countrymen who did not adopt his System, a Trip in this Affair, as to the Evidence he brings in Support of the Authority of this Account of *de Fonte*, would have given them an Advantage which they would not have neglected, and have done Justice to the Publick, by letting them know there was little of Truth in this Account; but as no Reflections have appeared, we have no Reason to question the Veracity of Monf. *de Lisle* in this Relation, on any Surmises of Strangers, on no better Authority than meer Opinion, without a single Reason produced in Support of what they insinuate.

This Letter, when published in 1708, was considered only as an Account that was curious; was looked on as of no Importance, and did

not engage the Attention of the Publick until the Difcovery of the North-weft Paffage became the Topick of common Converfation, and would have lain, without having any further Notice taken of it, had not the Attempts to difcover a North-weft Paffage been revived. It is from their being produced in a proper Seafon, that Accounts of this Sort become permanent, affifting in fome favourite Defign, being thus ufeful they are preferved from Obfcurity and Oblivion. We have an Account, the Author Captain *Don Francifco de Seixas*, a Captain in the *Spanifh* Navy, and is frequently quoted by the *Spanifh* Writers, though he is little known amongft us.—He fays, P. 71. ' *Thomas Peche*, an *Englifhman*, having been
' at Sea twenty-eight Years, and made eight Voyages to the *Eaft-Indies*
' and *China* during fixteen Years of that Time, fpent the other twelve in
' Trading and Piracies in the *Weft-Indies*, from whence he returned to
' *England* in 1669; and, after continuing there four Years, in 1673,
' with other Companions, fitted out at the Port of *Briftol* one Ship of
' five hundred Tons, with forty-four Guns, and two light Frigates of
' one hundred and fifty Tons, and in each eighteen Guns, giving out
' that he was bound on a trading Voyage to the *Canaries*; whence they
' bore away with the three Veffels, and went through the Streight *Le
' Maire*, with two hundred and feventy Men, which he carried directly
' to trade at the *Moluccas* and *Philippinas*.

' And after continuing in thofe Parts twenty-fix Months and fome
' Days, it appearing to the faid *Thomas Peche* that from the *Philippinas*
' he could return to *England* in a fhorter Time by the Streight of *Anian*
' than by the Eaft or Streight *Magellan*, he determined to pafs this
' Rout with his large Ship, and one fmall one, the other having loft
' Company by bad Weather, or worfe Defign in thofe who com-
' manded it.

' And having, as he fays, failed one hundred and twenty Leagues
' within the Streights of *Anian*, relates, that as the Month of *October*
' was far advanced, in which the northerly Winds reign much, and drove
' the Waters from the North to the South, that the Currents of the faid
' Streight of *Anian* were fuch, and fo ftrong, that had they continued
' longer they muft, without Doubt, have been loft; wherefore, finding
' it neceffary to return back, failing along the Coaft of *California* (after
' having failed out of the Channel of *Anian*) and thofe of *New Spain*

' and

' and *Peru*, he went through the Streight of *Magellan* into the North
' Sea in sixteen Hundred and seventy-seven, with the Vessels and much
' Riches, great Part whereof was of a *Spanish* Vessel which they took on
' the Coast of *Lugan*.'

Wherefore passing over all the rest of what the Author says in his Voyage, only mentioning what regarded the Currents, he relates, that when he entered into the Streight of *Anian* he found, from Cape *Mendocino* in *California*, for above twenty Leagues within the Channel, the Currents set to the N. E. all which and much more the Curious will find in the Voyage of the said *Thomas Peche*, which in sixteen Hundred and seventy-nine was printed in *French* and *English*, in many Parts of *Holland*, *France*, and *England*, in less than twenty Sheets Quarto: And (he adds) further I can affirm, that I have seen the Author many Times in the Year eighty-two, three and four in *Holland*, who had along with him a *Spanish* Mestize born in the *Philippinas*, together with a *Chinese*.

It can scarce be imagined the Whole is without Foundation, though no such Voyage is at present to be come at, *Seyxas* publishing his Work soon after the Publication by *Peche*, to which he particularly refers, seems to obviate all Doubt of his Sincerity; and there are too many Circumstances, which are collateral Evidence, mentioned, to imagine he could be entirely deceived. He published his Work at *Madrid* in sixteen Hundred and eighty-eight, dedicated to the King, as President in his Royal Council of the *Indies*, and to the Marquis *de los Velez*; the Work intituled, *Theatro Naval Hydographico de Los Fluxos*, &c. This Account was received as a true and faithful Relation of a Voyage performed, as it was published in various Languages; yet the Want of this Account is a Particular, some Reason for Exception with us, that we cannot receive it as a Certainty. And we are more suspicious as to the Truth of any Accounts that we have received relating to the Northwest Part of *America*, than to any other Part of the Globe. Our Opinion being in a great Measure influenced by the System we embrace, as, Whether there is a North-west Passage, or not? And for this Reason only, no Part of the Globe hath more engaged the Attention of the Geographers, and with respect to which they had more different Opinions.

Those whose Opinion it was that *Asia* and *America* were contiguous, had, for many Years, their Opinion rejected, but now confirmed to be true by the *Russian* Discoveries; and we may conclude they had a good Authority for what they advanced, which was not transmitted down to us, as they had such an Assurance of what they had advanced, as they supposed there could never be the least Doubt of it. Those who advanced that there was Passage between the *Atlantick* and Southern Ocean, by a Streight in the Northern and Western Parts of *America*, and very likely on a good Authority, have their Opinion opposed, all Accounts of Voyagers treated as fabulous, and for the same Reason that the Opinion of *Asia* and *America* being contiguous was rejected, as they could produce nothing further for it than Tradition, and as to which the Tradition now appears to have had its Foundation in Truth. Soon after *America* was discovered, and the *Spaniards* had settled in *New Spain*, the Report of there being a Streight prevailed, the Truth of this Report hath not been disproved, and we have no just Reason to reject this Tradition for positive Assertions which are produced without any Evidence, but that our Attempts have not succeeded. Which is an Inference deduced from a false Principle, for our not having had the expected Success hitherto, doth not imply that we may not succeed hereafter, as we proceed in our future Attempts; and all that hath been said, as to there being no North-west Passage, is not adequate to the Tradition of there being such a Passage. This Tradition is also supported by a few Accounts, which we reject too absolutely. These Accounts are given by various Persons, at different Times, without any Concern, Connection, or even Acquaintance the one with the other; which Accounts shew that the Opinion of their being such a Streight prevailed. These Accounts were given by Foreigners; we could not receive them from any other, as we did not frequent those Seas, and at present have no ready Access to them. And as it was but occasionally that any Persons went into those Parts, it is but by a few Persons only we could receive any Information respecting thereto. Nor could we attain such Information as we have in another Manner, than from what our own Countrymen accidentally picked up, as a regular Publication of such Account was not permitted, and as some thought themselves interested to keep the most material Part a Secret, in hopes to turn it to Advantage, by being employed, or receiving a Gratuity for their Discovery. And Allowances

should

should be made, without declaring a Person immediately too credulous, who reports what he hears only in Conversation from another; he may, in such Conversation, omit many Circumstances which it would have been necessary for him to be informed of, in order to give that Satisfaction to others to whom he reports this Information, which he himself received of the Truth of what was related to him at the Time of the Conversation. And we have no Reason to censure those as too credulous who have published these Accounts, until we get a more perfect Information as to the North-west Parts of *America*, which at present remain unknown. A Dispute arises as to the Situation of such a Streight; and Accounts given by *Indians* are produced to prove that the Streight cannot be in such a Part, where it is supposed to be so far to the Southward as to have its Entrance from the South Sea, in Latitude 51; whereas, on a little Examination, it would appear that those *Indians*, whose Accounts are produced, are almost equal Strangers as to those Parts with the *Europeans*. They do not seek inhospitable Countries, where there is little Produce, no Plenty of Fuel, great and frequent Waters, Mountains and Swamps, having no Inducement from Trade or on Account of War, as they would not go into those Parts to seek their Enemy, whom, with less Hazard and a greater Certainty of finding them, they could attack when returned from their Summer hunting and fishing to their Retirements, where they live more comfortably than in those Parts into which, by Necessity, they are obliged to go on Account of the Chace, as they could not otherwise subsist themselves and Families. And on due Examination it will appear all the Accounts we have from the *Indians* are erroneously made use of, to evince that there is no Streight in the Part that is contended for. Instead of too severe a Censure on the Credulity of others, we should be cautious that our Diffidence does not lead us into an unreasonable Incredulity, and prevent our using such Testimony as is presented to us so candidly as we ought to do, and prevent our getting a true Insight into an Affair of such Importance; and the utmost that can be said of it is, that it is a Point yet undetermined, whether there is a North-west Passage or not.

As to the original Letter of *de Fonte*, we interest ourselves in the important Matter it contains, and therefore become more suspicious and
diffident,

diffident, as to its Authenticity, than upon a due Use of our Reason it will appear that we ought to be. As we have no Reason, as is apparent from what hath been said, that the original Letter should ever come to our Hands; and if it appear, as we proceed, that it is rather to be attributed to inevitable Accidents, than there not having been such a Letter, that we cannot attain any particular Information respecting thereto. If it is considered that we have a Publication of such Letter, the Deficiencies in which are not, as it will appear, any other than the Errors of the Translator and Printer. That there are a great many concurring Circumstances in Support of and conformable with what the Letter contains. And the Account is composed of such Particulars as exceed the Industry and Ingenuity of those who employ their Fancy in composing ingenious Fictions. These various Branches of Evidence cannot be rejected, if we make a fair Judgment in this Matter: There must be a Prepossession from common Fame, a Prejudice from a prior Opinion, or an Interest and Design to support a particular System, that prevents our accepting of it, as a Probability next to a Certainty, of this being a true Account; and there is only wanting, to our receiving it absolutely as such, that the Copy be produced from which the Translation was made, or a full and compleat Evidence as to what is become of such Copy.

Why we cannot obtain a particular Information as to the original Letter of *de Fonte*, appears from the Account, which shews that the Court of *Spain* had a secret Intelligence of this Undertaking. And as that Court would not openly declare that they had such an Information, or how they intended to defeat the Design, the Orders sent, and consequently the Account of the Execution of those Orders, and whatever related thereto, would be *secret* Papers, and as such kept in a Manner that few Persons would have a free Access; and by those few who had, as the publick Business did not require it, might never be taken in Hand, unless they accidentally catched the Eye of some who was particularly curious. Thus neglected, in a Century of Time it might not be known, if the Subject was revived, where they were deposited, and being so few in Number would take up but a small Space, which might make it difficult to find them.

The Politeness and Civility which prevail in this Age, will not admit of such a Complaisance to curious Inquirers as to gratify them in that, which, in Policy, from good Reasons of State, might as well be omitted. There are Instances of late Discoveries being made, as to the Whole of which, from particular Views, as it is said, the Curious have not been gratified. And if this Expedition of *de Fonte* was remembered, and the Papers relating thereto could be brought to light, it might immediately encourage us to proceed on making a further Attempt for the Discovery of a North-west Passage, therefore we can have no Reason to expect the Court of *Spain* would assist us with what might determine us to a Proceeding at which they must take Umbrage, as we are now become the only Power who share *North America* with them, from the Advantages that such a Discovery would give us in case of a future Rupture between the two Crowns; though our present Intention is to increase our Commerce, by opening a Trade to *Japan*, and carrying on a Trade in a more advantageous Manner to *China*.

We cannot be assured, if full Permission was given to find these Papers, and more particular Pains and Application used, than is customary with People in publick Offices, when the Occasion of the Search being to little other Purpose than satisfying Curiosity, whether such Search might not be rendered unsuccessful, by such Papers being burnt amongst many other State Papers, in the Fire in the *Escurial*, the common Depository for State Papers at that Time.

If we consider the Changes that have happened, as to the Succession to the Crown of *Spain*, the Changes in the Ministry, Foreigners introduced into their Ministry, there must have been many Particulars, not only of this but of other Kinds, which they are not at present acquainted with, the Ministry having no Occasion to give themselves any Concern about them. *Don Olivarez*, who was the Minister at this Time, was known to do his Business by Juntos of particular People, as the Resolutions of Government thereby remained an inviolable Secret, which was not always the Case when the Business was managed by publick Councils. They also gave their Advice in a particular Manner, by written Billets, which were handed to the King, that every Thing was conducted in a very mysterious Manner during the Time that he was in

the

the Miniftry, contrary to the former Practice, and which was alfo difufed afterwards.

If Inquiry hath been made by the moft intelligent amongft the *Spaniards* as to this Expedition, and the Commands of the Monarch to make Difcovery of thefe Papers, and the Orders relating thereto, have been duly executed, but they cannot be found. The Reafons are apparent, the Voyage being fcarce fpoke of at the Time, went foon out of Remembrance, and whatever may be in private Hands relating thereto, is not immediately recollected by the Poffeffors, and the Originals, if not fecreted or miflaid, are burnt in the *Efcurial* in the Year 1671, the ufual Refidence of the Court, and therefore where this Letter may be fuppofed to be received and lodged. For the Evidence relative to this Account, which the Diftance of Time or other Accidents could not deface, yet remains. If *de Fonte* was Governor or Prefident of *Chili*, from the Nature of his Office it muft appear, amongft fome Records or Inftruments of Writing, and we accordingly are informed, that there was a Perfon in that Office named *Fuente*, which is fynominous. That we have not more minute Particulars, is by reafon that the Account is from thofe Parts where we have not a free and ready Accefs to make our Enquiries, and from a People, excepting a few Individuals, who are not very communicative to Foreigners. But where we have not laboured under the like Difadvantage, we have found that there was one *Gibbons*, alfo *Shapley*, Perfons exactly circumftanced as the Letter mentions, upon the Authority of Records, the Tradition of antient Men, in thofe Parts where they had lived, and alfo other Accounts, fupporting the Authenticity of this Letter, as will be fhewn when we proceed to confider of the Subject of the Letter. There is therefore juft Reafon to conclude, was it poffible to have the like Pains taken in *New Spain* or *Peru*, we might meet with Particulars refpecting this Matter, which would put the Truth of this Account out of all Doubt; and any Failure in the Inquiries there, may be owing to their not having been made with an equal Induftry, and which it is not in our Power to procure in thofe Parts fo diftant and inacceffable.

The Circumftances of the Inhabitants of *Bofton*, and the neighbouring Provinces, during this Period of Time fince the Expedition of *de Fonte*, have been very different, they have not been fubjected to the like fatal Accidents with the People of *Lima*, and that Neighbourhood, who several Times have had their City laid in Ruins, and almost entirely depopulated by Earthquakes, particularly in *April* 1687, and in the Year 1746. The Buildings becoming an entire Heap of Ruins, and many People perishing, must lessen the Force of Tradition, and affect, in some sort, the publick Records; and if the Marine Office was at the *Calloa* of *Lima*, the *Calloa* having been twice overwhelmed by the Sea, then there is no Reason to expect from *New Spain* an authenticated Account of the Equipment of this Fleet under the Command of Admiral *de Fonte*.

Those who argue against the Authenticity of this Account, must admit that he was a Person of Capacity and Abilities who composed it, and should assign us some Reason, if a Fiction, why a sensible Person should undertake it, as there could be no Inducement either in Point of Reputation or Profit: For, if a Fiction, it is neither entertaining or instructive. Neither can any political Motive be urged for this Undertaking, as the Subject must then have been treated in a Manner entirely different; so managed as to shew that a North-west Passage was absolutely impracticable, and to let nothing be introduced that would afford the least Incitement to Adventurers to come into those Parts. But it is apparent, that in this Account the Facts are related in a plain and simple Manner, without any Violation of Truth, as they are related without any Consideration of their Consequences. The Representations made, as to the Tides, as to the different Sorts of Fish that came into the Waters from Westward and Eastward, would have been an Encouragement to a further Trial as to a North-west Passage, had such Account been published; and if the Phænomena as to the Tides, and the Difference as to the Fish, was not from its communicating with the *South Sea*, and the Attempt had proved successless as to the Discovery of a North-west Passage, yet to countervail, in some Measure, that Disappointment, there was a Prospect of a lucrative Trade, in all Appearance to be carried on in those Western Parts where *de Fonte* is represented to have been in, with greater Convenience than that which had been carried on by the *Boston* People from the East before and at this Time in *Hudson's* Bay; and the *English* might be invited, if successful in their Trading, to make a Settlement, an Event which the *Spaniards* were apprehensive

E

prehensive of, and earnestly desirous to prevent. These are Defects which the Capacity and Abilities of the Author would not permit him to run into, if he was writing a fictitious Account, as he must easily see that such Representations to destroy the Notion of a North-west Passage, and prevent the *English* settling there, were absolutely contrary to his Purpose. To give a greater Plausibility to a fictitious Tale, the Scene may be laid in distant Parts, by this Means introducing, more securely, Names and Characters of Persons as real who never were; and though this Account mentions Persons who lived at a great Distance, and in an obscure Part, yet there were such Persons as the Account mentions. Also the Period of Time when this Voyage was performed, so corresponds with their Transactions, as the Author could fix on no other Period so agreeing with the Circumstance of Major *Gibbens* being so long, and at that very Time, absent from home; and his Absence can be attributed to no other Cause than his being out on a Voyage. Here is more Plainness and Consistency than is usual in Fiction, with such a Variety of Particulars, and so circumstanced, as would perplex the most pregnant Fancy to invent, which can be no Way so naturally accounted for as by admitting that the Letter contains a genuine Account of a Voyage made by Admiral *de Fonte*, not a Forgery to support political Views; or that it is the Production of a sporting Fancy to contrast some other Performance, or in order to expose the Credulous to publick Ridicule.

The Editors of this Letter, whose Business it was to know whether this Account was authentick, gave an entire Credit to it as being authentick, not only as they assured the Publick in a general Way, and with respect to all their Pieces that they should publish, that they would only exhibit such as were of unquestionable Authority, but by their annexing an Advertisement to the Letter, have given us a particular Assurance of the Account being authentick; and we have just Reason to conclude they *could* have given us that further Satisfaction we *now* desire; but what they have done was thought by them sufficient, as they had no Idea of the *Importance* of the Subject. They comprehended not further of this Account, *Than that it contained many curious and unknown Discoveries; and they humbly presumed*, being Strangers to any further Merit that it had, *that it would not, on that Account, be unacceptable to the Publick.* Had this Letter been publifhed at a Time a North-weft Paffage was under Confideration of the Publick, there might be fome Sufpicion that the Editors had fome further Defign. But as to a North-weft Paffage after the Voyage of Captain *James*, and after the Difcovery was entrufted to a Company, and no Succefs confequent, it was generally received, many Years before this Letter was publifhed, that to find fuch a Paffage was a Thing impracticable. The Opinion of there being fuch a Paffage was treated as a Chimera: And the Affair of a North-weft Paffage lay in a State of Silence and Oblivion near thirty Years after the Publication was made. We may obferve, that there is no Art in the Compofition of this Advertifement; it was inferted by Men of Honour and Veracity, who had no other Intention in publifhing thefe Memoirs than the Advancement of Science; who, from their general Knowledge, could not be impofed on, and cannot, from their known Characters, be fuppofed to have a Defign to impofe on others. And what further or other Evidence than that which they have given could be expected from the Editors, unlefs they had been acquainted with the Importance which the Letter now appears to be of? It was all that was at that Time neceffary, as they did not expect that there would be any invidious Imputation of Forgery, for then they would have vindicated it from all Sufpicion in a more particular Manner than they have done. They thought it a fufficient Proof of its Authenticity their receiving it into their Collection. As to that mean Reflection that this Account is a Forgery of fome *Englifhman*, it is thoroughly obviated if we confider on what a Foundation fuch a Suppofition muft be grounded, which is, That fome *Englifhman* compofed this Account, tranflated it into *Spanifh*, though there were but few and very indifferent Linguifts at that Time in *England*, to be again tranflated by the Editors, the better to impofe on them and the Publick. The Publick is a Name which comprehends many Perfons of Curiofity and Sagacity, for whom chiefly thefe Memoirs were publifhed; and by thefe Perfons, as well as by all others, the Account was received at that Time as genuine, without the leaft Sufpicion of there being any Fraud or Impofture.

The principal Object or Defign of the Publication was, that the Account contained a Difcovery made of thofe Parts, as to the Knowledge of which the Geographers were at that Time very deficient; and the Editors being satisfied as to the Authenticity, all they thought necessary was to give a Translation of the Letter. And, from their Avocations to their own private Affairs, did not consider it in so minute a Manner as it required, as is plain from their Apology made as to the Stile of the Letter, not being *altogether so polite, being wrote like a Man whose Livelihood depended on another Way, and with an Abundance of Experience.* Whereas the Politeness of Stile would have been an absolute Objection as to the Authenticity of the Account. That as it was a Letter wrote by Admiral *de Fonte* to lay before the Court of *Spain*, what had passed in the Course of the Voyage, though *de Fonte* might express himself in proper and well chosen Terms, yet he was to use a Stile that was natural and simple. On the several Lights in which the Editors have been considered, as to the Part which they undertook, it must appear that they are unjustly reproached with Want of Integrity; they acted consistently, having no Occasion to say more with respect to this Account than they have done. Their Neglect was not from Want of Penetration or Design. Their genuine Characters were such as they could not suppose it would be ever suspected, that they could have any Inducement to impose a spurious Account on the Publick.

Those who censure this Account of *de Fonte* as a Cheat and a Forgery imposed by some one on the World, have produced no Evidence from Facts, or urged any Thing to shew the Improbability of this Account; as to the Argument they so strongly insist on that the Original was never produced, it is highly improbable that the Original ever should be produced in these Parts; and there is a Uniformity in the Circumstance that a Copy only came to the Hands of the Editors, which turns the Argument against the Objectors. The Suspicion of there being any Deceit or Forgery, hath arose from there having been different Systems advanced by Geographers respecting these Parts: Those in whose System this Account is not adopted have been the Occasion of such Suspicions being raised, and have given some Countenance to such their Suspicions from the imperfect Manner in which this Account hath been exhibited; though that is not to be attributed to the Account in its genuine Dress, but as broken and disfigured by the Translator and Printer. The Glosses and Comments added by the Person who took the Copy, and those added by the Translator in Explanation of the Text, are inserted in the same

Character,

Character, and without any Distinction from the Text, and those by the Translator ignorantly introduced. Marginal Notes are inserted as Part of the Narration; Courses are omitted; others mistaken from the Translator's Inattention to the *Spanish* Compass; Dates misplaced by the Printer: The Translator also deviates from the Mode of Expression, and renders, in an inaccurate, confused and obscure Manner, a very material Part in this Account. Many of these Faults we may attribute to Precipitation, from the Translator wanting due Time to study the Letter, occasioned by a Persecution of the Printer, who pressed him to finish that the Printer might compleat his monthly Number, and, from the same Necessity, the immediate Publication, it may be that the Faults of the Press are so many. Such numerous Defects make it evident that this Account could never have been originally constructed in this Manner; and it is on these Defects only that they rely, or from which their principal Arguments are drawn to invalidate the Authenticity of this Account. They might have perceived that a Relation, so mutilated and impaired, must have had a more uniform or regular Shape at one Time or other: And the Editors, in their Index, when the Year's Numbers were compleated, stile it *an original and very entertaining Letter of Admiral de Fonte*, by which they mean for the Curious; and by stiling it an Original, they not only to be understood that it was never before published, but also that it was wrote by *de Fonte*; which implies that they had a *Spanish* Account, and of which, as being consistent with their Purpose, they gave only a Translation: Also the Impression of the first Part, being so uncorrect and full of Faults, the second Part more correct, and the Mode of Expression resumed, shews that the first Composition is not their own, but that it is a Translation which the Editors have given us. The Defects and Imperfections of which being pointed out, we shall comprehend what little Reason there is to dispute the Authenticity of this Account, from the Disfigurements which have prevented our seeing it in its proper Shape, and for suspecting those Persons to be Authors of the Fiction who meant well; but their Fault consisted in their Inattention to the Translator, who did not therefore give a successful Conclusion to their good Design, as by rendering the Account obscure and unintelligible, he afforded Matter for Cavil and Dispute as to this Account of the Voyage, whether credible or not, and which a just Translation would have confirmed to be true.

(30)

As to the Name *Bartholomew de Fonte*, we may obferve that when the Tranflator can render the Names in the *Spanifh* by *Englifh* Names which are anfwerable thereto, he doth not infert the *Spanifh* Names, but the *Englifh*. Thus, as to the Ships, he calls one the King *Philip*; but when they cannot be rendered by a refembling Denomination in the *Englifh*, and the Name hath its Original from the *Latin*, he paffes by the new Name, or as it is wrote in the *Spanifh*, and gives us the antient Name, or according to the Latin *St. Spiritus, St. Lucia, Rofaria*, for *de Efpiritu Santo, Santa Lucia, del Roferia*. Hath rendered *Bartholomew de Fonte, Philip de Ronquillo* both in *Englifh* and *Latin*. From which Management of the Tranflator, in giving the Name according to the *Latin* and not giving it as it hath been transformed or changed agreeable to the *Spanifh* Orthography, there is juft Reafon to conclude the Name which is here rendered *Fonte*, was *Fuente* or *Fuentes* in the Original. But if it was wrote *Fonte*, it was in the provincial Dialect, different from the Manner of writing the good Writers introduced, which did not immediately prevail in all Parts alike, but was gradually received. For Inftance, they wrote *Fuenterabia* in *Caftile*, when the *Bifcayners* continued to write *Fonterabia*; and it is as often fpelt the one Way as the other in our Books and Maps.

Fuente and *Fuentes* are not of one Termination. *Fonte* or *Fuente*, in the Titles of the *Marquis Aguila de Fuente*, fo in *de Fuente de Almexi*, is of the fingular Number, or the Title is taken from the Water of *Almexi*. But *Fuentes*, in the Titles of the *Marquis de Fuentes*, and in *Conde Fuentes de Valde Pero*, or of *Don Pedro Enriques Conde de Fuentes*, expreffes a plural Number, which the Tranflator, through his Indifference as to the Subject which he was employed to tranflate, might not obferve.

Don Pedro Enriques Conde de Fuentes was raifed to the Honour of being a Grandee by *Philip* the Third, in the Year 1615, in refpect to his great Services in the Wars; was defcended from a Branch of that illuftrious Family the *Enriques*. Nine of which Family were fucceffively Admirals of *Caftile*; and the ninth, *Don Joan Alonfo Enriques*, was in that high Poft at the Time of this Expedition. There were Intermarriages between the Families of *Enriques* and *Valafco*; and *Don Pedro* was fucceeded in his Eftate and Title by *Don Luis de Haro*, of the principal

Houfe

House of *Valasco*, and Son-in-Law to *Don Olivarez*. These Circumstances considered, we have a further Reason to suspect that the Name *de Fonte* is not duly rendered by the Translator, as there is a Consistency in a Relation of the *Conde de Fuentes* being advanced to be Admiral of *New Spain* and *Peru*, which coincides with what is reported from *New Spain*, of the Name being *Fuentes* of the Person who was President of *Chili*. It was also apparent that *de Fonte* was a Man of Family, from those who took the respective Commands under him. *Pennelossa*, of whom more particular mention is made in the Letter: *Philip de Ronquillo*, seemingly allied to *John de Ronquillo*, who did considerable Service in the Year 1617, and was Governor of the *Philippine* Islands. There was also *Ronquillo* a Judge, sent to reduce the Insurgents at the City of *Segovia*, in the Time of the Civil Wars in *Spain*. *Pedro de Bonardæ*, who is afterwards called Captain *Barnarda*: Of him we must have the least to say; and we could not expect to be any Way successful in our Inquiries from this Inaccuracy. He seems not to have had so distinguished an Alliance as the others, and employed on this Expedition on the Account of his Abilities, being allotted to a Service not like that of *Pennelossa*, or *Ronquillo*, disagreeable in respect to the Climate, fatiguing and hazardous. That he was a Gentleman by his Descent, is evident from his being named *de Bonardæ*.

The *Spanish* Fleet was but in a mean Condition at the Conclusion of the Ministry of the Duke of *Lerma*; but when an Expedition was set out to recover *St. Salvador* in the Year 1626, was much improved; the *Portuguese* had twenty-six Sail, but the *Spanish* Fleet were now numerous. It doth not appear that the Fleets from *Lisbon*, when *Portugal* was under the Crown of *Spain*, were sent otherwhere than to the *East Indies*, *Brazil*, and the Perlieus; and those from *Old Spain*, that sailed from *Cadiz*, went to *New Spain*, and the Islands under that Dominion. In the Year 1596, when Sir *Francis Drake* took *Cadiz*, he burnt the Fleet that was lying there bound for *Mexico*; and Mr. *Gage*, in the Year 1625, sailed with a Fleet of sixteen Sail, all for *Mexico*, and to the *West Indies* seventeen Sail, besides eight Galleons for a Convoy, all under two *Spanish* Admirals.

The

The Inconsistency that *de Fonte*, a *Portugueze*, should be in such a Post as *Admiral of New Spain*, a great Objection to the Authenticity of this Account, is removed by the Observations that have been made as to the Name *de Fonte*, by which it appears that he was not a *Portugueze*, and their having Sea Commanders, *Spaniards* by Birth, with whom they could supply the principal Posts in the Marine, without being under the Necessity of applying to *Portugal* for Persons qualified to fill those Stations.

As to *de Fonte* being afterwards President of *Chili*, it is meant of the *Audience of Chili*, subordinate to the *Viceroy of Peru*.

REMARKS

ON

The LETTER of Admiral DE FONTE.

THE Viceroys of *New Spain* and *Peru*, having Advice from the Court of *Spain*, and not from *the Court* and the *Council of Spain*; which latter is the common Form of Expression used in any Matter which had been under the Consideration of the *Supreme Council of the Indies*, implies that such Advice must have proceeded from the Secret Council, or from the King through his Minister, that the Design of the Equipment of the four Ships, and the Attempt of the Industrious Navigators from *Boston* might remain a Secret.

The Appellation of Industrious Navigators was conformable to the Characters of *Gibbons* and *Shapley*. Sir *Thomas Button*, in the Extract which there is from his Journal, gives *Gibbons* a great Eulogium as to his being an able Navigator; and this was the Character of *Shapley* amongst his Cotemporaries.

The Court of *Spain* knew that this Attempt to discover a Passage between the *Atlantick* and the *Western Ocean*, was intended by the Northward and Westward; and though they allude to all the Attempts to make such Discovery which had been at any Time made, by mentioning the several Reigns in which any such Attempts were made, yet they hint more particularly, that they expect this Attempt will be by *Hudson*'s Bay, as they mention expresly in their Advice the two Voyages of *Hudson* and *James*. For what is here said, *That the several Attempts*, &c. is a Recital from the Advice sent by the Court to the Viceroys, or from the Orders that *de l'onte* received.

(34)

This Expedition from *Boston* particularly commanded the Attention of the Court of *Spain*, as Captain *James* had not abfolutely denied there was a North-weſt Paſſage; and *Fox*, though not mentioned here, had publiſhed an Account in 1635, by which he had poſitively declared that there was a North-weſt Paſſage; and Sir *Thomas Button*, who kept his Journal a Secret, was very confident of a Paſſage, and is ſaid to have ſatisfied King *James* the Firſt. The Death of his Patron *Prince Henry* prevented his being fitted out again. *Gibbons*, his Intimate, had made the Voyage with him: Afterwards had made a ſecond Attempt by himſelf, but loſt his Seaſon by being detained in the Ice. And now, though a married Man, had a Family, a Perſon in Truſt and Power where he reſided, engages in a third Attempt from *Boston*.

The ſecond, third, and fourth Year of the Reign of King Charles refers ſolely to the Voyage of Captain *James*; to the Time he was engaging Friends to fit him out; and the Time when ſuch Voyage was concluded on. As the *Engliſh* uſed the *Julian*, and the *Spaniards* the *Gregorian* Account, theſe Tranſactions which refer to Captain *James*'s Expedition, could not be made to coaleſce as to the Time, from the Difference there was between theſe two Computations, in any other Manner than by putting the Year of the King of *England*'s Reign. As King *Charles* began his Reign the 27th of *March* 1625, two Days after the Commencement of the Year, according to the *Julian* Account, and the ſecond Year of his Reign would not begin until the 27th of *March* 1626, two Days alſo after that Year commenced, but according to the *Gregorian* Account, the Year 1626 began in *January*; from the 1ſt of *January* to the 27th of *March*, the Year 1626, according to the *Gregorian* Account, would correſpond with the firſt Year of the Reign of King *Charles*. As to this Expedition from *Boston*, it is mentioned to be in the Year 1639, and in the fourteenth Year of the Reign of King *Charles*; but the Year 1639, according to the *Julian* Account, is the fifteenth Year of that King's Reign; but according to the *Gregorian* Account, the Year 1639 correſponds from *January* to *March* with the fourteenth Year of that King's Reign.

The Times mentioned in this Letter do not refer to the Times when the Voyages were actually ſet out on, but when undertaken or reſolved on, as it is expressed in the Letter, *undertaken* by some industrious Navigators from *Boston*. Captain *James* did not sail until the Year one Thousand six Hundred and Thirty-one, not getting the King's Protection early enough in one Thousand six Hundred and Thirty, to proceed that Year, or in the fourth Year of the King's Reign. That is, he did not get it early enough in Spring to be ready by the latter End of *March*, as he must have been to proceed that Year; so the fourth Year of the King well agrees with this Proceeding. And *de Fonte* did not sail until one Thousand six Hundred and Forty, which was a Year after the Court of *Spain* had received Intelligence of such Undertaking from *Boston*. Which they would use the first Opportunity to transmit to *New Spain*; *de Fonte* therefore had at least six Months for the Equipment of the four Ships to go on this Expedition; a Time sufficient, in so fine a Climate, and every Thing that was necessary to be done was enforced by Orders of the Crown. Had this Equipment been executed in a much smaller Space of Time, there would have been nothing so admirable in it: Therefore the Objection, as to the Impossibility that Ships should be fitted between the Time the Court received this Information, and their sailing, drops to the Ground.

It is not any way strange that this Design, as it appears to have been, was made known to the Court of *Spain* the Year before that it was set out on; as that Court entertained a continual Jealousy of these Undertakings, as is apparent from their sending Vessels to intercept *Davis*; their having Informations as to Captain *James*'s Voyage also, and the Consequences of it, as may be collected from this Letter.

Major General *Gibbons*, if he had not the King's Protection, yet he had Friends at the Court of *England* who made Application for him to be Captain of the Fort at *Boston*, and one of the Council, the latter End of the Year one Thousand six Hundred and Thirty-eight, or in the Beginning of the Year one Thousand six Hundred and Thirty-nine. That the most secret Affairs of the Court were at that Time betrayed, I believe will be admitted, and the Secret of his designed Attempt might be known, by his applying for Leave of Absence from his Post during the Time that he should be engaged in this Undertaking. Or the Persons with whom he corresponded in *England* might be apprized of his intended Voyage, as he could not, at that Time of Day, be supplied with every Thing that was necessary thereto in *America*; and as he intended to trade, he would be for procuring his Goods from *England*. By some of these Means probably his Design perspired, and was secretly and unexpectedly, transmitted to the Court of *Spain*.

There are several Reasons to be assigned why both Viceroys should be informed, not only the Viceroy of *Peru*, in whose District the Ships were to be fitted, but the Viceroy of *New Spain* also. That if a Passage was made by any other Way than where the Ships were to be stationed to intercept the *Boston* Men, or they accidentally passed such Ships, the Viceroys might order a Look-out also to be kept. And such a Provision being made, it would be scarce possible, if a Passage was obtained, that the *Boston* People should get clear out of those Seas, and not fall into the Hands of the *Spaniards*. Another Reason is, that such Particulars as *de Fonte* was to put in for on the Coast of *Mexico* might be ready, that *de Fonte* might not meet with the least Delay, as such Delay might occasion the Disappointment of his Design.

The Letter proceeds, ' Upon which, I Admiral *de Fonte*, received ' Orders from *Spain* and the Viceroys to equip four Ships of Force.' These Words, *upon which*, I understand not to allude to the Advice given the Viceroys, but refer to the Attempt intended from *Boston*, and as to which he had received his Orders from *Spain*. But from the Viceroys he received Orders only as to the Equipment of the four Ships, as Orders of that Nature would regularly proceed from them. If it was otherwise, and he had also received his Orders from them, containing Instructions as to the Conduct of his Voyage, he would have made his Report to the Viceroys as to the Manner in which he had conducted his Voyage, and they would have reported it to the Court.

De Fonte mentioning the Viceroys so simply and plainly, without any respectful or distinguishing Additions, is an Instance that this Letter was wrote to the Court of *Spain*, it not being proper, in a Letter so addressed, to mention the Viceroys in any other Manner; and as it is also evident from the Expression, *I Admiral de Fonte*, that he did not write

this

this Letter in his private Capacity, but as an Admiral, therefore this Letter could not be otherwhere addressed than to such Court, to transmit an Account how he had executed these Orders, which he had received immediately from *Spain*.

De Fonte mentioning that the Advice which the Viceroys received was from the Court of *Spain*, and that the Orders he received were from *Spain*, carries a Distinction with it as though the Advice and the Orders were not transmitted from the same Persons. Those who transmitted the Advice to the Viceroys were not seemingly in the Secret, as to the particular Orders or Instructions which were sent to *de Fonte*, as to the Manner in which he was to conduct his Voyage. It was the Province of the Admiral of *Castile*, who was stiled Captain General of the Sea, who was subject to no Controul but the King's, to issue all Orders relative to maritime Affairs, and therefore *de Fonte*'s Orders might come from him. Or otherwise these Orders were immediately transmitted by the *Conde de Olivarez*, who was on ill Terms with the Admiral, and regarded no Forms, under the Sanction of the Favour he had with the King, whom he influenced to authorize all his Measures. It is also consistent with the Conduct of *Don Olivarez* that this Affair should be managed in this Manner, who was always mysterious, confided in his own Judgment, singular in his Manners, and therefore was called a Lover of Projects, and supposed a meer Visionary in some of them. He did not want for Persons of the greatest Abilities to assist him, and the Accuracy with which the Orders are composed that were sent to *de Fonte*, (as may be collected from the Manner in which the Voyage is conducted, and in which it cannot be supposed *de Fonte* was left to his Discretion) is an Instance there had been no Want of the Assistance of able, sagacious and experienced Persons in the composing of such Orders and Instructions.

The Design of this introductory Part is to shew the Proceedings in this Affair previous to his Voyage; that the Advice was received, and the Orders subsequent were obeyed; and it is drawn with peculiar Care and a Concisenesss which would be censured in a Voyage Writer, but is used with the greatest Propriety on this Occasion.

The Names of the Ships are agreeable to the Manner that the *Spaniards* name theirs; and by Ships of Force is not meant either their Caracks or Galeons, but Country Ships, which the Equipment seems to imply,

imply, made defensible against any Attacks of the Natives, and to have nothing to fear from the *Boston* Men, and these Ends could be obtained in Vessels which had no great Draught of Water, as the Rivers they were to pass up and the Lakes required, and of a Tonnage suitable to those Northern Seas, therefore *de Fonte* only expresses their Names, and their Commanders, says nothing of their Rates.

De Fonte, in his Course from the *Callao* of *Lima*, and in all his subsequent Courses through the Voyage, computes his Distance after the Marine Manner, from that Land from where he takes his Departure to the Land made when he enters a Harbour, or the Termination of the Land which makes such Harbour to Seaward; and here takes his Departure from the extreme Part of the *Callao* of *Lima*, which is in the Latitude 11° 5' S. Longitude 80° 39' W. and from which to *St. Helena*, being North of the Bay of *Guiaguil*, in Lat. 2° 5' S. Long. 84° 6' W. is two hundred Leagues; and there is no Fault in the Impression, as hath been supposed. Though these Words, *on the North Side of the Bay* of *Guiaguil* seem to be an Interpolation.

The Distance said to be run between the *Callao* of *Lima* and *St. Helena* is not reconcileable with the Accounts published by *Dampier*, *Wood Rogers*, or the Accounts in general, excepting with a Copy of a *Spanish* Manuscript, of the Latitudes and Longitudes of the most noted Places in the *South Seas*, corrected from the latest Observations, by *Manuel Monz. Prieto*, Professor of Arts in *Peru*, whose Computation of Longitude is from the Meridian of *Paris*; but he fixes *Lima* at full eighty Degrees. I use *Prieto*'s Tables in this, and principally in all my subsequent Computations, though *de Fonte* no where mentions the Longitude in this Letter, as he only regards the Difference of the Meridian of *Lima*. And it by no Means invalidates but favours the Authenticity of this Account, that *de Fonte* differs in his Computation from the *English* and *French* Accounts at, and after those Times, which also differ from each other, as they only ranged along the Coasts of those Seas, judged of their Distances according to their Journals, and must have made many vague Observations, as to the Latitude of Places, by Inspection of the Land from Sea, and which Land they might not certainly know. Their best Directions they got from Manuscript Journals,

or

or Sea Waggoners, composed for their own Use by Coasters. But the navigating of the King's Ships were better provided for in this respect; and we may well suppose that *de Fonte* was not, on this Occasion, deficient in Artists well versed in the Theory as well as the Practice of Navigation, and under this Character of an Artist we may consider *Parmentiers*. The Truth, as to the Latitude, once fixed is not variable by Time; and in this respect *de Fonte* and *Prieto* must agree, though a Century between the Time of their Computations.

The Expression, 'anchored in the Port of *St. Helena* (in *Spanish, Santa Elena*) *within the Cape*,' hath something more particular in it than appears on a transient View. The Point of *St. Helena* is thus described in the sailing Directions in the *Atlas Maritimus*, published in 1728. 'The Point itself is high, but as you come nearer in there is a lower Point runs out sharpening towards the Sea.' And there are two distinct Anchorages within this Port, one within the lower Point, here Vessels ride without Shelter, and amongst Banks and Shoals. Under the high Land, there is the other Anchorage, deep Water, and secure riding.' Under this high Land, being called the Port within the Cape, is a Distinction which I do not find made by the Voyage Writers, or in any other of the sailing Directions for these Parts that I have seen; and *de Fonte* particularly mentions, as it may be supposed, being in Conformity with his Instructions.

De Fonte taking in the *Betumen* must have been in pursuance of his Instructions, and there provided for him by Order of the Viceroy.

That which follows, called vulgarly Tar, &c. seems to be an Interpolation, or additional Comment, though not distinguished as such; and it may be observed here is a different Mode of Expression, and a Want of that Conciseness which apparently precedes. If with these Words took *a Quantity of Betumen*, we connect *on the 10th we passed the Equinoctial*, then that Conciseness and Simplicity of the Narration is preserved. It is inconsistent that *de Fonte* should inform the Court, that it was not for Want of Tar that he put into this Port, and that he did not procure this *Betumen* to use instead of Tar, but to make Use of it as Medicine. The taking the *Betumen* aboard sufficiently intimated his Compliance

with

with his Inftructions. The Expreffion, *we took it in for Medicine*, hath fomething particular in it, feems to be a Note or Memorandum added by fome Perfon who made the Voyage, to inftruct a Friend for whom he made, or to whom he gave, a Copy of this Letter.

The one Degree feven Minutes of Latitude is mifplaced, Cape *St. Francifco* being by no Geographers or Voyage Writers placed in that Latitude; the one Degree feven Minutes is the Latitude of the River *St. Jago*, and which *Prieto* lays down in one Degree eight Minutes.

As to the Courfes and Diftances eighty Leagues N.N.W. and twenty-five Leagues E. and by S. which were placed in the Margin in the firft Edition, but are fince crept into the Text. N.N.W. is a Courfe entirely contrary, and inftead of one there is two Courfes, North and North Eaft, and which two Courfes are confiftent with the E. and by S. Courfe twenty-five Leagues, as that Courfe will then terminate in the Latitude and Longitude of the River *Jago*. This Error of North Weft for North Eaft may be accounted for by remarking, that in the *Spanifh* Compafs North Eaft and North Weft are rendered *Nord Efte* and *Nord Oefte*: The Omiffion of the *O* in *efte* is a Fault which may be committed even by a careful Tranfcriber, or may be a Miftake in the Tranflator, for Want of due Attention to the Compafs.

In the Paffage from *St. Helena* he would keep the Coaft aboard, for the Benefit of a fair and frefh Wind, and which he would have without any Interruption from the Land Breezes, and by ftanding N.W. to clear the Iflands of *Solango* and *Paita*, and then ftand North Eafterly would form a North Courfe of one Hundred and Thirty-two Miles, or forty-four Leagues, and then be off Cape *Paffao*, in N. Lat. 8'. Long. 83° 59' W. and well in with fuch Cape, as it is evident he was from the Expreffion in the Letter by the Cape *del Paffao* with a North Eaft Courfe, thirty-fix Leagues, they would be in Lat. 1° 23' North, Long. 82° 50', and fo have paffed Cape *Francifco*, N. Lat. 50', Long. 82° 55', and with an Eaft and by South Courfe twenty-five Leagues, would be in the Lat. 1° 8', Long. 81° 36', the Latitude and Longitude of the River *St. Jago*.

There was not such a Provision Country, it appears from later Accounts, on any Part of the Coast between this and *Lima*; nor could the Ships be any where brought up with greater Safety: *St. Helena* is described as a poor and barren Part of the Country.

The Health of his People, liable to scorbutick Disorders in the northern Climates whither he was going, was an Object that must be attended to, in order that the Voyage should meet with the desired Success. Therefore after the *Betumen*, he recruits what he had consumed of his fresh Provision in his run from *Lima*, and lays in a great additional Store, as is apparent if we consider that their Consumption in this respect is not proportionable to ours, from their Mode of dressing it. And we may judge from having so great a Quantity of Fowl ready, with Goats and Hogs, the People had received Orders to be thus provided against the Ships Arrival; the Sailors would be a great Assistance in curing the Provisions, the Flesh as well as the Fish, and would do it in the most suitable Manner for the Sea Service; a Number of Hands, gave an Expedition so as the Provisions would not be spoiled by the Heat of the Sun; and his Victualling detained *de Fonte* four Days.

Six Miles and a half, or the Left Hand the River is navigable for small Vessels, and all that follows seems by Way of Comment, and to be a spurious Interpolation, as also, *which are there wild and in plenty*.

' The 16th of *April* we sailed from the River of *St. Jago* to the Port
' and Town *Raleo*, 320 Leagues W. N. W. a little westerly, in about
' 11 Decrees 14 Min. of N. Latitude, leaving Mount *St. Miguel*, &c.'

The Point of *Yeaxos*, or the *Sandy Strand*, in Lat. 11° 58', Long. 93° 31', which covers the Port of *Raleo* (or *Realejo*) is three Hundred and twenty Leagues from the River *St. Jago*; but the Course N. 47° 30' W. or N. W. almost a Quarter West, and by the Expression *a little* Westerly, the W. N. W. seems to mean, he steered first West from the River *St. Jago*, until he made the high Land, and then North-west, a little Westerly.

Between Mount *Miguel* and Point *Cazarnina* (rightly *Caravina*) is the Entrance in the Bay of *Amapalla*, which is to the Northward of the Port of *Realejo*; therefore the leaving Mount *St. Miguel* on the Larboard, &c. being an abfolute Contradiction to *de Fonte* entering the Port of *Realejo*, is an Interpolation and not inferted by the Perfon who wrote the Letter, but a Comment very injudiciouſly added by Way of Explanation. From this Circumſtance the Truth of my Aſſertion appears, as to there being Gloſſes and Comments added to the original Text, and that I had good Reafon to believe ſeveral Places in the preceding Part of this Account to be Interpolations added by Way of Comment.

The great Ships that are built in *New Spain* are built in *Raleo* is diſpoſed in the Margin in the firſt Edition; but in all the ſubſequent Editions hath crept into the Text. We may ſuppoſe the W. N. W. Courſe hath crept into the Text in the firſt Edition to make room for this Comment, as may be judged from the Courſe between *St. Helena* and *St. Jago* being placed in the Margin: And there is an apparent Reafon for the Courſe and Diſtances being ſo placed, for when inferted in the Text, they interrupt the Attention; and as the Courſes and Diſtances were all that was neceſſary to be mentioned, the Latitudes have been ſince added by ſome injudicious Perſon.—The Latitude of *Paſſao*, of Cape *St. Francifco*, is not mentioned, and the Latitude of *Raleo* is wrong, which the Courſe and Diſtance ſhews, and its Latitude is in moſt Maps agreeable to the Courſe and Diſtance here given. The Run, allowing *de Fonte* eight Days, would be but one hundred Miles in twenty-four Hours, which is very moderate going. Nor can there be any Objection, as to the Truth of this Account, from the Time that *de Fonte* is ſailing between the *Callao* of *Lima* to *St. Helena*, from *St. Helena* to *St. Jago*.

All that belongs to the original Letter I take to be this, The 16th of *April* we ſailed from the River *St. Jago* to the Port and Town of *Raleo*; here we bought (which probably might as well be rendered procured) four long well-ſailed Shallops, built expreſs for ſailing, riding at Anchor, &c. The 320 Leagues W. N. W. a little Weſterly, I ſuppoſe to have been placed in the Margin.

It

(43)

It cannot be suppofed that Boats fo fitted, and four of them, could be procured in fo fmall a Time as *de Fonte* ftaid here, it implies they were previoufly provided before that he arrived, to be ready at the Arrival of the Ships.

'The 26*th* we failed from *Raleo* for the Port of *Saragua,* or rather of
'*Salagua,* within the Iflands and Shoals of *Chamily,* 480 Leagues
' N. W. and by Weft, a little Wefterly from *Raleo.* From the Town
' of *Saragua,* a little Eaft of *Chamily* at *Saragua,* and from *Compoftilo* in
' the Neighbourhood of this Port, we took in a Mafter and fix Mari-
' ners accuftomed to trade with the Natives for Pearl the Natives
' catched on a Bank in 19 Degrees of Latitude North from the *Baxos*
' of *St. Juan* in 24 Degrees of North Latitude, 20 Leagues N. N. E.
' from Cape *Saint Lucas,* the South-eaft Point of *California.*'

The Point of *Yeaxos* is laid down in Lat. 11 Deg. 58 Min. Long. 93 Deg. 31 Min. and with a Courfe North-weft and by Weft, a little Wefterly, Diftance four Hundred and eighty Leagues, *de Fonte* would be at the Iflands of *Chiametlas,* in Lat. 22 Deg. 10 Min. Long. 114 Deg. 29 Min.

The Port of *Saragua,* or rather of *Salagua* (which is properly *Zuelagua*) is thus defcribed. ' The Mount of *Sant Jago* is in the Port of
' *Zuelagua.* There are two very good Harbours which have good an-
' choring Ground, and will hold a great many Ships, by reafon they are
' great and are called the *Calletas.* On the North-weft Side of the faid
' Bay is another very good Port, which is called likewife the Port of
' *Zuelagua.* You will find in it a River of frefh Water, and feveral Plan-
' tations. At the Sea Side is a Pathway that leads to the Town of *Zue-*
' *lagua,* being four and a half Miles from the Port within Land. Be-
' tween the Port of *Zuelagua* and the white Ferrelon (or Rock) is a very
' good Port, in which you are Land-locked from all Winds.'

From this Defcription it is eafy to comprehend what is *de Fonte*'s Meaning as to the Port of *Zuelagua,* where he took in his Mafter and Mariners on the North-weft Side of the Bay, and which he expreffes by, at *Saragua* a little Eaft of *Chamily*; and which Mafter and Mariners were not promiscuously taken, but were chosen Men, as they were taken both from *Zuelagua* and *Compostilo*, in the Neighbourhood of the Port. *Zuelagua* seems originally the City which was called *Xalifco*; but from its unhealthy Situation, *Compostilo* was built more within Land; yet the former continuing to be a Port, some Inhabitants remained there.

The Islands and Shoals of *Chiametla*, which the Translation renders *Chamily*, which is a Name given to Islands South of Cape *Corientes*. But the Distinction is the Islands to Northward of Cape *Corientes* are called *Chiametla*, those to Southward *Chametla* and *Camilli*. *Prieto* agrees with *de Fonte*'s first mentioning the Islands of *Chiametlas* in Lat. 22. 10. Long. 114. 29. and then *El mal Pays y mal outradu*.

This Master and Mariners were accustomed to trade with the Natives for Pearl, which the Natives catched on a Bank in nineteen Degrees of Latitude, being North from the *Baxos of St. Juan*, or the Bank of *St. John*, which is in twenty-four Degrees of North Latitude, and twenty Leagues North North-east from Cape *Saint Lucas*, the South-east Point of *California*; and this Account *de Fonte* had either from themselves, or the Character that was sent with them, to shew the most proper Persons had been provided to answer the Purpose for which they were procured. And all that belongs to the Text is, which the Natives catched on a Bank North from the *Baxos St. Juan*, twenty Leagues N. N. E. from Cape *St. Lucas*.

' The Master Admiral *de Fonte* had hired, with his Vessel and Mari-
' ners, who had informed the Admiral that, 200 Leagues North from
' Cape *St. Lucas*, a Flood from the North met the South Flood, and
' that he was sure it must be an Island, and *Don Diego Penneloffa* un-
' dertook to discover whether it was an Island or not, with his Ship and
' the four Shallops they bought at *Raleo*, and the Master and Mariners
' they hired at *Zuelagua*.'

Here the Thread of the Letter is broke, and the Translator proceeds as with a common Narrative of a Voyage. The Master might be easily deceived as to the Tide, as Time hath shewn in many Instances as to other Persons having been deceived in like Manner in other Parts.

That

That we have no Account of what was the Event of this Expedition *Penneloſſa*, who had undertaken the Charge, being no more to join *de Fonte*, as it was unneceſſary and to no Purpoſe, *Penneloſſa* would return firſt and ſend his Account to Court. *De Fonte* could in this Caſe do no further than ſhew he had ſent him on this Service, it muſt be ſuppoſed, agreeable to his Inſtructions. Which, from the Boats brought from *Realejo*, (and muſt be of a particular Conſtructure, the like of which were not to be any where elſe on the Coaſt) and the Maſter and Mariners hired here, it is evident, was before propoſed, that *Penneloſſa* ſhould go on this Part of the Expedition, not on the Maſter's declaring that there was a Tide from the Northward, and ſo *California* an Iſland. This was only mentioned by *de Fonte*, to ſhew what Intelligence he had got in this Affair.

The Account given of *Penneloſſa* could be evidently no Part of the Letter. What is ſaid as to his Deſcent, his being a Nobleman, his Addreſs to Coſmography, and the Undertaking of this Diſcovery, muſt evidence as already ſaid, whoever inſerted the Account was ſatisfied as to their being ſuch a Perſon ſo accompliſhed, and who aſpired to undertake this Part of the Expedition. A Diſcovery of theſe Parts would carry, at this Time particularly, great Reputation and Honour with it, and by this Opportunity to intercept Perſons on a Deſign ſo prejudicial to the Intereſts of the Court of *Spain* in thoſe Parts, as it was then thought, had *Penneloſſa* ſucceeded; he would have had no ſmall Share of Merit; or if he did not ſucceed, the Merit of the Attempt would be accounted of, and not unjuſtly, it would be a Means of his Promotion through the Connections he had, as they would urge he did not purſue thoſe Sciences for Speculation only, but to carry them into Practice for the Service of his Country. And according to the Regulations Don *Olivarez* had made, there was no Preferment but what was in conſequence of Service.

Siſter's Son of *Don Lewis de Haro*, and a young Nobleman, expreſſes as of the Time preſent, when the Copy was taken from which we have the Publication; and *Don Haro, Prime Miniſter of Spain*, was a Gloſs added by another Hand. Neither is *Don Luis de Haro* the Perſon here meant, for he does not ſeem to have been of an Age to have had a Siſter who could be Mother to *Don Ronquillo*; but *Don Lopez de Haro*

is

is the Perfon meant, *Marquis de Carpio*, the Father of *Don Luis*, who was at that Time Gentleman of the Chamber to the King, and afterwards Prime Minifter, and muft be underftood the Son of his Wife's Sifter, who was a Daughter of *Olivarez*, married to the *Marquis de Valderiabano*.

' But Admiral *de Fonte*, with the other three Ships, failed from them within the Iflands of *Chamilly* the 10th *May* 1640, and having the Length of Cape *Abel* on the W. S. W. Side of *California*, in 26 Degrees of N. Latitude, 160 Leagues N. W. and W. from the Ifles *Chamilly*; the Wind fprung up at S. S. E. a fteady Gale, that from the 26th of *May* to the 14th of *June* he had failed to the River *Los Reyes*, in 53 Degrees of North Latitude, not having Occafion to lower a Topfail, in failing 866 Leagues N. N. W. 410 Leagues from Port *Abel* to Cape *Blanco*, 456 Leagues to *Riolos Reyes*, all the Time moft pleafant Weather, and failed about 260 Leagues in crooked Channels, amongft Iflands named the *Archipelagus de St. Lazarus*; where his Ships Boats always failed a Mile a-head, founding to fee what Water, Rocks, and Sands, there was.'

De Fonte and *Penneloffa* both put out to Sea together; but as their Courfes were various, one to the Weftward of *California*, and the other to enter the Gulf. They parted within the Shoals of *Chiametla* the tenth of *May* 1640; and *de Fonte* attaining the Length of Cape *Abel* in Latitude 26, one Hundred and fixty Leagues North North-weft and Weft from the Ifles of *Chiametla*, he then meets with a fair Wind from South South-eaft. By the Latitude of Cape *Abel*, and the Diftance run, it is apparent that the Iflands *Chiametla* mentioned, are the Iflands here meant.

De Fonte, after running one Hundred and fixty Leagues from the Ifles of *Chiametla*, in Lat. 22 Deg. 10 Min. and Long. 114 Deg. 29 Min. attaining the Length of Cape *Abel* in Latitude 26, his Courfe could not be North-weft and Weft, but North-weft by Weft wefterly, or 61° 22′. and, inftead of, *by*, may be fuppofed an Error of the Prefs.

Dr. *Heylin* mentions a convenient Haven named *St. Abad*, who wrote near thefe Times. But it is *Chriftabel*, or *Chrifteval*, the Name of a Cape

Cape the Extremity of the Land, which forms a Harbour or Port of the same Name *Chriſtabel*. *Prieto* mentions no Place on the main Land but the three Iſlands of *Caſonas*, which lie off at Sea, ſo more to Weſtward than this Cape. They are in Lat. 26 Deg. Long. 122 Deg. 24 Min. the Longitude of Cape *Abel* I make in 122 Deg. 11 Min. and he lays down the Point of *Madelena* in 26 Deg. 30 Min. and the Long. 123 Deg. 24 Min. which ſeems to be the northermoſt Land of ſuch Harbour. By *de Fonte* mentioning the Latitude of this Cape, and not any other, he may be ſuppoſed to take from hence a new Departure, as was uſual with the *Spaniards* when they came to this Length in theſe Seas, ſo *Prieto* mentions *Las Bajas de los Abraja*, *Primier Meridiano*. Lat. 25°, 15'. Long. 121 Deg. 54 Min. from *Lima*.

De Fonte in his Run from *Chiametla* met with contrary Winds; but when the Length of Cape *Abel*, he had Wind and Weather rather unexpected in thoſe Parts; and the Spring not being much advanced, he rather expected to have been, at Times, under his Courſes, which is meant by the Expreſſion afterwards uſed, that he never had occaſion to lower a Topſail, and is conformable with its being a ſteady Gale, or did not overblow. As the Run to *Los Reys* terminated the fourteenth of *June*, *de Fonte*, for the whole eight Hundred and ſixty Leagues, ſailed after the Rate of forty-five Leagues in twenty-four Hours, which is conſiſtent with and agreeable to the Seamens common Experience, when favoured with ſuch Wind and Weather. Amongſt the Iſlands would have the Aſſiſtance of the Floods, and Wind enough to ſtem the Ebbs.

The Computation of the eight Hundred and ſixty-ſix Leagues is four Hundred and ten Leagues to Cape *Blanquial*, to which there is a Courſe aſſigned North North-weſt; and as to four Hundred and fifty-ſix Leagues to *Rio los Reys*, no Courſes are added, which we may aſſign to the Courſes being originally in the Margin, when one was introduced into the Copy the other was neglected. And we have juſt Reaſon to ſuſpect the Careleſſneſs here, as it is firſt called *Cape Abel*, then *Port Abel*, and the River *Los Reys* in 53 Degrees, and afterwards *Rio los Reys*, as tho' they were diſtinct and ſeparate. With the N. N. W. Courſe *Rio los Reys* could not be in the Latitude *de Fonte* mentions.

Port Abel, Latitude 26, Long. 122° 11', and the *Callao* of *Lima*, being laid down Longitude 60 Weſt from the firſt Meridian of *Fero*, and hitherto we have carried on our Computation of Longitude 80 from *Paris*, we ſhall hereafter compute from *Fero* and *London*; and Cape *Chriſtable* we compute 102° 11' from the Meridian of *Fero*, or 119° 46' from the Meridian of *London*.

The Courſe four Hundred and ten Leagues North North-weſt, *de Fonte* made Cape *Blanquial* in Latitude 45, Longitude from *London* 129° 28', from the Meridian of *Fero* 111° 53', to Northward and Weſtward of the Entrance of *Martin Aquilar*. Sufficient Obſervations have not been made to determine by the Geographers as to the true Latitudes and Longitudes of theſe Places, and, until they attain more perfect Informations, muſt diſagree.

The Courſe from *Blanquial* is not inſerted, but is to be determined by the Diſtance two Hundred and ſixty Leagues, ending in Latitude 53 at *Rio los Reys*. *De Fonte* had, during the whole Time between *Abel* and *Los Reys*, the Wind in his Favour. Therefore his Courſe muſt have been to the Northward of the Eaſt; and if he run two Hundred and ſixty Leagues, with a Courſe Eaſt 52° North, he would make 2 Deg. 1 Min. Latitude, and 20 Deg. 24 Min. Longitude. To correſpond with which *de Fonte* muſt, for the one Hundred and ninety-ſix Leagues, made his Courſe North 52 Deg. Weſt, which would determine in Latitude 50 Deg. 59 Min. and in Long. 141 Deg. 12 Min. from *London*, in 123 Deg. 27 Min. Weſt from *Fero*. *De Fonte* would then be about thirty Leagues from the Land, agreeable to the *Ruſſian* Diſcoveries, tho' this Voyage was made ſo many Years before that Attempt; a great Evidence of the Authenticity of this Account. His Conduct alſo in this Caſe was neceſſary, conſiſtent with the Character of a good Seaman, not to make the Coaſt direct, or immediately engage with this *Archipelago*, to which he was a Stranger, and in Parts unknown, or where he had no ſailing Directions but to form ſuch Courſe as gradually to fall in with the Land, and, as the Wind was, if he ſaw Occaſion, could at any Time ſtand off.

De Fonte by this Courſe, agreeable to the Latitude of the *Sueſta del Eſtrech D'Anian*, which is laid down by *Prieto* in Latitude 51, would be

to

(49)

to the Southern Part of the Entrance into such *Archipelago*, had he been Northward, as the Wind was, he would have regained it with great Difficulty and Loss of Time.

As this Table of *Prieto* was composed before the *Russian* Discoveries, and this Land, the *Suesta del Estrech D'Anian*, is computed in Longitude 141 Deg. 47 Min. computing *Lima* at 80 Deg. answerable to 238 Deg. 13 Min. East Longitude from *Fero*, it is a little singular that these Accounts should agree so well, as to the Longitude of this Part of *America*; is an Instance that *Prieto* did not proceed upon vague Calculations; had acquired a more exact Account than could be even supposed in these unfrequented Parts, and from his Care and Exactness, as to the more known Parts, we have no Reason to doubt but he hath laid down the Latitude and Longitude of the *Suesta del Estrech de Anian*, with the greatest Certainty that he could attain to.

I shall not controvert it whether these are the proper Streights of *Anian*. This Entrance was commonly called amongst the Navigators into those Parts by that Name, as is evident from former Accounts; and *Hornius*, from his Maps, which may be seen in *Purchase*, lays it down in the same Manner. My Intention is answered in producing an Authority from the *Spaniards* of *New Spain*, that there is an Entrance here agreeable to the Account in this Letter; also, in all Appearance, a superior Entrance to that of *Martin Aguilar*, which *Prieto* doth not expresly mention; neither could he properly; but inserts Cape *Escondido* in Lat. 43, and Cape *Blanquial* in Lat. 45, an intermediate Distance of one Hundred and twenty Miles. Again mentions the Port of *Salagua* in Lat. 46, and then the Port of *Salado* in Lat. 48; in which Interspace the Entrance of *de Fuca* is supposed to be.

By the Name *Archipelago*, *de Fonte*, who would give the Name with Propriety, expresses it to be a Sea; and on his Return says, he sailed down the River *Los Reys* to the North-east *Part* of the *South Sea*; after that returned home. Where the Word *Part*, properly speaking, or to use the Word as it really imports, can be no otherwise understood than as an Arm or Branch of the *South Sea*. Had he steered eight Hundred and sixty-six Leagues North North-west, he must necessarily have tra-

H   versed

versed the Courses of those brave Discoverers Capt. *Beering* and *Tschirikow*, which were from Lat. 45 in *Asia*, to Lat. 56 and 58 in *America*, and who were not interrupted by any such Islands. Capt. *Tschirikow* positively says, the Coast was without Islands where he was in Lat. 56; by Capt. *Beering*'s Account in Lat. 58, the Islands lay only *along* the Coast; and *de Fonte* in his Account mentions, that he sailed in crooked Channels, amongst Islands. These various Descriptions shew that these Accounts relate to various Parts. As *de Fonte* could not, in the whole Extent between *Asia* and *America*, meet with such Islands, and yet was under a Necessity to pass up crooked Channels, with no small Hazard, as the Boats being a-head express, his Course must have been to the Eastward of where Captain *Tschirikow* fell in with the Land, and for the Distance of the two Hundred and thirty Leagues before *de Fonte* came to a River, to *Los Reyes*, was then passing up the North-east Part of the *South Sea*, as he terms it, and in some Part of which there were Islands, which he names the *Archipelagus of St. Lazarus*. There is a Singularity of Expression in the Letter, *where* his Boats always sailed a-head, the Word *where* limits the Islands to a certain Space, and that they were not extended the whole two Hundred and thirty Leagues, which is consistent with the Expedition he made, as otherwise the Ships must have often shortened sail, and it could not be avoided, and must have frequently brought up at Night.

As *de Fonte* did neither make the South or North Shore of this Streight, the most comprehensive Way of expressing himself was to say, he passed up these Islands, by which those who had composed his Instructions well knew the Parts he meant. It must be considered *de Fonte* was not as to this Part on Discovery, the Whole would be pointed out to him by his Instructions, which being to fall in with the Islands, or Entrance in such a Latitude, to mention either the North or South Limit of the Entrance would be improper; whereas the contrary was the Case as to Cape *St. Helena*, *Francisco*, *Passao*, and Cape *Abel*, as his Instructions were express, as to the making these Lands.

As *de Fonte* made a true Course East 81° North, subtract the Longitude 20 Deg. 24 Min. from the Longitude 141 Deg. 12 Min. from *London*, and from the 123 Deg. 27 Min. from *Fero*. The Entrance to the

4   River

River *Los Reys* lies in Lat. 53 Deg. Long. 120 Deg. 48 Min. from *London*, and 103 Deg. 3 Min. Weſt from *Fero*. And that his Courſe was now Eaſterly is plain from the ſubſequent Words of the Letter, *as they ſailed more Eaſterly*. It was alſo conſiſtent with the Purpoſe they were ſent on, to meet a Veſſel from *Boſton*.

' The 22d of *June* Admiral *de Fonte* diſpatched one of his Captains
' to *Pedro de Barnarda*, to ſail up a fair River, a gentle Stream, and
' deep Water, went firſt N. and N. E. N. and N. W. into a large Lake
' full of Iſlands, and one very large *Peninſula* full of Inhabitants, a
' friendly honeſt People in this Lake, he named Lake *Valaſco*, where
' Captain *Barnarda* left his Ship; nor all up the River was leſs than
' 4, 5, 6, 7, and 8 Fathom Water, both the Rivers and Lakes abound-
' ing with Salmon Trouts, and very large white Perch, ſome of two
' Foot long; and with three large *Indian* Boats, by them called *Periagos*,
' made of two large Trees 50 or 60 Foot long. Capt. *Barnarda* firſt
' ſailed from his Ships in the Lake *Valaſco*, one Hundred and forty
' Leagues Weſt, and then 436 E. N. E. to 77 Degrees of Latitude.
' Admiral *de Fonte*, after he had diſpatched Capt. *Barnarda* on the Dis-
' covery of the North and Eaſt Part of the *Tartarian Sea*.'

We may ſuppoſe, from the Manner in which this Part was managed, that there was a great Neceſſity to get the Tranſlation finiſhed in any Manner. As the Difficulties of the Tranſlation increaſed, the Deſign of this Account being only Amuſement, the Tranſlator thought it would anſwer the Purpoſe to give the Account in groſs.

The Date, the 22d *June*, is an apparent Error, by reaſon *de Fonte* did not enter into Lake *Belle*, as will be ſhewn hereafter, until that Time.

Admiral *de Fonte* diſpatched one of his Captains to *Pedro de Barnarda*, to ſail up a fair River, gentle Stream, and deep Water. Then the Tranſlation breaks off abruptly, and the Tranſlator renders the following Part as an Account of *Bernarda*'s Voyage, not obſerving how juſt a Connection there is with *de Fonte* diſpatching one of his Captains to *Bernarda*; and what follows being the Orders ſent by him, and the Inſtructions for *Bernarda*; inſtead of being *Bernarda*'s Account of his Ex-pedition, and not obſerving how conſiſtent it is with being a ſummary Recital of thoſe Inſtructions theſe Words are which follow, Admiral *de Fonte*, after he had diſpatched Captain *Bernarda* on the Diſcovery, &c.

As to his diſpatching one of his Captains, he muſt be ſuppoſed to have beſides the Captain of the Ship he was in, alſo one called an Admiral's Captain. The Inſtructions were of ſuch Conſequence, that a leſs Perſon might not be ſo properly employed, nor conſiſtent with the Reſpect due to *Bernarda*.

De Fonte and *Bernarda* were Strangers here; but theſe Parts had been already diſcovered, as it is expreſly ſaid that *two Pater Jeſuits* had been here two Years, and made Obſervations as far as the Latitude 66. From their Diſcoveries we may conclude, that theſe Inſtructions were formed which *Bernarda* received, and thoſe of the whole Courſe of the Voyage; and it was neceſſary that *de Fonte* ſhould not only mention that he had diſpatched *Bernarda*, but ſhould alſo, with the Brevity due to a Letter, mention the Orders with which he diſpatched him. And further from what is expreſſed in thoſe Orders, as to the River, the Courſe and Soundings, what Fiſh were in the River and Lake, the Road or Harbour which was to be found in the Lake, the Temper and Diſpoſition of the Inhabitants, it evidently appears that there had been a prior Diſcovery of theſe Parts, and Obſervations made of every Thing worthy of Conſideration, and neceſſary alſo at this Time to be mentioned to *Bernarda*. To let him know that his Ship could paſs up the River, would find a Harbour in the Lake, he had nothing to fear from the Natives, and would meet with Proviſions. There leaving his Ship he might be furniſhed with *Periagos* to proceed. And I underſtand his Directions to ſteer firſt North and North-eaſt, then North and North-weſt, that he might make no Miſtake by purſuing or entering into any other Openings which might preſent themſelves in his Courſe up, and which from their Appearance might perplex him, as to which of them he was to enter; no uncommon Thing, as thoſe who have been to Northward on like Undertakings will allow.

' The

' The Admiral failed up a very navigable River, which he named
' *Rio los Reys*, that run nearest N. E. but on several Points of the Com-
' pass 60 Leagues, at low Water, in a fair navigable Channel, not less
' than 4 or 5 Fathom Water. It flowed on both Rivers near the same
' Water, in the River *Los Reys*, 24 Feet Full and Change of the Moon;
' a S. S. E. Moon made high Water. It flowed in the River *Haro*, 22
' Feet and a half Full and Change. They had two Jesuits with them,
' that had been on their Mission to 66 Degrees of North Latitude, and
' had made curious Observations.'

De Fonte, having dispatched *Bernarda*, sets out on his Part of the Expedition, and proceeds up the River *Los Reys*, at the Entrance of which he had arrived the fourteenth of *June*. During his Stay, until *Bernarda* was dispatched and sailed, he seems to have taken an accurate Account of the Tides in both Rivers. The Distance up the River was more than sixty Leagues, and though a good navigable Channel, yet would require a great Precaution in his Proceeding with the two Ships; Tide Times and the Night would make it necessary for him to bring too; for had he touched the Ground with either of them, the Delay that might have followed on such Accident, might have defeated this Part of the Undertaking, and the most important, and which, therefore, was allotted to him to execute.

Their having had two Jesuits with them seems an additional Note. That two Jesuits should be sent into those Parts to make Observations, is but consistent with the general Practice of the Jesuits to go on Missions into all Parts of the Globe, engaged by a special Vow, not injoined any other Order, to be always ready to go and preach whithersoever they shall be sent.

These Jesuits are by no Means a singular Instance of the People of that Order being great Adventurers, when we consider those who ventured to the *Philippinas* and *Japan*, enforced by the Vow, puffed up with the Vanity of popular Applause, the Favour of the President, and the Hope of being acceptable to the rest of the Order on their return from such Mission, expecting by such Mission to add to the Wealth or Reputation of the Order. The Effect of this Mission seems to have been they had acquired

quired the Favour of the Natives. Had made some Observations of the Country, but principally to Northward, as to which they seem not to have got a perfect Account; though they did a great deal for the Time, the Unseasonableness of the Winter, and the melting Weather in the Spring considered; nor is it strange they should not get a perfect Account, in a Country so intermixed with Waters, which hide themselves in their Courses between inaccessible Mountains; and in many Places where they are to be come at, are deceitful in their Appearance, as to what they really are, whether Lakes, Gulphs of the Sea, or Inlets. As they proceeded to the Northward, they thought it the Part that principally claimed their Observation. Were of Opinion as to the Southward, that it was Part of the Continent of *New Spain*, or they would not have lead *de Fonte* to *Los Reys*, but caused him to proceed up that Streight which separated the Part they had been in from *New Spain*. As to this Mission not being known to the Publick, these Jesuits must have been sent from *Europe* into *New Spain*; and they would so far regard their Obedience to the Pope, as to pay due Respect to the King of *Spain*'s Authority, in observing the established Maxim of the Time, as to keep their Discoveries a Secret from the Publick or other Nations. And as to all Missionaries who went into *New Spain*, the King of *Spain* hath a Power to call them to Account, by the Pope's Permission, though not permitted in *Old Spain* to meddle with ecclesiastical Affairs, or ecclesiastical Men.

' A Letter from Captain *Barnarda*, dated the 27th of *June* 1740, that
' he had left his Ship in the Lake *Valasco*, betwixt the Islands *Barnarda*
' and the Peninsula *Conihasset*, a very safe Port; it went down the River
' from the Lake 3 Falls, 80 Leagues, and fell into the *Tartarian* Sea
' in 61 Deg. with the Pater Jesuits, and 36 Natives, in three of their
' Boats, and 20 of his *Spanish* Seamen; that the Land trended away
' North East; that they should want no Provision, the Country abound-
' ing with Venison of three Sorts, and the Sea and Rivers with excel-
' lent Fish (Bread, Salt, Oil, and Brandy they carried with them) that
' he should do what was possible. The Admiral, when he received the
' Letter from Captain *Barnarda*, was arrived at an *Indian* Town called
' *Conosset*, on the South Side Lake *Belle*, where the two Pater Jesuits on
' their Mission had been two Years; a pleasant Place. The Admiral,
' with his two Ships, enter'd the Lake the 22d of *June*.'

The

The Letter from *Bernarda* being dated the 27th of *June*, it is impoſſible he ſhould finiſh all that Buſineſs in four Days, which he gives *de Fonte* an Account of: This alſo confirms its being a Miſtake as to the 22d of *June*, being the Time he received his Diſpatches. It might well take *Bernarda* from the fourteenth of *June* to the twenty-ſeventh to receive his Diſpatches, to paſs up the River, and to the Peninſula in Lake *Valaſco*, procure the Natives, who were not under his Command, get all Things fitted, and ſet out. And what this Letter contains, makes it evident it could be no Account of his Voyage that was before-mentioned.

This Letter is apparently an Anſwer to the Diſpatches *Bernards* received from *de Fonte*. He mentions, that he had left his Ship, agreeable to Orders, and in a ſafe Port; gives an Account how he was equipped to proceed; the Number of the Perſons he had with him; that he had thirty-ſix of the Natives, which is conformable to the Character given of them, a friendly honeſt People, and ſhews the Influence of the Jeſuits. Theſe Natives, by joining in the Expedition, were Hoſtages for the good Behaviour of the others towards his People left behind, and an Aſſurance to *Bernarda* for the Security of his Ship left at the Port, were of great Uſe as Pilots as to the Coaſt, and alſo in ſailing and managing their *Periagos*. Their having theſe *Periagos* implies they had a Country abounding with Waters; and it was their uſual Way of paſſing from one Part to another, Time and Experience had made them expert in the Management of them; and by ſhifting from one Part to the other as the Seaſons required for hunting or fiſhing, and by Excurſions out of their own Country either for War or Curioſity, as is the Nature of *Indians*, they were become acquainted not only with the inland Waters, but alſo the Sea Coaſts.

De Fonte had ordered Captain *Bernarda* that he ſhould ſail one Hundred and fifty Leagues Weſt (but is rather to be believed a Miſtake from not underſtanding the Compaſs, *Oeſte* and *Eſte* being ſo ſimilar) and then four Hundred and thirty-ſix Leagues Eaſt North Eaſt to 77 Degrees of Latitude. In Anſwer to which *Bernarda* here mentions, that from the Lake *Valaſco* there was a River in which there was three Falls, eighty Leagues in Diſtance, and fell into the *Tertarian Sea*, in Latitude

61; that the Land trended away North East, and that he would do what was possible. By which Expression it is plain, that he did not pursue the exact Course that *de Fonte* directed; probably that Course was pointed out to *Bernarda* by which the Jesuits had travelled to Latitude 66, but pursued a Course more immediate and direct to attain to Latitude 77, the Back of *Baffin*'s Bay, as to which the Natives had informed him; and that though he did not pursue the Course directed by *de Fonte*, which he found not to be so consistent with the Design he was sent on, yet he would do all that was possible to answer that Design. And the Expression also implies, that he was sensible he should meet with Difficulties, which he might expect from the Climate, the Ice, and the Fatigue; but as to the Article of Provisions, was in no Fear on that Account. As to what is mentioned as to Venison of three Sorts, they were the small Deer, the Moose, and the Elk, all which are in the Northern Parts about *Hudson*'s Bay, and the *Labarador* Coast.

The Name of *Haro* given to the River is a particular Compliment to *Don Haro*, who was the Head of the Houses of *Valasco*; and the Name of *Valasco*, in Compliment to the other Houses, of that Family. Which Respect shewn by *de Fonte* seems to indicate a particular Connection with, or his being related to that Family, as already mentioned. *Valasco*, as here wrote, with a *va*, as those Families did write it at that Time, and one of that Family, who was Constable of *Castile*, in his Titles is named *John Ferdinandes de Vallasco*, Constable of *Castilia*, &c. now Lord of the Houses of *Vallasco*, &c. and by the Orthography in the Letter being so conformable with that which was used at that Time, and not with a *ve* as at present, we have very good Reason to suppose, that the Letter was not only wrote in *Spanish*, but also by *de Fonte* on his return from his Voyage. Don *Ferdinandez* was living in 1610, and succeeded by his Son, in his Title and Honour of Constable of *Castile*, Don *Bernardino*, who was living at the Time of the Voyage.

' The Admiral entered the Lake an Hour before high Water, and
' there was no Fall or Cataract, and 4 and 5 Fathom Water, and 6 and
' 7 Fathom Water generally in the Lake *Belle*. There is a little Fall
' of Water half Flood, and an Hour and Quarter before high Water
' the Flood begins to set gently into Lake *Belle*: The River is fresh at

' 20 Leagues Diſtance from the Mouth or Entrance of the River *Los*
' *Reyes*. The River and Lake abounds with Salmon, Salmon Trouts,
' Pikes, Perch and Mullets, and two other Sorts of Fiſh peculiar to
' that River, admirable good; and Lake *Belle* alſo abounds with all
' thoſe Sorts of Fiſh large and delicate: And Admiral *de Fonte* alſo ſays,
' the Mullets catched in *Rios Reyes* and Lake *Belle*, are much delicater
' than are to be found, he believes, in any Part of the World.'

De Fonte was not inactive from the 14th to the 22d of *June*. Various
Courſes, contrary Winds, waiting for the Tides at times; from the Circumſtance of the Tide as to Lake *Belle*, that there is a Fall until half
Flood, and it is an Hour and Quarter only before high Water that
the Flood makes in, evidences that there was a Current againſt him;
and it is further evident, as on his return he was but two Days running
from *Conoſſet* to the Entrance of the River *Los Reyes*.

De Fonte is very particular in his Account, being now to take a Survey of the Parts through which a Paſſage was expected, and in which
Parts he now was. He mentions the Trial of the Tides at *Los Reyes* and
Haro; gives a particular Account of the Navigation up *Los Reyes*, and
to Lake *Belle*; that it was freſh Water after they were ſixty Miles up the
River; and what is no immaterial Circumſtance in this Affair, ſhews
how far the Waters from Weſtward flowed up, which he inſtances in the
Account of the Fiſh. That ſuch as came out of the Sea into the Land
or freſh Waters to ſpawn at thoſe Seaſons, and afterwards return to the
Sea, went no further than Lake *Belle*; for here he found the Mother
Fiſh, as he deſcribes them, large and delicate, ſuperior to thoſe in the
River, and indulges his Fancy, ſo delicate as, he believes, they are not
to be exceeded in any other Part of the World. *De Fonte*, in his Orders
to *Bernarda*, ſhewed it was freſh Water in Part of *Haro*, and in the Lake
Conibaſſet, from the Salmon and Perch, in which he means Sea Perch,
which come into freſh Waters at this Seaſon of the Year.

' The firſt of *July* 1640, Admiral *de Fonte* ſailed from the reſt of his
' Ships in the Lake *Belle*, in a good Port, covered by a fine Iſland, be-
' fore the Town of *Conoſſet*, from thence to a River I named *Parmen-*
'   *tiers*,

' *tiers*, in Honour of my induſtrious judicious Comrade Mr. *Parmentiers*,
' who had moſt exactly marked every Thing in and about that River.'

We now proceed to conſider the Remainder of Admiral *de Fonte's* Letter, which was publiſhed in *June* 1708.

Admiral *de Fonte*, when he received the Letter from Capt. *Bernarda*, was arrived at an *Indian* Town called *Conoſſet*, in the Lake *Belle* ; and as he entered ſuch Lake the twenty-ſecond, probably arrived at the Town the ſame Day ; ſtaid eight Days, and then ſailed the firſt of *July*. That *Bernarda* ſhould write, as to the Situation of his Affairs, muſt have been before concerted between them, they having been informed by the Jeſuits or *Parmentiers*, that it was practicable for *Bernarda* to ſend ſuch Meſſage, that the Admiral might know whether *Bernarda* had met with any Accident as to his Ship, or any other Obſtacle to his Proceeding, as he might aſſiſt him from thoſe Ships Companies then with the Admiral. How the Letter was conveyed is not expreſſed ; probably by a Seaman with an *Indian* Guide (the Diſtance between the Admiral and *Bernarda*, at this Time, will be conſidered hereafter) who would uſe all poſſible Expedition both by Land and Water : Had the Advantage of very ſhort Nights. *De Fonte* would not proceed until he received this Account, though ready as ſoon as he received it. As *de Fonte* ſailed on the firſt of *July*, that Account muſt have come to his Hand the thirtieth of *June*.

The Ships being ſecure in a good Harbour, and the Command left with *Ronquillo*, the Admiral proceeds to the River *Parmentiers*, ſo named in Honour of Monſ. *Parmentiers*, whom he ſtiles his Comrade, and commends his Induſtry and Judgment in the Survey of ſuch River, and the Parts adjacent. From his being ſtiled his Comrade, he was in no Command, as he could not have a Commiſſion without having been bred in the Service, and a Native of *Spain*. Therefore being a Perſon immediately neceſſary for to have on this Occaſion, he is introduced under the Character of a Friend and Companion. Mr. *Gage* mentions, Chap. xv. of his new Survey of the *Weſt Indies*, one *Thomas Rocalono*, a *Frenchman*, a Prior of the Cloiſter of *Cemitlan*, who, with himſelf, was the only Stranger in that Country, by which he means in that Part where he was;

and it implies there being others in other Parts, which falsifies the Assertion that no *Frenchman* was ever admitted in *Peru*.

The Countries of *Quivira* and *Anian* were represented, at that Time, to be barren or desolate; as is also evident from the Description of the Inhabitants eating raw Flesh, drinking Blood, and in all Respects suitable to the Character of the *Eskemaux Indians*, who by Choice, not Necessity, make Use of such Diet when out a hunting or travelling, which expresses those Parts to be very inhospitable, and where the *Indians* only frequent at certain Seasons, in Pursuit of the wild Game, and for fishing. And *Cibola* is represented as a Country which hath a Cultivation, where the *Indians* constantly live, and seem a different People from those of *Quivira* and *Anian*. This is agreeable to the Accounts given at that Time, which is sufficient to shew that the Jesuits could not expect that they should be able, or would undertake to pass through such a Country as *Quivira* and *Anian* in Pursuit of their Discoveries to Northward; therefore must have taken some Opportunity of being conveyed there, which could only be by some Persons who had been on these Coasts, and had, through Necessity, Interest, or Curiosity, passed up these Waters, and surveyed the adjacent Country in Pursuit of something which might turn out to their private Emolument: Nor were such Attempts unprecedented, even on our Parts, though the Hazards were much greater. The private Trade carried on by the People from *Boston*, in *Hudson*'s Bay, before there was a Grant to the Company; which Trading might not have come to the Knowledge of the People in *England*, or been known to the Publick for a Series of Years, had it not been for an Accident which happened to Captain *Gillam*, who thereupon made a Discovery of this Trade. Nor is there the least Improbability but that *Parmentiers* had, on some Occasion, introduced himself into these Parts, had invited the Jesuits to a Mission there, who, on other Missions, had undertaken what hath been much more hazardous, and succeeded. There were sufficient Motives for that Undertaking; the Northern Bounds were then unknown, so that they could not affirm *America* to be Continent, nor certainly to be an Island distinguished from the old World. This is the Account Mr. *Gage* gives us, Chap. xiii. and mentioning that he will not write, as many do, by Relation and Hearsay, but by more sure Intelligence, Insight and Experience. He says *Quivira* is seated on the most Western Part of *America*, just over against *Tartary*; from whence, being not much distant, some suppose that the Inhabitants came into this new World. The West Side of *America*, if it be not Continent with *Tartary*, it yet disjoined by a small Streight. Here then was a sufficient Matter to encourage a Mission of this Sort, and to keep a Progress to the Eastward, or in *America*, with the Discoveries that were going on by the Missionars sent to *Japan*; and there was a Propriety in this being done, as the Coasts of both were supposed to be at no great Distance from each other: And this was expresly the Purpose of their Mission, as it is said they had been to Latitude 66, and made curious Observations, on which Account they were with *Bernarda*. As *Parmentiers* went to the Eastward with *de Fonte*, who must have had a different Motive from them for coming into those Parts, he must have had his own private Emolument in view, his better Success in which depended on his Secrecy, as he thereby prevented others from interfering; which Consideration would prevail with him, as with all Traders, superior to any Satisfaction the Publick might have from his Informations; and as Trade would be carried on most successfully where the Inhabitants were more numerous, we find he had found his Way to Eastward, apparently the most populous, as the Jesuits had gone to the Northward and Westward, principally as most consistent with their Plan; tho' *Conasset* was where the Jesuits had been first introduced, where their courteous Behaviour and Management of the Natives, would be of Advantage to *Parmentiers*. In searching for the most popular and inhabited Part of the Country, he would become acquainted with the Geography of those Parts necessarily, Depths of Water, Shoals, Tides, which his own Preservation, and the better conducting of himself would naturally lead him to observe; but there might be a more particular Reason for his Observation of the River *Parmentiers*, and of all the Parts about it; and therefore he had been so exact as to the Falls, which were the Obstruction of the Ship Navigation through to the Eastern Sea, that lay beyond the Streights of *Ronquillo*, for his own private Advantage; by opening a new and extensive Trade, he would have greatly promoted it if he had found this Communication practicable for Ships of Burthen.

The People that Captain *Tchirikow* met with on the Coast is no Objection to the Character given of those within Land in this Letter, as it

is

is from Experience known that the *Eskemaux*, who are along the Coast of the *Labrador*, are cruel and thievish; but that *Indians* of a different Disposition live within Land.

As to *Parmentiers* being the general Interpreter for all, he is not said to be so. He would, for the Benefit it would be to him in his Trade, endeavour to learn the Language, and would of course acquire something of it unavoidably, as he frequented amongst the *Indians*: And it must be observed, though there are many different Nations, and there is a Difference in Dialect, yet there is a Language which all those Nations will understand, called the Council Language.

That Voyages had been made to these Parts more than once is evident, as the Jesuits staid there two Years, therefore did not return with the same Opportunity by which they came there, but another; and it is probable that there had been a Voyage prior to that, which had encouraged them to undertake it.

In what Manner *de Fonte* proceeded, the Boats and Number of Persons he had with him, the Translator hath omitted. It is mentioned, that *de Fonte* sailed from the rest of his Ships; the River *Parmentiers* hath Falls of thirty-two Feet perpendicular Height from its Source to where it issues into Lake *de Fonte*; so again, on the South Side Lake *Belle* on board our Ships; and had it been with his Ship, his Inference that there was no North-west Passage would have been unjust, as his meeting with this Ship the Vessel from *Boston*, would have effectually proved the contrary.

‘ We passed eight Falls, in all 32 Foot, perpendicular from its Source
‘ out of Lake *Belle*; it falls into the large Lake I named Lake *de Fonte*,
‘ at which Place we arrived the 6th of *July*. This Lake is 160 Leagues
‘ long, and 60 broad; the Length is East North East, and West South
‘ West, to twenty or thirty, in some Places sixty Fathom deep; the
‘ Lake abounds with excellent Cod and Ling, very large and well fed;
‘ there are several very large Islands, and ten small ones; they are co-
‘ vered with shrubby Woods; the Moss grows six or seven Foot long,
‘ with which the Moose, a very large Sort of Deer, are fat with in the
‘ Winter,

'Winter, and other lesser Deer, as Fallow, &c. There are Abundance
'of wild Cherries, Strawberries, Hurtleberries, and wild Currants; and
'also of wild Fowls, Heath Cocks and Hens; likewise Partridges and
'Turkeys; and Sea Fowl in great Plenty. On the South Side the Lake
'is a very large fruitful Island, had a great many Inhabitants, and
'very excellent Timber, as Oaks, Ashes, Elm and Fir Trees, very
'large and tall.'

We here again see the Form of the Letter, *de Fonte* expressing himself, as in the first Part of the Letter, *I named Parmentiers, my industrious*; and there are other Instances.

The River *Parmentiers*, which is the Communication by which the Waters of Lake *Belle* are conveyed into the Lake *de Fonte*, so named we may suppose not in Compliment to himself, which would be absurd, but of his Family, as the Expression is, *I named Lake de Fonte*, though it almost deserves the Name of a Mediterranean Sea; but from having a superior Water near it, with which it communicated, *de Fonte* calls it a Lake. It is not a casual naming of Places, or Waters, as *Hudson*'s Bay, given to that great Mediterranean Sea, and continued, but the Names of the Waters he passed through, would be given with Exactness and Propriety. In the Lake *de Fonte* there was a great Depth of Water, also Banks, as there is said to be in some Parts twenty or thirty Fathom Water, as is also evident from the Cod and Ling there, and which instance it to be a Salt Water Lake. It was the Season when these Fish come to the Northward to spawn. The shrubby Wood on the Islands, the Moss for the Subsistence of the Deer hanging on the Trees, the wild Cherries and other Fruits ripening at that Season of the Year, are all corresponding Tokens of his being advanced to the North-east Part of *America*, is agreeable in all the above Respects to the Country Northward and Westward in *Canada*, about the River *St. Lawrence*, to the interior Parts of the Country of *Labrador*, in Lat. 56; but as you proceed further to Northward, the high rocky Mountains, which in this Part are only confined to the Coast, then extend more inland, increase in their Height, and in Lat. 59° and 60°, the whole Country, as far as *Baffin*'s Bay, seems to consist only of Ridges of barren Mountains, intersperfed with Waters; and the Progress of the Productions, as to Trees

and

and Plants, gradually decreases from a more flourishing to an inferior Sort, as you proceed to Northward; in Lat. 59, on the Western Side of *Hudson*'s Bay to the Northward of *Seal* River, there is no Wood, only Grass and a small Shrub of about a Foot in Heighth, which continues, as far as it is known to Westward; and a thin Soil, with a hard rocky Stone just below the Surface, and very frequently there are large Ponds of standing Water.

De Fonte seems to have made a Stop at the Island at the South of Lake *de Fonte*, to take Refreshment, and make Inquiry as to the *Boston* Ship, it being out of his Course, or on any other Account to go there.

' The 14th of *July* we sailed out of the East North-east End of the
' Lake *de Fonte*, and passed a Lake I named the *Estricho de Ronquillo*,
' thirty-four Leagues long, two or three Leagues broad, twenty, twenty-
' six and twenty-eight Fathom of Water; we passed this Streight in ten
' Hours, having a stout Gale of Wind, and a whole Ebb. As we sailed
' more Easterly the Country grew very sensibly worse.'

What follows, ' as it is in the North and South Parts of *America*,' appears to me an additional Comment.

De Fonte mentions, as he went more Easterly the Country grew worse; from which it may be supposed he found the Alteration to begin when he was come to the Eastern Part of the Lake, and more so, as he passed the Streights of *Ronquillo*.

Where the Streight of *Ronquillo* terminated *de Fonte* makes no mention; gives us no Account of the Soundings or Tides; but his Silence here, and the preceding Circumstances, sufficiently prove that he thought himself then in some Branch of the *Atlantick Ocean.* And it is to be observed there is the same affected Silence here as to the Part he was come into, as when he had left the Western Ocean and entered the North-east Part of the *South Sea* to pass up to *Los Reys*.

' The 17th we came to an *Indian* Town, and the *Indians* told our In-
' terpreter Monf. *Parmentiers*, that a little Way from us lay a great Ship,
' where there never had been one before.'

The *Indian* telling the Interpreter *Parmentiers*, which expresses a Kind of Acquaintance made between them, and *de Fonte*'s passing out of the Lake into the Sea, coming to a Town, and *Parmentiers* knowing the Language, is an Evidence of *Parmentiers*' having been there before. And we may suppose, that from the Time they left the River *Parmentiers*, *de Fonte* had been on the Inquiry, it being now Time to expect the People from *Boston*; and what the *Indian* told him was in pursuance of such Inquiry.

' We sailed to them, and found only one Man advanced in Years, and a Youth; the Man was the greatest Man in the Mechanical Parts of the Mathematicks, I had ever met with; my second Mate was an *Englishman*, an excellent Seaman, as was my Gunner, who had been taken Prisoners at *Campechy*, as well as the Master's Son; they told me the Ship was of *New England*, from a Town called *Boston*. The Owner and the whole Ship's Company came on board the thirtieth; and the Navigator of the Ship, Captain *Shapley*, told me, his Owner was a fine Gentleman, and *Major General* of the largest Colony in *New England*, called the *Maltechusets*; so I received him like a Gentleman, and told him my Commission was to make a Prize of any People seeking a North-west or West Passage into the *South Sea*; but I would look on them as Merchants trading with the Natives for Bevers, Otters and other Furs and Skins, and so for a small Present of Provisions I had no need on, I gave him my Diamond Ring, which cost me twelve Hundred Pieces of Eight (which the modest Gentleman received with difficulty) and having given the brave Navigator *Captain Shapley*, for his fine Charts and Journals, a Thousand Pieces of Eight, and the Owner of the Ship, *Seimor Gibbons*, a quarter Cask of good *Peruan* Wine, and the ten Seamen, each twenty Pieces of Eight, the sixth of *August*, with as much Wind as we could fly before and a Current, we arrived at the first Fall of the River *Parmentiers*.'

De Fonte makes no Delay, but immediately proceeds as the Case required; finds an old Man aboard, the Man (as being a great Mechanick might be very useful on such an Expedition) and a Youth, might venture to stay, their Age would plead as to any Severity that might be intended by *de Fonte*; and through the Fear of which Severity the others retired

retired into the Woods, where they could manage without being sensible of those Difficulties which *Europeans* apprehend. To leave the Ship without any one aboard, *de Fonte* could of Course have taken her as being deserted; and by their Retirement into the Woods, his Pursuit of them there would have alarmed the *Indians*, and more especially if he had attempted any Severity, it might have been fatal to him and his Company, from the Resistance they might have met with, not only from the *Boston* People, but the *Indians* assisting them, as they would have considered it as an Insult, an Exercise of Power which they would apprehend he had no Right to use in those Parts, as to a People who were trading with them, and been the Occasion that the *Spaniards* would have been no more received as Friends in those Parts.

De Fonte had particularly provided himself with some *Englishmen*, who, by a friendly Converse with the People from *Boston*, might endeavour to learn their Secrets, and prepare them the better by what they would be instructed to tell them to come to a Compliance with the Admiral's Intentions. The Result of this Affair *de Fonte* only mentions; but they would not have staid away so long, would have returned sooner aboard, had they only left the Ship on Account of Trade. Trade was only a secondary Object, the Discovery was the principal, and they would not have staid in one Place, at this Season, had they not been necessitated through a Fear of *de Fonte* so to do. It may be supposed the *Englishmen* who were with *de Fonte*, two of whom were from *Campechy*, and the other become Catholick, as he was married to the Master's Daughter, they would not act either with much Sincerity or Truth as to their own Countrymen, but managed with the old Man to bring the Owner, Navigator, and rest of the Crew aboard. .

On their return the Navigator of the Ship was the first who waited on the Admiral, and he calls him Captain *Shapley*, his Name *Nicholas Shapley*, who was famous as a Navigator, for his Knowledge in the Mathematicks and other Branches of Science, that the common People supposed he dealt in the Magick Art, and had the Name given him of *Old Nick*, not by the People of *Boston*, but by a Set of Libertines as they termed them, and who had separated from the People of *Boston*, and gone to live by themselves at *Piscatua*, where he was settled at a

K   Place

Place called *Kittery*, in the Province of *Main*; the Name of *Kittery* given by his Brother *Alexander Shapley*, to a Tract of Land he had settled on there; and they write the Name *Shapley* exactly in the Manner in which it is wrote in the Letter. The Brother *Alexander* was a Cotemporary at *Oxford* with Captain *James*, who went on Discovery, and his Acquaintance. The Descendants of *Alexander*, a genteel People, were not many Years since living at *Kittery*; but *Nicholas Shapley* retired to *New London*, where he had a Son that was living in the Year one Thousand seven Hundred and fifty-two, a Fisherman. The Family at *Kittery* were very shy as to giving any Information as to what they knew in this Affair, upon an Application by the Author of these Observations, or looking into *Alexander*'s Papers, as an officious Person had got beforehand, and discouraged them from giving any Gratification of this Sort, under Pretence, if their Papers were seen, it might give some Insight into a Lawsuit depending between the Branches of the Family, or expected to be commenced; and that there was a great Reward for the Discovery of a North-west Passage, which, if the Account was attained from them they would be intitled to a Part, which by this Means they would be deprived of. Jealousies of this Kind raised by a pretended, at least an ignorant Friend, against the Application of a Stranger, who assured them he was superior to any Trick of that Sort, and would give them any Satisfaction in his Power as they should propose, occasioned a Disappointment. The Son of Captain *Nicholas*, upon an Application made by the Author likewise, had nothing but his Father's Sea Chest, in which there were once a great many Papers, and which his Mother, the Wife of Captain *Nicholas*, made a great Account of; but the Son being an illiterate Man, had made Use of them in the Family as waste Paper. I have mentioned him as illiterate, but he was a well meaning Man, and he had heard his Mother talk something about such an Affair; but I shall not lay a Stress upon the Account he gave, as he may be supposed prompted by the earnest Manner of the Inquiry to give grateful Answers, in Expectation of a Reward. The Number of Settlers in all *Piscatua*, the Province of *Main* included, did not at that Time exceed four Hundred People, but is now become a well settled Country; yet there was amongst the antient People about *Kittery*, a Tradition of Captain *Nicholas* having been on such a Voyage, and as to which, on proper Application to Persons who have Influence, and will make due Inquiry, it appears to me the Publick

will

will receive a farther Satisfaction than they may at prefent expect. A confiderable Merchant who lived at *Falmouth* in *Pifcatua*, a Man of Character, no Way biaffed for or againft a North-weft Paffage, but as he is fince dead, I may take the Liberty to fay, married a Daughter of his late Excellency Governor *Weymouth*, mentioned an Anecdote refpecting his Father, who was a very antient Man : That when the Difpute was between the late Governor *Dobbs* and Captain *Middleton*, he faid, Why do they make fuch a Fuzz about this Affair, our *Old Nick* (meaning Captain *Shapley*) was through there? And this antient Gentleman had been an Intimate of Captain *Shapley*'s.

Early in the Year before this Voyage Major General *Gibbons* went with others over to *Pifcatua*, to have a Conference about Church Matters; and Mr. *Alexander Shapley* was one on the Part of the Settlers in *Pifcatua*, and who had but returned from *England* the Fall before. At this Meeting, probably, they fixed on the Time and Manner of executing the Defign, which they had before concerted. This whole Affair was concerted in an obfcure Part, the Affair not known to the People of *Bofton*, as it was more to the Purpofe of thofe who undertook it to keep it a Secret; and probably Major *Gibbons* was more inclined it fhould be fo, as he had before met with two Difappointments. The Characters of the Perfons were fuch, as by whom it is very reafonable to fuppofe fuch an Expedition might be undertaken. Mr. *Alexander Shapley* was a Merchant, a lively, active, enterprifing Man; fufficient to this Purpofe hath been faid of his Brother: And we may add to the Character of Major General *Gibbons*, it was faid of him, that he was much of a Gentleman, a brave, focial and friendly Man, had the latter End of the Year 1639 a Commiffion to be Captain of the Fort, was one of the Council, alfo concerned in Church Matters, as appears from Records. But during the Time that this Voyage was making, as that worthy Paftor of *Bofton* and great Antiquarian Mr. *Prince*, who, from a generous Difpofition to get at the Truth, ufed extraordinary Induftry in this Affair, by fearching the Records in the old Church there in the Year 1752, could not find his Hand fet to any Thing, or any Matters relating to Major General *Gibbons*, tho' he found Papers figned by him frequently before, and other Tranfactions in which he is mentioned to be concerned, alfo after the Time of this Voyage, and the only Objection that he could find was, that

that the Wife of Major General *Gibbons* muſt have had a ſeven Months Child, if he went on ſuch Voyage, as it was a Cuſtom in the Church of *Boſton*, at that Time, that the Child ſhould be brought to be baptized the *Sunday* after it was born; and by the Regiſter it appears that this was the Caſe, according to the Time that it muſt be ſuppoſed he returned.

The Name was *Edward Gibbons*; and *Seimor* is a Miſtake of the Tranſlator, not obſerving that as *de Fonte* reſpectfully ſtiles *Shapley* Captain, he would not mention the Owner by his Chriſtian Name only, a fine Gentleman and a Major General, but ſtiles him agreeable thereto after the *Spaniſh* Manner *Sennor*; and this Miſtake of the Tranſlator, as to the Name, and not obſerving that the *Major General* and the Owner were one and the ſame Perſon, ſhews that the Tranſlator and Editors knew nothing of the Perſons mentioned.

What is ſaid of the largeſt Colony in *New England*, called the *Mattechuſets*: The Dominions of *New England* conſiſted, at that Time, of the Colonies of *Plymouth*, *Maſſachuſets*, and *Connecticut*, of which *Maſſachuſets* was the largeſt, as *New Hampſhire*, *Piſcatua*, and the Province of *Main*, were under its Juriſdiction: And it is a little remarkable that the Admiral ſhould call it the *Maltechuſets*; he apprehended it a Miſtake, though ſo exact as to the Names *Shapley* and *Gibbons*; ſeems to have given the Alteration agreeable to his own Ideas, and that it muſt have Reference to *Malta*.

The old Man told them the Ship was of *New England*, from the Town called *Boſton*, which was the only Place where they could fit out properly or conveniently, the Part where *Shapley* lived conſiſting only of a few ſcattered Houſes, and as it was very frequent from *Boſton* to make Voyages to the Northward, their true Deſign for further Diſcoveries might remain a Secret to all but themſelves.

De Fonte's Addreſs to *Gibbons* as the Owner, repreſented ſo on this Occaſion to ſerve the Purpoſe, though the Veſſel ſeems to have been *Alexander Shapley*'s, implies that he underſtood, or took the Advantage on finding they had been trading with the *Indians*, that they had two Purpoſes in their Undertaking, to diſcover a Paſſage, and to trade. As to the firſt, *de Fonte* tells him he had an Order to make a *Prize of any People*

People seeking a West or North-west Passage, speaking in general Terms, not of them only, so concealing the Advice he had received as to their particular undertaking of this Discovery; nor could it be peculiarly understood as to the Subjects of *England*, for the *Danes* also, to their immortal Honour, had before attempted the same Discovery; and in Consequence let him know that the Part he was in was of the Dominions of the Crown of *Spain*, as his Commission could be of no Force beyond the Extent of that Dominion. *De Fonte*'s Address likewise implied, that as he would consider them only as Traders, that he would not make Prisoners of them on that Account; but expected after this Adventure that others would learn to keep nearer home, for Fear of falling into a like Accident, and meeting not with the same favourable Treatment. Nevertheless he takes effectual Measures to embarrass them on their Return, and obliges them to stay no longer in those Parts, as he takes from them what *de Fonte* calls a small Present of Provisions, which he had no Need on, but he knew they might, and as to which, the Affair of Provisions, he gave such an Attention to, through the Course of his Voyage; and though small what he accepted in respect to the Subsistance of those he had with him, yet as the Sequel will shew, was afterwards the Occasion of infinite Distress to the *Boston* People. The Gift in return, which is pompously mentioned at twelve Hundred Pieces of Eight, when we consider the Price Things bore of this Sort where he purchased it, in *Peru*, as he estimates by Pieces of Eight, the Manner of Valuation in those Parts, would not be to *Gibbons* a Hundred Pounds Sterling; and the Present to the Seamen must be considered as in lieu of these Provisions; and by this Means of mutual Presents countenanced what was absolutely extorted by Force, as was the Case with *Shapley*, as to his Charts and Journals, which he would not have parted with, but constrained through Fear; and by his *English* Seamen *de Fonte* could let them know that the Provisions, Charts, and Journals would be acceptable. He executed his Design in this Manner, that if the *Boston* People returned there could be no proper Foundation for the Court of *England* to take Umbrage at his Proceeding.

The Generosity of *de Fonte* so exceeding what their Present and the Charts and Journals could be worth, would be considered as to make them some Satisfaction for their Disappointment; for the Fears they had

been

been put into, and their being detained there ; the Gift of Wine, might be from a Respect to *Major General Gibbons*, as an Officer, whom *de Fonte* stiles modest, tho' he might perceive it to be the Effect of his Uneasiness on being thus intercepted. In all other Respects, what he gave was a Debt which the Crown of *Spain* would pay, would be considered as Money advanced in their Service; a Sum of no Consideration with them, as he had met with these People, procured their Charts by which they got into the Secret, by what Way they had advanced so far, and probably very particular Charts and Journals of the other Voyagers whom *Gibbons* was acquainted with; and he would endeavour to be furnished with all Materials which he could probably procure before that he set out. It would be greatly commended by the Court of *Spain* the artful Management of *de Fonte* in distressing these People, and not with a seeming Intention, and giving an absolute Discouragement to other Adventurers, who would be afraid of falling into the *Spaniards* Hands, whom it would be supposed constantly frequented those Parts.

De Fonte only mentions the Issue of this Affair, what would be immediately necessary for the Court to know; he mentions no intervening Circumstances, nor what Time there was between their Examination and the Presents, whether he or they sailed first, but it must be supposed they were more than a Day together, and that *de Fonte* would see them out of those Parts, as, if they had staid longer, they might probably have supplied themselves well with Provisions, and proceeded further; but as they were circumstanced, they would be put under a Necessity to set out for home, would be glad to leave him the first Opportunity; and as *de Fonte* seems to be waiting for a Wind, which he had the sixth of *August*, and it had in the interim been fair for the *Boston* People, they were certainly gone before that *de Fonte* set out on his Return.

In the Ecclesiastical History of *New England*, by the Reverend *Cotton Mather*, published at *London* in 1702, in Folio, in his Account of wonderful Sea Deliverances, Book the sixth, is *The wonderful Story of Major Gibbons*.

'Among remarkable *Sea Deliverances*, no less than three several
' Writers have published that wherein Major *Edward Gibbons* was con-
' cerned

' cerned. A Veffel bound from *Bofton* to fome other Parts of *Ame-*
' *rica,* was, through the Continuance of contrary Winds, kept fo
' long at Sea, that the People aboard were in extreme ftraits for Want
' of Provifion, and feeing that nothing here below could afford them
' any Relief, they looked upwards unto Heaven, in humble and fervent
' Supplications. The Winds continuing ftill as they were, one of the
' Company made a forrowful Motion that they fhould, by a *Lot,* fingle
' out *One* to die, and by Death to fatisfy the ravenous Hunger of the
' reft. After many a doleful and fearful Debate upon this Motion, they
' came to a Refult, that *it muft be done!* The *Lot* is caft; one of the
' Company is taken; but where is the Executioner that fhall do the ter-
' rible Office upon a poor Innocent? It is a Death now to think who
' fhall act this bloody Part in the Tragedy: But before they fall upon
' this involuntary and unnatural Execution, they once more went unto
' their zealous *Prayers*; and, behold, while they were calling upon God,
' he anfwered them, for there leaped a mighty Fifh into their Boat,
' which, to their double Joy, not only quieted their outrageous Hun-
' ger, but alfo gave them fome Token of a further Deliverance: How-
' ever, the Fifh is quickly eaten; the horrible *Famine* returns, the hor-
' rible Diftrefs is renewed; a black Defpair again feizes their Spirits :
' For another Morfel they come to a fecond *Lot,* which fell upon ano-
' ther Perfon; but ftill they cannot find an Executioner: They once
' again fall to their importunate Prayers; and, behold, a fecond An-
' fwer from above; a great Bird lights, and fixes itfelf on the Maft;.
' one of the Men fpies it, and there it ftands until he took it by the
' Wing with his Hand. This was a fecond *Life from the Dead.* This
' Fowl, with the Omen of a further Deliverance in it, was a fweet Feaft
' unto them. Still their Difappointments follow them; they can fee
' no Land; they know not where they are: Irrefiftable Hunger once
' more pinches them: They have no Hope to be faved but by *a third*
' *Miracle:* They return to another *Lot*; but before they go to the
' Heart-breaking Tafk of flaying the Perfon under *Defignation,* they re-
' peat their Addreffes unto the God of Heaven, their former *Friend in*
' *Adverfity*; and now they look and look again, but there is nothing :
' Their Devotions are concluded, and nothing appears;. yet they hoped,
' yet they ftaid, yet they lingered: At laft one of them fpies a Ship,
' which put a new Hope and Life into them all: They bear up with
" their

' their Ship; they man their Long-boat; they go to board the Veſſel,
' and are admitted. It proves a *French* Pyrate: Major *Gibbons* Petitions
' for a little Bread, and offers all for it; but the Commander was one
' who had formerly received confiderable Kindneſſes of Major *Gibbons*
' at *Boſton*, and now replied chearfully, Major *Gibbons*, not an Hair of
' you, or your Company, ſhall *periſh if it lies in my Power to* preſerve
' *you*. Accordingly he fupplied their Neceſſities, and they made a com-
' fortable End of their Voyage.'

There are nine other Accounts, in each of which the Places the Perſons were bound to are particularly mentioned. In this Account (the Deſign being only to ſhew the wonderful Deliverance of *Gibbons*) Dr. *Mather* could not mention the Place to which the Voyage had been made in any other Manner, than *to ſome other Parts of America*, which hath an exact Correſpondence with the Voyage in which Major *Gibbons* was intercepted by *de Fonte*; for that Voyage was properly to ſeveral Parts, not being to one particular Part of *America*; which Parts were, at that Time, nameleſs. It is ſaid further, that their Misfortune was occaſioned by contrary Winds. *De Fonte* had a fair Wind from the ſixth of *Auguſt* to the fifth of *September*, and for a longer Time, ſo contrary to the *Boſton* Ship; afterwards they had the Wind again contrary, when they came into the Ocean, being North-weſt or to Weſtward of it, as they could ſee no Land; the Land expected to be ſeen may be ſuppoſed the Land of *Newfoundland*, or they were to Eaſtward and Southward of the Gulph of *St. Lawrence*: And which Account of the Weather is agreeable to the Time of the Year that they were there, the latter End of *September*, or Beginning of *October*, being the Equinoctial Gales. Alſo as to the Fiſh which muſt have been a Sturgeon, which Fiſh frequently jump into Boats; and ſhews, as the Boat was out, that they had then moderate Weather, but contrary; though a hard Gale ſucceeded, as one of the Birds of Paſſage, which are alſo then going to Southward, was blown off the Coaſt and tired, reſted on the Maſt. Far be it from me to reckon theſe as mere Accidents, and not the Aſſiſtances of the Almighty, but a Relief which the Almighty ſent them by Contingencies which are natural: And as to the Ship, which was a *French* Pirate, ſhe had probably come with a freſh Wind out of the Gulph of *St. Lawrence*, and ſtanding to Eaſtward of *Sables* to clear that Iſland and *Nautuchet*,

for

for which she had a fair Wind; and it is said the Commander had an Acquaintance with Major *Gibbons*, and received Favours from him at *Boston*; but I must add an Anecdote, to shew that there might also be another Reason assigned, which would not be suitable to be published with that Account; *Alexander Shapley* had used to hold a Correspondence with these Kind of Gentry, as is evident from a severe Censure on him on that Account, recorded in the Council Book at *Boston*. It was a *Ship* that Major *Gibbons* was in when intercepted by *de Fonte*; and this Account also mentions a Ship. After the Death of *Major Gibbons*, his Family, according to the Account of a very antient Gentlewoman at *Boston*, removed to *Bermuda*; which Lady, who was near ninety Years of Age, had some traditional Account of the *Major* having been such a Voyage to discover a new Way to the *East Indies*, and suffered much from the Snow and Ice, went through a great many Hardships, and, she said, she thought it was from *Boston* that he set out. The Persons discovered by Monsf. *Groseliers*, at what he calls an *English* Settlement, near Port *Nelson*, as it is now termed, were *Benjamin* the Son of Captain *Zachary Gillam*, and some others, from *Boston*, who were the same Year taken to *Canada*, whose Journal of that Voyage the Author hath seen, and this Circumstance is mentioned in it, which Persons have been mistaken for Major *Gibbons* and his Company.

' We arrived at the River *Parmentiers* the 11th of *August* 86 Leagues,
' and was on the South Side Lake *Belle* on board our Ships the 16th of
' *August*, before the fine Town *Conosset*, where we found all Things well,
' and the honest Natives of *Conosset* had, in our Absence, treated our
' People with great Humanity, and Capt. *de Ronquillo* answered their
' Civility and Justice.'

We have been before told, that the Admiral went sixty Leagues up *Los Reyes*, which I take to be the whole Distance between the Entrance of *Los Reyes* to *Conosset* in Lake *Belle*; and if we transpose the above Words, ' arrived at *Parmentiers* the eleventh of *August*, and was on the ' South Side Lake *Belle* eighty-six Leagues on board our Ships the six- ' teenth of *August*,' then we have the Distances respecting every Part of *de Fonte*'s Course thro' Land, from *Los Reyes* to *Conosset* sixty Leagues, from *Conosset* to Lake *de Fonte* eighty-six Leagues, from the Entrance of Lake

L   *de de Fonte* to the Streight of *Ronquillo* one Hundred and fixty Leagues, from the Entrance of the Streight of *Ronquillo* to the Sea thirty-fix Leagues. The Time that *de Fonte* was paffing down the River of *Parmentiers*, and the Time he took to return, are equal, which is plainly owing to his being obliged to wait the Tides for getting over the Falls both Ways. The fixth of *July* they had entered the Lake *de Fonte*, and by the fifteenth were through the Streights of *Ronquillo*, and at the *Indian* Town the feventeenth, fo they were eleven Days from their Entrance into the Lake *de Fonte*; but in their return the fame Way only five, favoured by a ftrong Current which the Wind occafioned to fet into the Lake, and having as much Wind as they could fly before, and now came directly back; whereas in their Paffage out they had made fome Delays. The Courfe to *Conoffet* being nearest North-eaft, I compute it to be in Lat. 56 Deg. Long. 118° 2′ from *London*. The Entrance of Lake *de Fonte* (fuppofing the Courfe of the River *Parmentiers* and from *Conoffet* Eaft North Eaft) in Lat. 59° 4′. Long. 113°. The Entrance of the Streights of *Ronquillo* Eaft North Eaft, in Lat. 61 Deg. 8 Min. Long. 98 Deg. 48 Min. the Courfe through the Streights to enter the Sea North by Eaft, fuch Entrance to be in Lat. 62 Deg. 48 Min. Long. 98 Deg. 2 Min. which Courfe muft be confiftent with *de Fonte*'s Account that a ftrong Current fet in, as by this Courfe fuch Current muft be accelerated, if it fet to the Southward, by the Wind from the Northward, or if it was from the Southward, would be oppofed in going to the Northward.

De Fonte proceeds to give an Account of the good Eftate in which he found all Things on his Return; mentions the Honefty and Humanity of the Natives, and the prudent Conduct of Captain *Ronquillo*, who anfwered their Civility and Juftice. For they had, during the Time of *de Fonte*'s Abfence, procured, by dealing with the Natives, Store of good Provifions to falt, Venifon, Fifh; alfo one Hundred Hogfheads of *Indian* Maiz; befides the Service this would be of on their Return, procured purfuant to *de Fonte*'s Order, it employed the People, with the other neceffary Work about the Ships after fo long a Run, and kept them from brangling with the Natives. The Natives were alfo employed to their Intereft, which preferved them in good Humour; and a Juftice in dealing preferved their Friendfhip.

The

' The 29th of *August* an *Indian* brought me a Letter to *Conoffet*, on
' the Lake *Belle*, from Captain *Bernarda*, dated the 11th of *August*,
' where he sent me Word he was returned from his cold Expedition,
' and did assure me there was no Communication out of the *Spanish* or
' *Atlantick* Sea, by *Davis* Streight; for the Natives had conducted one
' of his Seamen to the Head of *Davis* Streight, which terminated in a
' fresh Lake, of about 30 Mile in Circumference, in the 80th Degree
' of North Latitude; and that there was prodigious Mountains North
' of it, besides the North-west from that Lake the Ice was so fixed, that
' from the Shore to 100 Fathom of Water, for ought he knew from the
' Creation; for Mankind knew little of the wonderful Works of God,
' especially near the North and South Poles: He writ further, that he
' had sailed from *Baffet* Island North East, and East North East, and
' North East and by East, to the 79th Degree of Latitude, and the
' Land trended North, and the Ice rested on the Land.'

The Orders *Bernarda* received were to sail up a River North and North East, North and North West, which River I suppose to have emptied itself near to *Los Reyes* into the South-east Part of the *South Sea*; and it is not uncommon, in *America*, that two great Rivers should have their Entrances contiguous to each other; and I suppose *Conabaffet*, afterwards called *Baffet*, to be in Lat. 58 Deg. 10 Min. to the Westward of *Los Reyes* in Long. 122 Deg. 9 Min. from *London*. The Course up the River *Haro* North 14 Deg. West; and as *Conoffet* is laid down in Lat. 56 Deg. Long. 118 Deg. 2 Min. the Distance from *Baffet* to *Conoffet* is one Hundred and seventy-seven Miles; the Course North 46 Deg. West. The Letter by the first Messenger was dated the 27th of *June*, and is received the fourth Day, as he could not come a direct Course, we may suppose he travelled fifty Miles a Day, which is an extraordinary Allowance, the greatest Part by Water, and Light most of the Night. We know he would go Part by Water in Lake *Belle*, and Lake *Belle* issuing its Waters both by *Los Reyes* and the River *Parmentiers*, must receive some considerable Influx of Waters by which it is formed, as well as to give a constant Supply of the Waters that issue from it, and which must be principally or only from the Northward, for it cannot be supposed to receive its Waters from the Southward, and discharge them there again, and which the Messenger would make Use of as soon as possible, and come down Stream. The second Messenger, who is expresly mentioned to be an *Indian*, is nine Days a coming. But *Bernarda* mentions nothing as to his Ship or People in this Account, only says he is returned from his cold Expedition, therefore probably he sent away the *Indian* as soon as he could after he entered the River, which ran into the *Tartarian* Sea, in Lat. 61. If this was the Case, we may suppose that the Waters which came into the Lake *Belle* head a great Way up in the Country.

 Bernarda had Directions, after he left Lake *Valasco*, to sail one Hundred and forty Leagues West, and then four Hundred and thirty Leagues North East by East to seventy-seven Degrees of Latitude. *Bernarda*, in his Letter of the 27th of *June* observes, there was a River eighty Leagues in Length, not comprehended in his Instructions or Orders, and emptied itself in the *Tartarian* Sea; and says, in his Letter of the 11th of *August*, that he sailed from the Island *Basset* North-east; with that Course, when he entered the *Tartarian* Sea, in Latitude 61, his Longitude would be 116 Deg. he then begins the Course *de Fonte* directed him, one Hundred and forty Leagues East North East; and he mentions on his Return he had steered that Course, keeping the Land aboard. So that *West* and the Land trending *North East*, are Mistakes in the Publication in *April*; but the mentioning how the Land trended, shews he was then entering the Sea; for to talk of Land, with respect to a River, is absurd; and with the Course and Distance he steered would be in Lat. 63 Deg. 39 Min. and Long. 110 Deg. from *London:* Then he steers four Hundred and thirty-six Leagues North East and by East, and that brings him into Latitude 79 Deg. Long. 87 Deg. from *London*. But the Land trending North, and with Ice, which would be dangerous for the *Periagos*; and as the Land trended North, where he was appearing to him to be the nearest Part he could attain to to go to the Head of *Davis* Streight; and as to the Distance over Land, and the Propriety of sending a Messenger, the *Indians* would inform him; he sends a Seaman over with an *Indian* to take a Survey of the Head of such Streights, by us called *Baffin*'s Bay; which Name was not at that Time generally received. Which Seaman reports, that it terminated in the eightieth Degree of Latitude, in a Lake of about thirty Miles in Circumference, with prodigious Mountains North of it, which indeed formed that Lake,

or

or is a Sound, as that of Sir *James Lancaster* and of *Alderman Jones*, and along the Shore, from the Lake North-weft, the Ice was fixed, lying a great Diftance out, which was very confiftent with there being no Inlets there, the Waters from which would have fet it off. The Diftance that the *Indian* and Sailor travelled would not exceed fifty Miles; and their mentioning the high Mountains to Northward imply, that they were in a more level Country where they were to take this View. Light all Night, the Snow off the Ground, and the Heighth of Summer there. It is no vain Conjecture to fuppofe that the Journey was practicable, even if performed all the Way by Land, and much eafier, which is not the leaft improbable, if they had an Opportunity of making Part of it by Water. *Bernarda* proceeding thus far in the *Tartarian* Sea, and entering in Latitude 61, is no Way contradictory to the *Ruffian* Difcoveries; and by the *Tartarian* Sea is meant, the Sea which wafhes the Northern Coafts of *Tartary*, and is fuppofed to extend round the Pole. Thofe Difcoveries are agreeable to the *Japanefe* Map, as to the North-eaft Parts of *Afia*, and North-weft Parts of *America*, brought over by *Kemper*, and in which Map there is expreffed a Branch of the *Tartarian* Sea or Gulph, extending to the Southward, agreeable to this Account of *de Fonte*. Who calls it, with refpect to *Afia*, the North and Eaft Part of the *Tartarian* Sea. Which compared with what *de Fonte* fays, as to failing down the River to the North-eaft Part of the *South Sea*, thefe Expreffions caft a mutual Light on each other, and that the *Archipelagus of Saint Lazarus* is a Gulph or Branch of the Sea, in the like Manner.

Places which are in one and the fame Latitude, have not an equal Degree of Heat or Cold, or are equally fertile or barren, the Difference in thefe Refpects chiefly confifts in their Situation. The Country of *Labrador*, which is to Eaftward of *Hudfon*'s Bay, in Latitude 56, almoft as high a Latitude as Port *Nelfon*, is a Country capable of being improved by Agriculture, and would fupply all the Neceffaries of Life, though intermixed with rugged and craggy Mountains. The Winter's not fo fevere as in the more Southern Parts of *Hudfon*'s Bay, as the Earth is not froze there, as it is in the fame and lower Latitudes about that Bay: Alfo People have wintered in the *Labrador*, wearing only their ufual Cloathing: Therefore drawing a Parallel between Port *Nelfon* and *Cenoffet*, as to the Infertility of one, therefore the other being in the same Latitude, could not produce Maiz to fupply *Ronquilio*, is an Objection which hath no Foundation in it. The higher the Latitude the quicker is the Vegetation; and as *Indian Corn* or *Maiz* may be planted and gathered in three Months in lower Latitudes, it may be in an equal or lefs Time in higher Latitudes, in a good Soil. As to Port *Nelfon*, or *York Fort*, in *Hudfon*'s *Bay*, it is a low Country through which two large Rivers pafs, with the Bay in Front, and nothing is certainly known of the more inland Parts.

The phyfical Obftacles that are produced againft our giving Credit to this Account of *de Fonte*, from the Depth of the Falls at the Entrance of Lake *Belle* in the River *Parmentiers*, and from the River *Bernarda* paffed up, are, from not underftanding what is expreffed by the Word Falls amongft the *Americans*. They mean by a Fall wherever there is the leaft Declivity of the Water; and the Fall of thirty-two Feet in the River *Parmentiers*, doth not mean a perpendicular Fall, as the Objector would have it underftood, however ridiculous to fuppofe it, but eight gradual Defcents, from the Beginning of which to the Extremity of the laft there was a Difference of thirty-two Feet, and which became level or even at the Time of high Water.

What *Bernarda* fays as to his cold Expedition, a Perfon ufed to the Climate of *Peru* might juftly fay fo, of the Nights and Evenings and Mornings, at that Time of the Year, in the Latitude of feventy-nine, though temperate in Latitude fifty-fix; and the whole Difpofition of the Country, the immenfe high Lands, their barren and defert Afpect, in Places their Summits covered with perpetual Snow, the Ice fixed to the Shores, Sheets of floating Ice in the Waters, the immenfe Iflands, frequently feeing Whales, Sea-horfe, and a great Variety of the Inhabitants of thofe Waters, which do not frequent the Southern Parts: The Whole a Scene fo different from the Verdure and Delights of the Plains about *Lima*, and from the pleafing Views that prefent themfelves on running along the Coafts of *Peru*, *Bernarda* might well be affected with fuch Scene as to exprefs himfelf, that Mankind knew little of the wonderful Works of God, efpecially near the North and the South Poles. But he was not fo ignorant as to report, that he faw Mountains of Ice on the Land, as well as in the Sea, though he might fee them forming between

Points of Land, which jetted out into the Sea; and such a Column of Ice would appear to him as something very curious.

That these Parts were inhabited does not appear, for it was a Native of *Conibaffet* that conducted the Seaman over the Land; and, at that Season of the Year, the fresh Waters are thawed, no Snow on the low and level Lands, only on the extreme Summits of the Hills.

What is objected as to the Affability of the Inhabitants, that it is not consistent with the Character of the *Indians*. Hospitality is the Characteristick of the *Indians* towards Strangers, until such Time as they are prejudiced from some ill Treatment; and by the Account given by Sir *Francis Drake*, as to the *Indians* of *California*, and by the *Spaniards* who surveyed the Western Coasts, and the Islands lying off, they are represented in general as a kind, tractable People, and of a docile Temper.

As to the Dispatch used by *Indians* in carrying Expresses, or their Runners as they term them, to carry Messages from one Nation to another, they will gird themselves up with the Rhind of Trees, and keep going incessantly great Distances with a surprising Agility Night and Day, taking little either of Sleep or other Refreshments, and keep a direct Course, and in the Night steer either by the Moon or Stars. Nor is there any Thing miraculous in these Journeys, which the Expresses performed, either as to Distance or as to Time, especially as they passed through a Country abounding with Waters, and which Country being inhabited they could be supplied with Canoes, or they would find Floats at the Places where they usually pass the Waters.

Bernarda meeting *de Fonte* at a Port up the River *Rio los Reyes*, shews he had Persons aboard who could direct him there, therefore must have been previously there; and they can be supposed to be no other than the Jesuits, which is a further Proof of the Jesuits having been before in these Parts. It was consistent that the Ships should join and return home together. From where *Bernarda* came to with his Ship was one Hundred and twenty Miles to *Conoffet*: His Letter from thence was dated the 29th of *August*, and *de Fonte* sailed the second of *September*: It may be supposed the Letter came to Hand the first of *September*, which is

four

four Days, and the Exprefs had now all the Way by Water, and moftly againft Stream. *De Fonte*, to fhew that he had preferved the Affection of the Natives, mentions that he was accompanied with them; and they were of Affiftance to him in the Pilotage down the River. *De Fonte* adds, he had fent a Chart with the Letter, which is mifunderftood, as if fuch Chart had come to the Hands of the Editors; *which will make this much more demonftrative*, were Words added by them; but it was ufual in all the Naval Expeditions to have Perfons aboard whom they called *Cofmographers*, to take Draughts of Places, and compofe their Charts, and at that Time a very reputable Employment.

Miguel Venegas, a *Mexican* Jefuit, publifhed at *Madrid* in 1758, a Natural and Civil Hiftory of *California*; a Tranflation of which was publifhed in *London* in 1759, in two Volumes; and Vol. i. P. 185, fays, ' To this Æra (the laft Voyage he mentions was in 1636) belongs the ' Contents of a Paper publifhed at *London*, under the Title of the Narrative of *Bartholomew de Fuentes*, Commander in Chief of the Navy in ' *New Spain* and *Peru*, and Prefident of *Chili*, giving an Account of the ' moft remarkable Tranfactions and Adventures in this Voyage, for the ' Difcovery of a Paffage from the *South Sea*, to that of the North in the ' Northern Hemifphere, by Order of the Viceroy of *Peru* in the Year 1640. ' This Writing contains feveral Accounts relating to *California*; but ' without entering into long Difputes, let it fuffice to fay, that little ' Credit is to be given to this Narrative. For the fame Reafon we have ' before omitted the Accounts of Voyages made from the *South Sea* to ' the North round beyond *California*, and thofe of a contrary Direction, ' of which an Account is given by Captain *Seixas* and *Lebero*, in *Theatro Naval*, in *Spanifh* and *French*; and particularly of that *Spaniard* ' who is fuppofed, in three Months, to have come from *Puerto de Navidad* and *Cabo Corientes* to *Lifbon*. Thefe and other Accounts difperfed in different Books, we defignedly omit, as they want the neceffary Authenticity.'

This Work was publifhed with a Defign to induce the Court of *Spain* to a further Conqueft of, an intire Reduction of, and the full fettling of *California*, as of the utmoft Importance to Religion and the State; and one of the Arguments is, for their immediate putting what he recommends

commends in Execution, the repeated Attempts of the *English* to find a Paſſage into the *South Sea*. And obſerves, ' Should they one Day ſuc-
' ceed in this, why may not the *Engliſh* come down through their Con-
' queſts, and even make themſelves Maſters of *New Mexico*, &c.' which
implies, that he did not look on ſuch an Attempt as void of all Hopes
of Succeſs ; and he again ſays, ' Whoever is acquainted with the pre-
' ſent Diſpoſition of the *Engliſh* Nation, and has heard with what Zeal
' and Ardour the Project for a North-weſt Paſſage has been eſpouſed by
' many conſiderable Perſons, will be convinced that the Scheme is not
' romantick, and it would not be ſurprizing if the Execution of it ſhould
' one Day come under Deliberation.' Thus artfully hints, ſhould the
Scheme come under Deliberation, the Event would be to be feared ;
and though he aſcribes his Opinion of its not being romantick, is, to
many conſiderable Perſons having eſpouſed the Scheme, yet he tacitly ap-
plies to their own Knowledge, to what the Court of *Spain* knows as to
this Paſſage. He then proceeds, ' If this ſhould ever happen,' the Deliberation, ' what would be the Condition of our Poſſeſſions ?' The
Deliberation would, from Conſequences that would follow on ſuch a
Deliberation, endanger our Poſſeſſions.

Don Cortez informed the King, by a Letter of the 15th of *October*
1524, that he was building two Ships, to get a Knowledge of the Coaſt
yet undiſcovered between the River of *Panaco* and *Florida*, and from
thence to the Northern Coaſt of the ſaid Country of *Florida*, as far as
the *Baccaloo*, ' It being certain, as he expreſſes himſelf, that on that
' Coaſt is a Streight running into the *South Sea*'—' God grant that the
' Squadron may compaſs the End for which it is deſigned, namely, to
' diſcover the Streight, which I am fully perſuaded they will do, be-
' cauſe in the Royal Concerns of your Majeſty nothing can be con-
' cealed ; and no Diligence or Neceſſaries ſhall be wanting in me to ef-
' fect it.' Again, ' I hereby inform your Majeſty, that by the Intelli-
' gence I have received of the Countries on the upper Coaſt of the
' ſending the Ships along, it will be attended with great Advantage to
' me, and no leſs to your Majeſty. But acquainted as I am with your
' Majeſty's Deſire of knowing this Streight, and likewiſe of the great
' Service it would be to your Royal Crown.' Vol. i. P. 130.

M Agreeable

Agreeable to this Letter several Attempts were made by Sea to discover whether *Florida* was Part of the Continent, or separated by a Streight; but whether *Cortez* pursued his Design by searching between *Florida* along the Coast of *Baccaloos*, *Newfoundland*, and the *Terra de Labrador*, for a Streight, by which there was a Passage from the *North* to the *South Sea* is uncertain. *New Spain* comprehended the Country from the Cape of *Labrador* to the Cape *de los Martires*, or of *Martyrs*, opposite to the Island of *Cuba*. From thence to the Streights of *Magellan* was called *Florida*.

The King of *Portugal*, with a View of finding a shorter Passage to those Parts of the *Indies*, which he had discovered, than by the Cape of *Good Hope*, sent, in the Year fifteen Hundred, *Gasper de Corte Real* to the North of *America*, who landed on the *Terra de Labrador*; also gave his Name to a Promontory on that Coast which he called *Promonterium Corteriale*. The Name of *Labrador* implies a fertile Country, and given in Distinction from the high barren mountainous Country to Northward, which *Gasper* discovered in Latitude sixty, and to the Southward of it. But this Distinction seems to have been soon lost, and the Name of *Labrador* is now given to the whole Coast.

From the Knowledge we have of these Parts we may conclude, that the *Promonterium Corteriale* was what we at present name *Cape Chidley*, and the Islands *de Demonios*, where *Gasper* lost a Vessel, those Islands now named *Button*'s Islands; and it was *Hudson*'s Streights to which he gave the Name of the River of the *Three Brothers*, though the Reason of his giving that Name is not known to us.

We may perceive from this Account of *Gasper*'s Voyage, who did not proceed to Westward to make a Passage, but coasted down the main Land, the Accounts of their being a *Portuguese* who made a Voyage through the Streights of *Anian*, calling a Promontory after his Name *Promonterium Corteriale*, hath had some Foundation in Truth; and in what is said by *Frisius*, an antient Geographer, calling it the Streights of *Three Brothers*, or *Anian* (which that Word imports) because three Brothers had passed through a Streight from the *North* to the *South Sea*. It is also apparent that the Name of *Anian* was first given by *Gasper Corterialis*

Corterialis (for some particular Reason unknown to us) to that Part, which is now *Hudson*'s Streights. Though in Time this became a proper Name to express a Streight by which there is a Passage from the *North* to the *South Sea*, and is contended for to be the proper Name of the Streight that divides *Asia* from *America*, by which there is a Communication with the *Tartarian* and *Southern Ocean*. After a Discovery of these Coasts had been made to Northward, the following Year the King of *Portugal* sent *Americus Vespusino* to Southward, to discover the Land there.

Cortez's Designs seem to have their Foundation in these Expeditions of the *Portuguese*; but it was not until after the Year 1513, that the *South Sea* was discovered, and the *Portugueze* had discovered the *Moluccas*, that the finding a Streight to the Northward, by which a Passage might be made to the *South Sea*, became a Matter of particular Attention, and was the first and principal Object of *Cortez*'s Attention after he had become Master of the Capital of *Mexico* in 1521; and this Opinion of a Passage to Northward continued during the Reign of *Charles* the Fifth. Who in the Year 1524 sent from *Old Spain* to discover a Passage to the *Moluccas* by the North of *America*, without Success; but *Esteven Gomez*, who was sent on that Expedition, brought some *Indians* home with him. Then in the Year 1526 *Charles* the Fifth wrote to *Cortez*, in Answer to his Letters, and orders him to send the Ships at *Zacapila* to discover a Passage from *New Spain* to the *Moluccas*.

From this Time, the Year 1526, the Opinion of there being a Streight was generally received, though on what Foundation does not appear. It was certainly on some better Reason than *Gasper*'s Discoveries; and a Consideration of the Importance such a Passage would be of to the King of *Spain* with respect to the *Spice* Islands. It is consistent with the Characters of the Emperor *Charles* the Fifth, and of *Cortez*, when there were so many other solid Projects to pursue and this was preferred, to suppose that they should go, at that Time, on a meer visionary Scheme.

The same Opinion of a Passage to Northward prevailed in the Time of *Philip* the Second, and in the Year 1596 he sent Orders to the Viceroy

roy of *Mexico* for discovering and making Settlements in proper Parts of *California*, and one Reason assigned was, ' There was much Talk about ' the Streight of *Anian*, through which the *South Sea* was said to com- ' municate with that of the *North*, near *Newfoundland*; and should the ' *English* find out a practicable Passage on that Side, our Dominions, ' which then included all *Portuguese India*, would be no longer secure, ' all the Coast from *Acapulco* to *Culiacan* being quite defenceless, and ' from *Culiacan* Northward, not one single Settlement was made on the ' whole Coast.' Hist. Cal. V. i. P. 163. That now not only the Opinion of there being a Streight prevailed, but it was also fixed as to the Part, and had the Name of *Anian*.

The Opinion of a Passage still existed in the Reign of *Philip* the Third; and the same political Motives induced him to order the Conquest of *California* to be undertaken with all possible Expedition; and one Reason assigned is, ' His Majesty also found among other Papers a ' Narrative delivered by some Foreigners to his Father, giving an Ac- ' count of many remarkable Particulars which they saw in that Country, ' when driven thither by Stress of Weather from the Coast of *Newfound-* ' *land*; adding, they had passed from the *North Sea* to the *South*, by ' the Streight of *Anian*, which lies beyond Cape *Mendocino*; and that ' they had arrived at a populous and opulent City, walled and well ' fortified, the Inhabitants living under a regular Policy, and were a sen- ' sible and courteous People; with many other Particulars well worth ' a further Enquiry.' It must be considered this is given us in the History of *California*, V. ii. P. 239, from the *Monarchia Indiana* of *Juan Torquemada*, a learned *Franciscan*, published at *Madrid* in 1613, and republished in 1723, Vol. i. P. 629, That a Paper of this Sort was found in the Cabinet of *Philip* the Second, was thought deserving the Attention of *Philip* the Third. However the Matter of it is represented here, for nothing could be published but what was first perused and altered, so as to make it consistent with the Interest of Holy Church, the State, or good Manners, before it was licensed, such Paper must have contained some material Intelligence as to a Passage; and it is said to have contained *some remarkable Particulars*. Neither would the Work have been licensed, if what is related as to their having been such a Paper, had not been true.

Torquemada,

(85)

Torquemada, Vol. i. P. 20, quotes *Francifco Lopez de Gomara*, deemed a careful Writer, and Author of the Hiftory of the *Indies*. Who fays the Snowy Mountains are in forty Degrees, and the furthermoft Land that is laid down in our Maps; but the Coaft runs to the Northward until it comes to form an Ifland by the *Labrador*, or as feparated from *Greenland*; and this Extremity of the Land is five Hundred and ten Leagues in Length.

As to what is faid as to the Latitude of forty Degrees in this Quotation from *Gomara*, *Torquemada* hath prefixed a Map to his Work, *agreeable* to that formed by the King's Cofmographers, in which he hath made the moft Weftern and Northern Part of the Land in almoft forty-feven Degrees, and then the Land trends to the Eaftward, and the *Serras Nevadas* are reprefented to extend a great Length along the Coaft, and to Latitude 57 Degrees. Mentions, Vol. i. P. 16, the Royal Cofmographers do not infert any Thing in their Charts of the Sea Coafts but what they have upon Oath, or from creditable Perfons; and ' They make ' a Supputation in the Northern Parts of Iflands, which do not lie near or ' contiguous to the Lands of *Europe*; as to which Iflands, not long fince ' difcovered, the one is called *Iceland*, the other *Greenland*, which are ' the Bounds, Limits, or Marks, that divide the Land of the *Indies* ' from any other Part howfoever fituated or difpofed;'. afterwards obferves, which Iflands are not far from the *Labrador*; from which it is plain he calls *America* an Ifland. And this is agreeable to what *Acofta* fays, in the Senfe which I underftand him, that *Quivira* and *Anian* extend to the Weftern Extremity of *America*; and that the Extremity of the Kingdom of *Anian* to the North extends under the *Polar* or *Artick* Circle, and, if the Sea did not prevent it, would be found to join the Countries of *Tartary* and *China*; and the Streight of *Anian* takes its Courfe through the Northern Region, under the Polar Circle, towards *Greenland*, *Iceland*, *England*, and to the Northern Parts of *Spain*. By *Greenland* I underftand the Land to Northward, which is the North Part of *Hudfon*'s Streights, and *Cumberland* Ifles; and that this Streight fhould determine here is agreeable to what *Cortez* fays he would fend to fearch as far as the *Baccallaos*, (which was a Name given by *Cabot* in 1496) for the Streight by which he expected a Paffage from the *North* to the *South Sea*. By *Iceland* is meant, as is apparent from a View of fuch Map hereunto annexed, the Land to Northward of Cape *Farewel*, or the *Proper Greenland*.

Gomara

Gomara mentions thefe Iflands had not been long difcovered. It is apparent from the Map, that they had a very imperfect Account of thefe Difcoveries, which were made by *Frobifher* and *Davis*, who alfo were far from being exact in their Computations of the Longitude.

In this Map prefixed to *Torquemada*'s Work, and here annexed, the Southern Part of *Newfoundland* is laid down in Lat. 55, nine Degrees more to the Northward than it ought to be, for which Reafon the *Labrador*, *Greenland*, and *Iceland*, are placed much further to Northward than they ought to be placed, and are made to extend beyond the Polar Circle. It is from this Suppofition of *Newfoundland* being in fo high a Latitude that *Acofta* fays, *the Streight of Anian* takes its Courfe through the Northern Region under the Polar Circle towards *Greenland* and *Iceland*. In the fame Map the extremeft Point of *California*, anfwerable to Cape *St. Lucas*, is laid down in Longitude 105 Degrees from the Meridian of *Ferro*, and the Extremity of the Land to Weftward a Cape to Northward of Cape *Fortunes*, but to which no Name is given, and in Latitude 47, is placed in 135 Degrees from the Meridian of *Ferro*; the Difference of Longitude is 30 Degrees. This Map, publifhed by *Torquemada*, was conftructed before the Year 1612, therefore prior to a Map publifhed in *Holland* in 1619, under the Title of *Nova Totius Orbis Defcriptio*, prefixed to the Voyage of *George Spilbergen*, in which the Errors of *Torquemada*'s Map, as to the Situation of *Newfoundland*, and the Places to Northward are corrected; yet great Errors are committed as to the Parts to Weftward of *America*, making eighty-five Degrees of Longitude between Cape *St. Lucas* and the Extremity of the Land to Weftward and Northward in Lat. 42; and ninety-five Degrees between Cape *St. Lucas* and the Extremity of the Land neareft to *Afia*. The Reafon of this Difference is plain, they both err with refpect to thofe Parts, of which they had not authenticated Accounts.

Cortez wrote to the Emperor that he had fent People on Difcovery, both by Land and Water, it was not defigned that their Difcoveries fhould be communicated, as *Cortez* intended to turn them to his own private Advantage. But when *Mendoza* fitted out two Armaments, one by Land under the Command of *Coronado*, and the other by Sea under *Alarcon*; *Alarcon* was ordered to Latitude 53, to join the Land Forces, and to make a Survey of the Coaft, and fee if

there

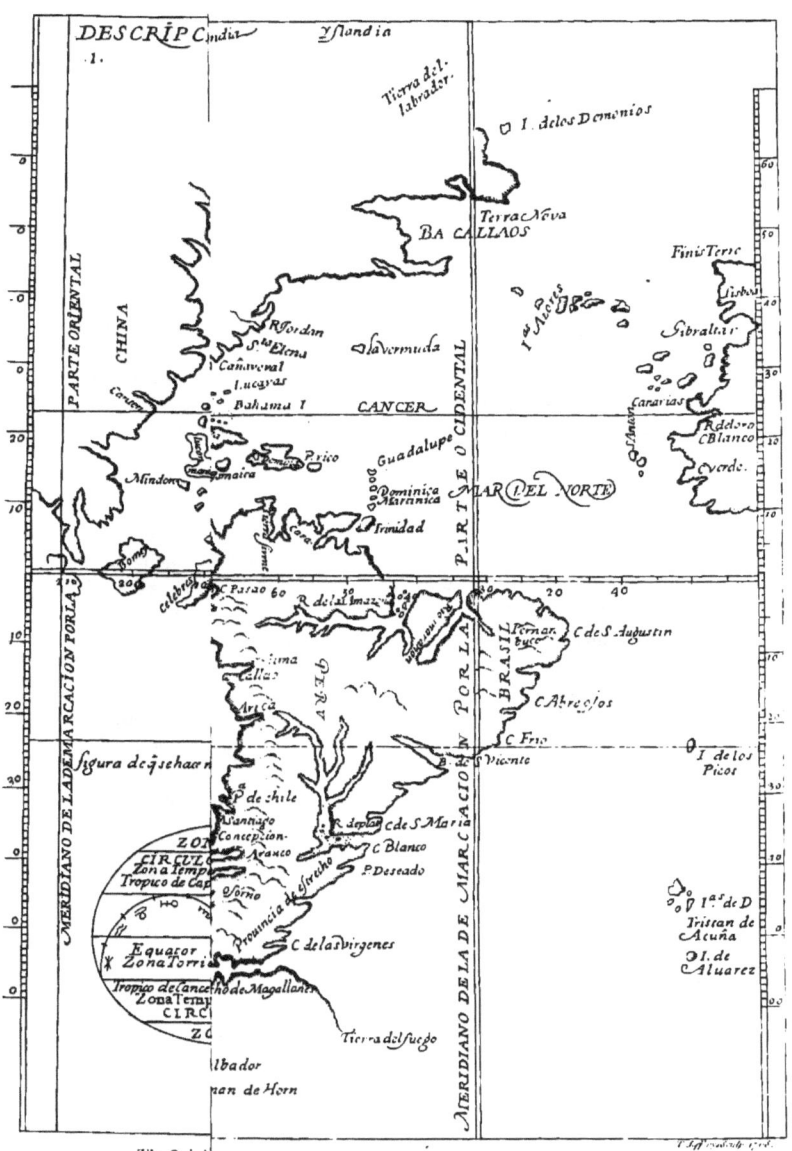

The Original Torquemadas MONARQUIA INDIANA. Vol I.

Gomara mentions thefe Iflands had not been long difcovered. It is apparent from the Map, that they had a very imperfect Account of thefe Difcoveries, which were made by *Frobifher* and *Davis*, who alfo were far from being exact in their Computations of the Longitude.

In this Map prefixed to *Torquemada*'s Work, and here annexed, the Southern Part of *Newfoundland* is laid down in Lat. 55, nine Degrees more to the Northward than it ought to be, for which Reafon the *Labrador, Greenland,* and *Iceland*, are placed much further to Northward than they ought to be placed, and are made to extend beyond the Polar Circle. It is from this Suppofition of *Newfoundland* being in fo high a Latitude that *Acofta* fays, *the Streight of Anian* takes its Courfe through the Northern Region under the Polar Circle towards *Greenland* and *Iceland*. In the fame Map the extremeft Point of *California*, anfwerable to Cape *St. Lucas*, is laid down in Longitude 105 Degrees from the Meridian of *Ferro*, and the Extremity of the Land to Weftward a Cape to Northward of Cape *Fortunes*, but to which no Name is given, and in Latitude 47, is placed in 135 Degrees from the Meridian of *Ferro*; the Difference of Longitude is 30 Degrees. This Map, publifhed by *Torquemada*, was conftructed before the Year 1612, therefore prior to a Map publifhed in *Holland* in 1619, under the Title of *Nova Totius Orbis Defcriptio*, prefixed to the Voyage of *George Spilbergen*, in which the Errors of *Torquemada*'s Map, as to the Situation of *Newfoundland*, and the Places to Northward are corrected; yet great Errors are committed as to the Parts to Weftward of *America*, making eighty-five Degrees of Longitude between Cape *St. Lucas* and the Extremity of the Land to Weftward and Northward in Lat. 42; and ninety-five Degrees between Cape *St. Lucas* and the Extremity of the Land neareft to *Afia*. The Reafon of this Difference is plain, they both err with refpect to thofe Parts, of which they had not authenticated Accounts.

Cortez wrote to the Emperor that he had fent People on Difcovery, both by Land and Water, it was not defigned that their Difcoveries fhould be communicated, as *Cortez* intended to turn them to his own private Advantage. But when *Mendoza* fitted out two Armaments, one by Land under the Command of *Coronado*, and the other by Sea under *Alarcon*; *Alarcon* was ordered to Latitude 53, to join the Land Forces, and to make a Survey of the Coaft, and fee if there

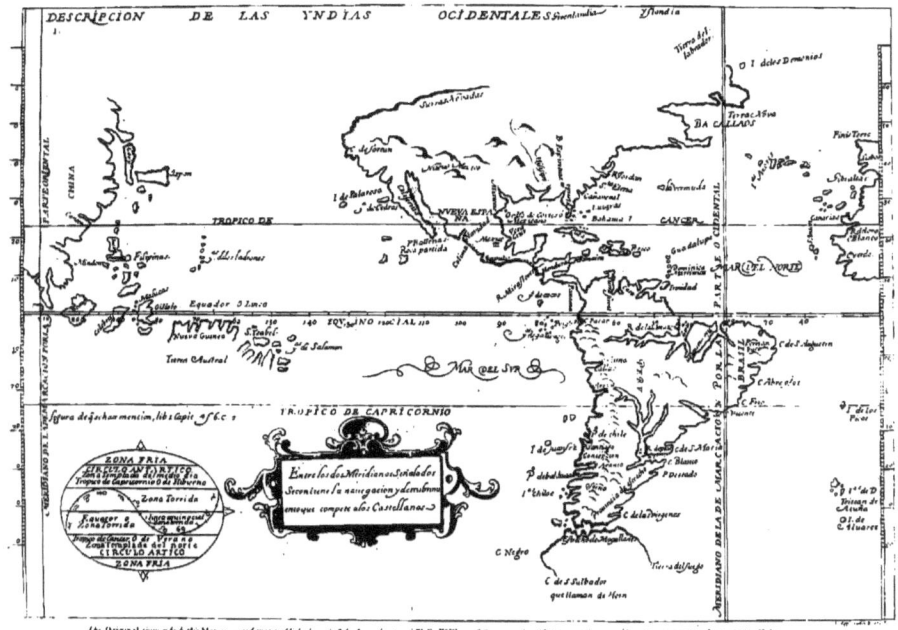

there was a Paffage or a Communication by Water through thofe Countries which *Coronada* was to difcover and fubdue, with the *South Sea*. As to *Coronado*, the *Francifcans* had been before in thofe Parts, and they gave Information and Direction as to his Part of the Expedition; but as to the Part that *Alarcon* had, on what Information he was ordered to go to Latitude 53, and what Probability there was that it was poffible for him to find fuch Paffage, and join the Land Forces, does not appear. But from his not finding fuch Paffage, not joining the Land Forces, and proceeding no further than the Lat. 36, though his Reafon for not going further is, that the Land then trended to the Northward, which he fuppofed would put him further off from the Army, whom he knew were in ten Days March of him, and the Excufe of Sicknefs and ill Condition of his Veffels, occafioned him to return before his Time; yet his Conduct threw the whole Difgrace of the ill Succefs of that Expedition on *Alarcon*, both with the Emperor and the Viceroy: And what he wrote to the Emperor was not attended to. He wrote to the Emperor, ' That it was for him only, and not in Subordination to " the Viceroy, that he had conquered, difcovered, and entered on the ' *Californias*, and all thofe Lands on the Coafts of the *South Sea*; that ' he had learnt that fome of thofe Lands were not far from the Coafts ' of *Grand China*; that there was but a fmall Navigation to the *Spice* ' Iflands, which he knew was wifhed for at that Time; that it engaged ' all his Thoughts, and was his moft ardent Defire to undertake fuch ' Navigation.' *Torquem.* Vol. i. P. 609.

On *Alarcon*'s Return *Juan Rodrique de Cabrillo* was fitted out, who went as far as Lat. 44. Sicknefs, Want of Provifions, and his Ships not being of fufficient Strength for thofe Northern Seas, obliged him to return, though he was defigned to go further to Northward. The Ships returning from the *Philippines*, which was alfo an Expedition in the Time of Viceroyfhip of *Mendoza*, fell in with the Land in Lat. 42, and found it all to be *Terra Firma*, from a Cape there, which they named *Mendocino* to the Port of *La Navidad*. In 1602 *Vizcaino* went, and then the Difcovery was made by *Martin de Aguilar*; and *Torquemada* tells us, Vol. i. Lib. 5. P. 725. That if there had not been, only fourteen healthy Perfons when they were at Cape *Blanco*, they were refolved to pafs thro' the Streight, which they named *Anian*, and which Streight is faid to be there; and P. 719, fpeaking of the Entrance of *Martin Aguilar*, it is

underflood

understood to be a River, by which you may pass to a great City, which the *Hollanders* discovered coming through the Streight, which is the Streight of *Anian*, and which City, he says, was named *Quivira*.

These Voyages, and we have Accounts of no others, could not have furnished the Cosmographers the principal Materials for composing their Map, and it must have been agreeable to those Materials, besides the Accounts of these Voyages sent to *Old Spain*, that they set down the utmost Limits of the Western Coast to be in the Longitude of 135 Degrees from the Meridian of *Ferro*. Therefore it was their Opinion at that Time that one Hundred and thirty-five Degrees was near the Difference of Longitude of the Entrance of the Streight of *Anian* in the *South Sea*, accounting the Longitude from the Meridian of *Ferro*. For which Reason the *Spaniards* can never be understood to mean by the Streight of *Anian* the Streight which separates *Asia* and *America*, now named *Beering*'s *Streight*, and by which there is a Communication between the Sea of *Tartary*, or the *Frozen Ocean*, and the *South Sea*.

It is something remarkable, and supports what hath been before said as to Deficiency of the *Spanish* Records, what Jesuit *Venegas*, the Author of the History of *California*, says, Vol. ii. P. 228, ' I was extremely
' desirous of finding Capt. *Sebastian Vizcaino*'s Narrative, and the Re-
' presentations of the Council to his Majesty *Philip* the Third, especially
' the Maps, Plans, Charts of his Voyage and Discoveries, in order to
' communicate the Whole to the Publick. Accordingly at my Request
' Search was made in the Secretary's Office of the Council of the *Indies*:
' But in this Intention of being serviceable to the Publick I have been
' disappointed.' And he again observes, on the Governor of *Cinaloa*
being ordered to pass over and take a Survey of the Coasts, Islands, Bays, Creeks, and the Disposition of the Ground of *California*, in the Year 1642, Vol. i. P. 188, ' There would have been little Occasion,
' says he, for this preparatory Survey, after so many others which had
' been continually making for above a Century, had the Reports, Nar-
' ratives, Charts, Draughts and Maps, which were made, or should
' have been made, by so many Discoveries still continued in being.
' But these are the Effects of a Want of a proper Care in preserving Pa-
' pers, a Fault to be regretted by Persons in Power, to whom they
' would be of Service in the Conduct of Affairs, and by private Per-
' sons,

' fons, on the Account of their Intereft, or as Entertainments of a com-
' mendable Curiofity.'—' But by the Lofs of fome Papers, either thro'
' a Change in the Government, or Irregularity in the Records, the whole
' Advantage of an Expedition is loft.'

From this Declaration by one who being a Jefuit, and of *Mexico*, compofing a Work entirely for the publick Service, under the Direction of the Jefuits ; by their Influence could attain the Sight of any Papers which were thought interefting as to the Work he was compofing; and his laft Reflection is not confined to the Records of *Old Spain* only; it is apparent what Uncertainty there is of attaining any Evidence from fuch Records, as to the Difcoveries made in the firft Century after the Conqueft of *Mexico*, and for a long Time after. The Narrative of *Vizcaino*'s Voyage, and every Thing thereto relating, as to any remaining Records might have become difputable, had not *Torquemada* collected it, and publifhed it amongft other Accounts ; yet what *Torquemada* hath preferved is but imperfect, as is apparent from a Journal of that Voyage, preferved in a private Hand at *Manilla*, and a Sight of large Extracts from which the Author hath been favoured by a Gentleman in *London*. It is owing to what *Torquemada* and fome others have collected of the Accounts which the Religious were the Authors of, that the Publick have the Accounts of thofe Parts ; but fuch Voyages and Accounts as have not met with the fame Means of being preferved, the Publick, from fuch Neglect, know nothing of them. It is plain from *Gomara*'s Account, alfo from *Acofta*'s, that great Difcoveries had been made in thefe Parts, but as to many of fuch Difcoveries, by whom is not known ; and *Venegas* fays, Vol. i. P. 30, the River *Santo Thome* was difcovered in the Year 1684 ; ' And tho' I do not find, fays he, in the Narratives of
' of that Expedition (of Admiral *Otondo*) that *Otondo* ever went afhore
' only to vifit the Harbours of the Eaftern Coaft and the Gulph ; yet
' from the ardent Curiofity of Father *Kino*, and the great Concern he
' had in the Affairs of *California*, I cannot think that he fhould be
' miftaken in any Particular relating to the Difcovery : That Father
' *Kino*, both in his large Manufcript Map, and likewife in the leffer Im-
' preffion, places the River of *Santo Thome* as rifing between the 26th
' and 27th Degrees of N. Latitude, and, after croffing the whole Penin-
' fula,

‘ fula, discharging itself into the *South Sea*, in the 26th Deg. and form-
‘ ing at its Mouth a large Harbour, which he calls *Peurto de Anno Neuvo*,
‘ being discovered in the Year 1685. On both Sides the River are
‘ Christian Villages, as is evident from their Names; *Santiago, Santo*
‘ *Innocentes, &c.* yet, in the Accounts of that Time, I do not meet with
‘ any Intelligence of this Discovery; to which I must add, that in the
‘ subsequent Relations no mention is made of any such River, Settle-
‘ ments or Harbours, though even little Brooks, are taken Notice of.'
And he observes many other Difficulties occur about this Coast. This
Harbour made by the River *Santo Thome*, is evidently that which *de
Fonte* and others call *Christabel*. Some Settlements had been made there,
as these Names were given, but either deserted from the Barrenness of
the Country, or had been only frequented by those who went out private
Adventurers, in order to trade with the Natives. But as to which River, Settlements and Harbour, were not the Names preserved by Father *Kino*, it would not have been known that any Persons had been in
those interior Parts of *California*, or that there were such Rivers and
Harbours. Father *Kino* looked upon it as a Thing so well known, as
he had no Occasion to defend himself, by giving the Reason of his
inserting those Names to protect himself from the Reproach of Posterity. And *Venegas* before tells us, that as to the Discoveries which had
been made for a Century passed, the Papers were lost.

Between the Year sixteen Hundred and eighty-five, and the Time of
Venegas's Publication, though in the Year sixteen Hundred and eighty-
five, it was well known that there was such a River as *St. Thome*, this River is exploded out of the Maps by the Geographers, on Account of the
Uncertainty; not duly considering that there was as full a Proof as could
be required with respect to so unfrequented a Part. The Account being
from a Person whose Business it was to make Observations there, who
had been so laborious and accurate as to discover, what had been so
long desired to be known, whether *California* was an Island or not, as
to which he was believed; and the Truth hath been confirmed by later
Observations of what he had reported, That it was not an Island. Therefore
there was no Foundation for any Uncertainty in this Case, the same as
with respect to the Letter of *de Fonte*, owing to the Neglect of a proper

per Enquiry into the Circumstances relating to it, by such an Inquiry the Uncertainty would have been removed.

What hath been said is to shew that the Argument on which so great a Stress is laid, that there is no Account of this Voyage amongst the *Spanish* Records, is an Argument of no Weight against the Authenticity of this Account; and that as a Publication of this Voyage was not permitted, an Account of such Voyage could not be perpetuated by the Religious, the only probable Means at that Time of preserving it from Oblivion. As it was intended what was the Effect of this Expedition should be kept a Secret, it is not consistent there should be many written Accounts of it; the Officers concerned would be cautious of letting Transcripts be made from their Journals; and it may be attributed to an extraordinary Accident, rather than to what could be expected, that a Copy of the Letter of *de Fonte* should ever come into the Possession of the *English*.

These Observations being previously made, we are better enabled to consider, what we have before inserted, the Objection of *Venegas* for not inserting this Account of *de Fonte*, as being of little Credit; but he seems rather to wish that we would be of his Opinion, than to imagine that he could convince us by any Arguments; therefore excuses himself as to the Length of the Dispute he might be engaged in. His Manner of expressing himself with respect to this Disappointment in the Secretary's Office, shews he hath a Manner of Address that his Words will admit of a further constructive Meaning than what is set down. The principal Object of his Writing is to incite the Court of *Spain* to prepare in Time against the ill Consequences of the *English* making a Discovery of a Passage; and he is to be understood, that it is not only his Opinion that the finding of such a Passage is practicable, but he apprehends it is of the Opinion of the Court also. Declares, that such Opinion hath prevailed from the first settling of *Mexico*, and that there really is a Passage in such a Manner as a Person who published an Account of this Sort would be permitted to express himself, to have it pass the Approbation of the Licenser; and does not desire to suppress the Account of *de Fonte*, as it is an absolute Contradiction to what he would infer, there being a

Passage,

Passage, and in such Letter it is declared there is no North-west Passage. For he must have had further and better Authorities for his Assertions of there being a Passage than such, as that single Assertion would prevail against. But desired to suppress this Account, as it was an Account which he knew it was more consistent with the Designs of the Court, it should be continued in Oblivion than revived. Mentions it therefore as the *Contents of a* Paper published in *London*, which contained a Narrative of little Credit; and to give the better Authority to what he says, as he could not trust to the Opinion that might be had of such Account on a fair Representation of the Title; to support the Character he gave of it, therefore uses Art, misrepresenting such Title; says it was *by Order of the Viceroy of* Peru, *in the Year* 1640, and *giving an Account of the most material Transactions and Adventures in this Voyage*. Was the Letter so entituled, the *Transactions* and *Adventures* of a Commander in Chief of the Navy, in *New Spain*, he would not be singular in his Opinion, but it would be understood by every one as a Romance, and not deserving of Credit.

This Misrepresentation is intentionally done; for if he never saw the Letter, or had not a right Account of it, on what Authority could he assert it was of little Credit; and that it would engage him in a long Dispute, a Dispute which his Sagacity would point out to him how to determine in a very few Lines, by proving that there was no such Person as *de Fonte*, Admiral of *New Spain*; which it was in his Power to do had it been the Case. But what he mentions is so far from a Denial of there being such a Person Admiral of *New Spain*, that he gives us the Name, and sets forth the Character *de Fonte* was in, in a more proper Manner than we have it expressed in the Title of the Letter. *Bartholomew de Fuentes, Commander in Chief of the Navy in New Spain and Peru, and President of Chili*; and he is to be understood not to mean that there was no such Person, but that the Narrative is not credible as to any such Voyage having been made by Admiral *de Fonte*.

By a Schedule of the King of *Spain* in 1606 to the Governor of the *Philippines*, *Vizcaino* was to be again fitted out to discover a Harbour on the Western Coast of *California*, for the Reception of the *Aquapulco* Ship;

Ship; but the Death of *Vizcaino* prevented that Defign being carried into Execution; as the Court had found fo many Difappointments, and fuch ill Succefs in thefe Undertakings, they did not think proper to entruft it to any other Perfon in the *Philippines* or *New Spain*. And *Venegas* fays, Hift of *Cal*. Vol. i. P. 180. ' During the fucceeding nine Years incon-
' fiderable Voyages only were made to *California*, and thefe rather to fifh
' for Pearls, or procure them by Barter, than to make any Settlement,
' and therefore they have been thought below any feparate Account,
' efpecially as in the fubfequent Royal Commiffions they are only men-
' tioned in general without any Circumftances.' Though Commiffions were given to go into thefe Parts, without any Account remaining to whom, and on what particular Occafion; it is not to be doubted as in all Commiffions of this Nature they would be under an Obligation to make a Report to the Court, and it is not to be underftood that thefe Com- miffions were continued for nine Years only; and therefore what hath been faid as to *Parmentiers* and the Jefuits, their having been in thefe Parts, is not the leaft improbable. By thefe Commiffions they were not confined to the Gulph of *California*, is evident from Father *Kino*, as already mentioned, giving Names in his Map to Villages, or occafional Settlements rather, on the River *Santo Thome*: And he fays, P. 299, what made Father *Kino* defirous of difcovering whether *California* was an Ifland or not, ' That all the Moderns had placed it as an Ifland,
' there being extant alfo fome Journals of Mariners, according to which
' they went round *California* through a Streight, and gave the Parts and
' Places through which they paffed their own Names.' It appears from this Account they were permitted, by thefe Commiffions, to rove about, though not to make Settlements, induced by their private Advantage, and the Advantage to the Government was from their Difcoveries. Alfo Vol. i. P. 182, he mentions, ' That a great many private Perfons, from
' the Coaft of *Culiacan* and *Chametla*, made Trips in fmall Boats to the
' Coaft of *California*, either to fifh for Pearls, or purchafe them of the
' *Indians*;' which is agreeable to *de Fonte*'s Account of the Mafter and Mariners he procured at *Zalagua* and *Compoftilo*. We may alfo obferve what the Miffionaries fay, as to the Tides at the Head of the Bay, which ftill adds to the Authenticity of this Account. ' In thofe Parts the Tide
' fhifts

' shifts every six Hours; the Flood, with a frightful Impetuosity, rises
' from three to seven Fathoms, overflowing the flat Country for some
' Leagues, and the Ebb necessarily returns with the same dangerous
' Violence.—However the Pilot went on Shore in the Pinnace, at seve-
' ral Parts, in order to make a complete Drawing of it for his Chart;
' was equally convinced that this Cape was the Extremity of the Gulph
' of *California*, and that the Waters beyond it were those of the River
' *Colorado*.' Therefore it was, from the exact Observation of the Tide
which this Pilot took so much Pains to make, an unsettled Point from
whence the Tide proceeded. Which, at the Time of *de Fonte*'s Expedition, was said to come from the Northward, agreeable to the then prevailing Opinion of *California* being an Island. According to the usual
Practice, though the true Cause of a Phænomena is unknown, to quote
that Phænomena that favours a System which there is a Desire to establish as a Truth, not only in support of but to confirm such System,
as to render the Truth of it unquestionable.

After *Vizcaino*'s Death, and though the Court of *Spain* was disappointed
as to finding able and sufficient Persons in *New Spain* whom they could
intrust, yet Adventures were made by private Persons, at their own Expence, both for Discovery and Settlements; yet these could not be undertaken without the Permission of his Majesty, who had taken it into
his own Hand to grant such Commissions, and mostly required a Voyage
to *Old Spain* to attain them; and the next Expedition that was made, at
the Crown's Expence, was conducted by an Admiral from *Old Spain*,
who arrived in *New Spain* in 1643, Admiral *Caſſanate*, with full Power
and Neceſſaries to equip a Fleet, and make Settlements in *California*;
and he sailed on such Expedition in 1644. By which it is apparent
that there were Ships at that Time in *New Spain* proper for such Expeditions. As he came into these Parts within three Years after *de
Fonte*'s Expedition, and took the Command as Admiral of *New Spain*
when he arrived, it is to be supposed the Expedition *Caſſanate* was sent
on was too fatiguing for *de Fonte*, who was therefore retired to his Government of *Chili*. In the Year 1649 Admiral *Caſſanate*, in Reward for
his Services, being after the same Manner promoted to the Government

of *Chili, de Fonte* muſt be dead at that Time. This Circumſtance fixes the Period in which the Copy of this Letter was taken.

As what *Venegas* ſays as to the Account (which Account hath been before mentioned) given by *Seyxas y Lovera*, as to its wanting the neceſſary Authenticity. Beſides the uſual Licences, wherein the Licencers declare there is nothing contrary to good Manners, and beſides being dedicated to the King in his Royal and Supreme Council of the *Indies*, *Seyxas*'s Book hath the Licence and Approbation of the Profeſſor of Divinity in the Univerſity of *Alcara*, Preacher to the King, and Principal of a College of Jeſuits in *Madrid*. Hath alſo the Approbation and Licence of the Profeſſor of Erudition and Mathematicks in the Imperial College of the Company of the Jeſuits at *Madrid*. What unfavourable Opinion ſoever we may entertain of the Principles of theſe Perſons, we muſt have ſuch an Opinion of their Prudence, that they would not ſign their Approbation to a Book while it contained an unneceſſary Lie, which could be eaſily expunged, or until they were ſatisfied as to the Authenticity of this Account which *Seyxas* gives of *Peche*'s Voyage, having been publiſhed in various Places. And it is indiſputable from the Countenance his Book received, he was looked on at that Time as a deſerving honeſt Man.

Venegas deſignedly omits other Accounts diſperſed in various Books for Want of neceſſary Authenticity; but it is not to be underſtood that he abſolutely denies that ſuch Accounts are true. Neither is there ſo great an Improbability in ſuch Diſcoveries having been made, as ſome of theſe Accounts mention, as is imagined, when ſuch Accounts are duly conſidered.

We have already mentioned one Account which engaged the Attention of the King of *Spain*, therefore muſt have been of ſome Authority. There is another Account (unleſs it be the ſame Account differently repreſented) of a Ship that, to the Northward of Cape *Blanco*, on the Coaſt of *California*, paſſed through the Streight into the *North Sea*, and to *Old Spain*, which was alſo made known to the King of *Spain*, mentioned by *Torquemada*, Vol. i. P. 725.

Moſt

Most of the Discoveries are reported to have been made by Ships coming from the *Moluccas*, or from the *Philippine* Islands to the Eastward, and which have met with bad Weather. And what, in those Times, Ships were necessitated to do, if there was a Continuance of hard Gales of Wind, we may learn from the Schedule of *Philip* the Third, History of *California*, Vol. i. P. 175, after mentioning a Harbour found by *Vizcaino*, on the Western Coast of *California*, adds, ' And lies very conve-
' nient for Ships returning from the *Philippine* Islands to put into, and
' thus, in case of Storms, avoid the Necessity of making for *Japan*, as
' they have several Times done, and expended great Sums of Money.
' Besides, they usually have Sight of the Coast of *China*, which is an
' additional Benefit, as knowing where they are, they will not as for-
' merly, in case of bad Weather, make for *Japan*, or those Islands, as
' the same Winds which would carry them thither, bring them into this
' Harbour. Again, P. 177, considering how much it concerns the Se-
' curity of Ships coming from those Islands, in a Voyage of no less than
' 2000 Leagues, on a wide and tempestuous Sea, that they should be
' provided with a Port where they might put in and furnish themselves
' with Water, Wood, and Provisions: That the said Port of *Monterey*
' lies in 37 Degrees, nearly about half Way the Voyage.'

A Ship flying before the Wind, and the People steering her towards the Coast of *America*, to avoid *Japan* and the Islands, making a Cape Land on the Coast of *California*, would run for what they supposed a Harbour, and the bad Weather continuing might proceed up the Bay or Opening they were then in, to meet with the Inhabitants, in order to obtain Refreshments, and to learn where they were, by which Means find a Passage. As Ships were distressed in hard Gales of Wind, in the Manner the Schedule mentions, there is no Improbability of a Passage being first accidentally discovered by a single Ship coming from Sea with a leading Wind into a large Opening, in Expectation of a Harbour, though such Discovery hath not been made by Ships intentionally sent along Shore for that Purpose.

It is to be observed, the People of the *Philippine* Islands are those who most talked of a Passage: They informed *Peche* and others; and it is easily accounted for why they should do so: For if the *Portugueze* made

the

the Discovery in a Ship from the *Moluccas*, there was a constant Intercourse between them and the People of the *Philippines*; and whether the Discovery was made by the *Spaniards* or *Portugueze*, some of the Company who were aboard such Ship as had passed through the Streight from the *South* to the *North Sea*, would return to the *Moluccas* or the *Philippines*; and others would meet their Acquaintance from thence in *Portugal* or *Old Spain*; who would take Pleasure in relating to them the Accounts of their Voyage, and which they who heard those Accounts would be equally fond of communicating to others, especially when they returned back to the *Indies*. By which Means it would be known that there had been such a Discovery; and it would be out of the Power of the King of *Spain* or *Portugal* to prevent its being so far known, but could prevent the Account of such Discovery being published, or the Particulars communicated to Foreigners.

In the Year 1568 *Salvatierra*, a Gentleman of *Spain*, who had accidentally landed in *Ireland* from the *West Indies*, gave an Account of a Passage having been made by one *Andrew Urdanietta*, and by the Circumstances of that Account it was about the Year 1556 or 1557. This *Urdanietta* was a Friar, was with and greatly assisted *Andrew Miguel Lopez de Legaspi* in the Expedition to the *Philippine* Islands in the Year 1564, and was called the celebrated Religious *Andrew de Urdanietta*. His being thus employed, and so serviceable in this Expedition to the *Philippine* Islands, as he is said to have been, implies, that he had a prior Knowledge of those Parts, and must have been there before; and the Character that *Salvatierra* gave of him to Sir *Hugh Sydney*, then Lord Deputy of *Ireland*, and Sir *Humphrey Gilbert*, was, that he was the greatest Discoverer by Sea that was in that Age.

Salvatierra said that *a North-west Passage* was constantly believed to be in *America* navigable; and that *Urdanietta* had shewed him at *Mexico*, eight Years before *Salvatierra* arrived in *Ireland*, a Chart made from his own Observations in a Voyage in which he came from *Mare del Zur* into *Germany*, through this North-west Passage, wherein such Passage was expressed, agreeing with *Ortelius*'s Map: That *Urdanietta* had told the King of *Portugal* of it as he came there from *Germany* in his return home;

home; but the King earneftly intreated him not to difcover this Secret to any Nation: *For that* (faid he) *if* England *had once a Knowledge and Experience of it, it would greatly hinder the King of* Spain *and me.* And *Salvatierra* was himfelf perfuaded of a Paffage by the Friar *Urdanietta*, and by the common Opinion of the *Spaniards* inhabiting *America*.

It was this Account with fome other that gained the Attention of the greateft Men of that Age to purfue the Difcovery of a North-weft Paffage. Neither would *Dudley, Walfingham*, or Sir *Humphrey Gilbert*, and other honourable Perfons about the Court, be deceived with fictitious Stories, and purfue a Phantom. Could the great Abilities and Penetration of a *Walfingham* be defective in this Refpect, which was fo perfect in all other Refpects, as to be the Admiration of the prefent Age. Thofe who condemn this Account, and fome other Accounts of this Sort, have not confidered, that upon a flight Surmife or Sufpicion only they put their Judgments in Competition with and in Contradiction to the Judgments of thofe great Men, who embraced no Opinion as to any Matter but what was founded in Reafon, and all the Circumftances relating to which they had firft fully confidered, and which Opinion they adhered to. As to a North-weft Paffage, making a Diftinction between the Difappointments as to the effecting the Difcovery of a Paffage, and the Probability there was of their being fuch Paffage. The King of *Spain* was equally fuccefslefs as to the Execution, and at the fame Time as much affured of the Practicability of making it; for which Reafon Secretary *Walfingham* was concerned at his Death, as the Attention of the Publick was drawn to a *North-eaft* Paffage, by which nothing more was propofed than a Trade to *Cathay* or *China*, and that a North-weft Paffage was neglected on the Part of the *Englifh*.

It was an Opinion received in *England* in the Year 1560, or earlier, that there was fuch a Paffage; and before the *Philippines* were fettled by the *Spaniards*. Soon after the Difcovery of *Urdanietta, Frobifher*, who fet out in 1576, is faid to have projected his Defign, and made an Application for fifteen Years before. Did not fucceed in the City probably, as they might not fee any certain Advantage; but when he applied to the Court he fucceeded. On what Plan he went is alfo evident, to find an Entrance to Northward of the *Labrador*; for when he fell in with the South-west Part of *Greenland*, it was supposed by him to be the *Labrador* Coast.

There is another Account on the Oath of *Thomas Cowles* of *Bedminster*, taken the 9th of *April* 1579, at a Time when Oaths were considered by all People as solemn and sacred Obligations to declare the Truth. He says that six Years before, he heard a *Portugueze* read a Book which he set out six Years before in print in the *Portugal* Tongue, declaring that he, *Martin Chacke*, had found, now twelve Years past, a Way from the *Portugal Indies* through the Gulph of *Newfoundland*, which he thought to be in Latitude 59° of the North Pole, by Means that he being in the said *Indies* with four Ships of great Burthen, and he himself being in a small Ship of eighty Ton, far driven from the Company of the other four Ships with a West Wind; after that he had passed along by a great Number of Islands, which were in the Gulph of the said *Newfoundland*, and after that he overshot the Gulph, he set no more Sight on any other Land, until he fell in with the North-west Part of *Ireland*; and from thence he took his Course homeward, and by that Means came to *Lisbon* four or five Weeks before the other Ships. But the Books were afterwards called in by the King's Order.

This Passage was made about ten Years after that of *Urdanietta*; and it is probable *Chacke* was encouraged to proceed through such Passage, from the Report or an Account which he had heard of such Passage having been before made. It is evident he met with some Difficulties in such Passage which delayed him, as the Ships were at *Lisbon* so soon after him, and as he expresses that he was far driven from the other four Ships he left them in a low Latitude, and being got to the Northward, without any Expectation of rejoining them, proceeded intentionally to make his Voyage by the Passage; which he would not have done to the Hazard of losing his Vessel and Cargo, for he was not on Discovery, but returning to *Lisbon* in Company with other loaden Vessels, from whom he was separated, unless he had been assured that what he undertook was practicable, and a Passage had been made by some Vessel before that Time. This Account was received as a Truth by the principal People of the Kingdom, who certainly made a due Enquiry as to the Character of the Person who made the Affidavit with respect to his Capacity;

Capacity; there would be a proper Precaution alfo, at the Time of adminiftering fuch Affidavit, that it was exact and only what he knew pofitively as to this Matter, tho' there might be other Circumftances which he was not fo pofitive in. And as this Account was at that Time believed, it muft have been on better Reafons than can be at prefent urged by any one to call the Veracity of this Account in Queftion.

Juan de Fuca (the Account is from *Purchafe* and *North-weft Fox*) was an ancient Pilot, who had been in the *Weft India* of *Spain* for near forty Years, and had failed as Mariner and Pilot to many Places thereof in Service of the *Spaniards*.

He was Pilot of three fmall Ships which the *Viceroy* of *Mexico* fent from thence, armed with a hundred Soldiers, under a *Spaniard* Captain, to difcover the Streights of *Anian* along the Coaft of the *South Sea*, and to fortify in that Streight, to refift the Paffage of the *Englifh* Nation, but by Reafon of a Mutiny which happened amongft the Soldiers, for fome ill Practices of the Captain, the Voyage was overfet, and they returned to *New Spain*.

The Viceroy fent *de Fuca* out again in 1592, with a fmall Caravel and Pinnace, armed with Mariners only, for the Difcovery of the faid Streights. Finding the Land to trend North and North-eaft, with a broad Inlet between 47 and 48, he entered it, and failing therein more than twenty Days, found the Land trending ftill, fometimes North-weft, fometimes North-eaft, and alfo South-eaftward, far broader Sea than at the faid Entrance; and paffed by diverfe Iflands in that Entrance.

He went upon Land in feveral Places, and faw fome People on Land, clad in Beafts Skins; and that the Land was very fruitful, and rich of Gold and Silver, and Pearls, and other Things like *Nova Hifpania*.

Being entered thus far in the faid Streight, and come into the *North Sea* already, and finding the Sea wide enough every where, and to be about thirty or forty Leagues wide in the Streight where he entered; he thought he had well difcharged his Office, and done the Thing he was fent to do; and that he not being armed to refift the Force of the

favage

savage People, that might happen to affault him, therefore fet fail and returned to *Nova Hifpania*, where he arrived at *Aquapulco*, *Anno* 1592, hoping to be well rewarded by the Viceroy for his Voyage fo performed.

The Viceroy received him kindly, and gave him Promifes; but after an Expectation of two Years the Viceroy wifhed him to go to *Spain*, where the King would reward him; and he accordingly went.

He was well received at Court; but after long Suit could get no Reward to his Content, fo ftole away and came to *Italy*, to live amongft his Kindred in his own Country, being very old, a *Greek* by Birth, born in the Ifland of *Sepholonica*, and his proper Name *Apoftollos Valerianos*.

De Fuca went firft to *Leghorn*, then to *Florence*, where he met one *John Dowlafs*, an *Englifhman*, a famous Mariner, ready coming for *Venice*, to be a Pilot for a *Venetian* Ship to *England*; they went in Company to *Venice*. *Dowlafs* being acquainted with Mr. *Lock*, at leaft a confiderable Merchant if not a Conful there; gave him an Account of this *de Fuca*, and introduced him to Mr. *Lock*, who gave Mr. *Lock* the preceding Account; and made a Propofal, if Queen *Elizabeth* would make up the Lofs which he had fuftained aboard the *Aquapulco* Ship taken by Captain *Cavendifh*, which was to the Value of fixty Thoufand Ducats, he would go to *England*, and ferve her Majefty to difcover the *North-weft Paffage* into the *South Sea*, and engage his Life for the Performance, with a Ship of forty Tons and a Pinnace. They had two feveral Meetings on this Occafion; and *Lock*, at *de Fuca*'s Requeft, wrote to the old Lord *Treafurer Cecil*, Sir *Walter Rawleigh*, and Mr. *Richard Hackluit*, the Cofmographer, defiring a Hundred Pounds for to pay his Paffage to *England*. His Friends wrote *Lock* Word, the Action was very well liked, if the Money could be procured. As no great Expectations were to be had from this Anfwer, *de Fuca* left *Venice* in a Fortnight after, purfued his Defign of going to *Greece*, and there died.

There is nothing in this Relation but what is very natural and fimple. *De Fuca*'s Demand was exceffive, for which Reafon, probably, as a Man who over-rated his Services, he was not rewarded by the *Viceroy* or the *King*; yet the *Viceroy* availed himfelf of him, by fending him to Court to give an Account of his Voyage, which he might be ordered to do, as another Expedition was defired, and a Reprefentation for that Purpofe made by the Viceroy *Luis Velafco*, as is mentioned in the Schedule of the King. Hiftory of *California*, P. 173.

It did not appear that he could certainly perform what he undertook, concluding he was in the *North Sea*, from fuch Sea returned back to *New Spain*, therefore had not acquired a Knowledge of the Entrance into the Streights from the Eaftward; which was the Difficulty that obftructed this Difcovery on the Part of the *Englifh*, and had been fo much fought after, but unfuccefsfully. His Age was alfo a very material Objection, that he would fcarce be able to bear the Fatigue of fuch a Voyage, his Defire to undertake which immediately proceeded from his Avarice: Nor was it confiftent that the Hundred Pounds fhould be fent over to bring him to *England*, if the other Part of the Terms could not be complied with; which feems to be the Meaning of the Expreffion, the Action is well liked of if the Money could be procured. And *de Fuca*, whofe Motive for propofing this Undertaking, was to be fatiffied for his Lofs by Captain *Cavendifh*, would not have altered his Defign of going into his own Country, and proceeded to *England*, unlefs he was affured of his being fo gratified on a Performance of what he undertook.

Dowlafs, who was a good Mariner, as he travelled with him, and kept his Company, would have had particular and frequent Converfation with *de Fuca*, and who, as a Mariner, was more capable of finding out if his Account was true, and was thoroughly fatisfied it was fo, as he fpoke to Mr. *Lock* about him. Neither *Lock* nor *Dowlafs* could have any finifter Views, but only animated by a publick Spirit to do their Country fo acceptable a Service, which it was thought to be in *England*, as it is faid the Action is well liked of.

As to *de Fuca* being taken Prifoner by Captain *Cavendifh*, and how did he efcape out of the Hands of the *Englifh*? When the Ship was taken all the People were put afhore on the Coaft of *California*, the Goods were taken out, and then the Ship was fet a Fire, which burnt to the Water Mark, the Wreck floated afhore, they erected Jury-mafts in her, and fortunately got to *Aquapulco*.

De

De Fuca says, the Cause he thought of the ill Reward he had of the *Spaniards* was, that they understood very well the *English* Nation had now given over all their Voyages for the Discovery of a *North-west Passage*, wherefore they feared not them to come any more that Way into the *South Sea*; and therefore they needed not his Service therein any more: Which is so far agreeable to the Accounts of those Times, that, after the Death of Sir *Francis Walsingham*, the Discovery of a North-west Passage had no Patron at Court; and Sir *Francis* had particularly interested himself in procuring *Davis* to go on his last Expedition. The Discovery was not re-assumed until the Year 1602, by the *Muscovy* Company, who had never engaged as a Company in this Discovery; but having made some successless Attempts, as to the North-east Passage, fitted out Capt. *George Weymouth* for the Discovery of a North-west Passage, which it is observable was the same Year with *Vizcaino*'s Expedition. And it is observable the next Expedition for the Discovery of a North-west Passage, was not until the Year 1606, when Mr. *John Knight* was fitted out; and the same Year the King of *Spain* orders *Vizcaino* on a third Expedition, but *Vizcaino* died, though in the interim *Vizcaino* had been to *Old Spain*, to make Application to make a fresh Attempt, at his own Expence, and he could not obtain Permission of his Majesty. As the Expeditions which the Court of *Spain* order peremptorily to be undertaken, correspond as to the Time with those from *England*, shews a Jealousy on the Part of the King of *Spain* that the *English* might succeed as to a Passage through the Streights. And though it is mentioned as the principal Design in the Expeditions by Order of the King of *Spain*, is the Discovery of a Harbour for the *Aquapulco* Ship, the Publick understood there was yet a farther Design, and as much may be collected from the King of *Spain*'s Schedule in 1606. Count *de Monterey*, ' by pursuing the Discovery intended by *Don Luis de*
' *Velasco*, wrote to me concerning, and was of Opinion that small Vessels from the Harbour of *Aquapulco* were the fittest; and that in the
' Discovery might be included the Coasts and Bays of the Gulph of *California*, and of the Fishery, to which, in my Letter of the 27th of
' *September* 1599, I ordered to be answered, that the Discovery, and
' making Draughts, with Observations of that Coast, and the Bays along
' it, having appeared to me *highly convenient*, it was my Will he should
' immediately

'immediately put it in Execution, without troubling himself about *Ca-*
'*lifornia*, unless occasionally—And *Sebaſtian Vizcaino* carefully informed
'himself of these *Indians*, and many others, whom he discovered along
'the Coast for above eight Hundred Leagues; and they all told him,
'that up the Country there were large Towns, Silver, and Gold;
'whence he is inclined to believe that great Riches may be discovered,
'especially as, in some Parts of the Land, Veins of Metal are to be seen;
'and that the Time of their Summer being known, a farther Discovery
'might be made of them by *going within* the Country, and that the
'Remainder of it may be discovered along the Coast, as it reaches be-
'yond 42 Degrees, the Limits specified to the said *Sebaſtian Vizcaino* in
'his Inſtructions.' Though these Orders were received in *Mexico* in 1699,
no Voyage was set out on until 1602, the Time that *Weymouth* sailed,
then probably enforced by additional Orders from the Court of *Spain*.
The Expedition which was overturned by the Mutiny of the Soldiers,
seems to have been about the Time of Captain *Davis*'s Expedition; for
de Fuca says, after the Voyage was so ill ended, the Viceroy set him out
again in 1592, which implies a Distance of Time between the firſt and
second Voyage.

The Inſtructions *Vizcaino* had in the firſt Voyage were given by the
Viceroy, for it was the Viceroy who appointed him, and were formed
according to the Opinion that the Land beyond forty-two Degrees took
a Course to Weſtward and Southward of Weſt. And the Maps were
conſtructed agreeable thereto, therefore the King says, '*Vizcaino* had
'repreſented to him that the Coaſt, as far as 40 Degrees, lies North-
'weſt and South-eaſt, and that in the two other Degrees, which makes
'up the 42 Degrees, it lies North and South,' and, as before mentioned,
says, ' and that the Remainder of it may be discovered along the Coasts,
' as it reaches beyond 42 Degrees, the Limits specified to the said *Se-
'baſtian Vizcaino* in his Inſtructions.' Therefore when *Martin Aguilar*
got to 43 Degrees and found an Opening, he concluded, as the Coaſt
was repreſented to be terminated to the Northward, by the Maps and
Charts in Uſe, that this muſt be the defired Streights; and therefore said
on their Return, ' they ſhould have performed a great deal more, had
' their Health not failed them; for it is certain that only fourteen Per-
' fons enjoyed it at *Cape Blanco*. The General and thoſe that were with
' him

' him had a mind to go through the Streight, which they call of *Anian*,
' and is said to be thereabouts. It had been entered by the foreign
' Ship, who gave Intelligence of it to the King, describing its Situa-
' tion, and how through that Passage one might reach the *North Sea*,
' and then sail back to *Spain*, along *Newfoundland* and the Islands of
' *Baccalaos*, to bring an Account of the Whole to his Majesty.' *Torquemada*, Vol. i. P. 725. But it is very plain the King had another Information of this Matter, and as to the Extent of the Land to Northward.
Luis de Velasco was the Viceroy in whose Time the Expedition of *de Fuca*
was; and the Expedition of *Vizcaino* was under the Direction of the
Count *de Monterey*, who was either not informed of what had been done
by *de Fuca*, or might not think *de Fuca*'s Account of sufficient Authority
to justify him, the Viceroy, in drawing his Instructions agreeable thereto;
contrary to the general Opinion of the Cosmographers at that Time,
and the Description they gave of the Coasts in their Maps.

It must appear from what hath been said that there are no such great
Improbabilities in the Accounts of *Salvatierra*, *Chacke*, or *de Fuca*, as
hath been represented. It is also evident that the *English* had great Expectations of succeeding; and the Court of *Spain* had great Apprehen-
sions we should meet with Success, and be enabled to attain a Passage by
the Streight of *Anian* into the *South Sea*; for which there must have been
some reasonable Foundation both on the Part of the one and the other.
The *English* were first induced to attempt the Discovery of such a Passage, from the Accounts which they had from *Spain* of there being such
a Passage. The Court of *Spain* entertained, as hath been shewn, an
Opinion of there being such a Passage from the Time they conquered
Mexico; and, agreeable to what *Torquemada* says, had a certain Account
of it, or at least an Account which appeared to the King to be authentick. What that Account really contained we do not know, nor was it
consistent that it should be made publick; therefore what is said as to
the Particulars of it are but Conjecture, and Representations upon Reports, for which the Reporters could have no real Authority. As *Vizcaino* regretted being prevented, by the Sickness of his People that he
could not go round the World, and have carried home to *Old Spain* his
Account of his Expedition. This firm Persuasion that he should have
accomplished his Passage to *Old Spain*, by the Streight of *Anian*, must
have

(106)

have been from some Information which he had received before he set out, that such Passage was practicable: Neither is it mentioned as if he proposed making a Discovery of it, but as of a Thing before done. It was the Opinion of all those who were with him, that it was practicable; which is agreeable to what *Salvatierra* informed Sir *Hugh Sydney*, and Sir *Humphrey Gilbert*, That a *North-west Passage from us to* Cathay *was constantly believed in* America *navigable*. *Vizcaino*, who is represented as a Commander of great Conduct and Discretion (and which the Account of his Voyage expresses him to have been) would not have attempted to make a Passage thro' such Streights, to the Hazard, perhaps entire Loss, of the King's Ships, and what he had before done rendered of no Effect, unless he had a discretionary Power either to pass to *Old Spain* by these Streights, or return to *Aquapulco*.

After the Expedition of *Knight* failed, and *Vizcaino* died, we hear of no other Expeditions at the Expence of or by the positive Order of the Court of *Spain* until that of Admiral *Cassanate*, who went the third Year after the Expedition of *de Fonte*, to make a Survey of the Coast of *California*; yet we have no Reason to conclude there were no other Expeditions, but it is rather to be supposed that, after the *English* had proceeded in their Discoveries as far as *Hudson*'s Bay, the Court of *Spain* thought it necessary, and found an effectual Way of keeping their Expeditions, both in respect to their Equipment and what was done on such Expeditions a Secret, by sending Officers from *Old Spain* to conduct them, and as to which the Religious would not think themselves at Liberty to make any Publication without the Permission of the Court.

Having no Intercourse by Trade with those Parts, we cannot be acquainted with what is transacted in those Parts, any further than what the *Spanish* Writers are permitted to inform us, and the imperfect and uncertain Intelligence of those who have been cruizing in those Seas. The *Spanish* Nation have been particularly cautious of keeping the Knowledge of their Coast secret: Neither was it known, in the Year 1746, that an exact Survey was made of those Coasts until *Pasco Thomas* annexed to his Account of Lord *Anson*'s Expedition, published in 1745, a Copy of a Manuscript, which Manuscript contained an Account of the Latitudes

tudes and Longitudes of all the moſt noted Places in the *South Sea*, corrected from the lateſt Obſervations by *Manuel Monz Prieto*, Profeſſor of Arts in *Peru*, and are compoſed with as much Preciſion and Exactneſs, as Tables of that Sort are uſually made; but when theſe Coaſts were ſurveyed to the Northward, to attain a Knowledge of which was formerly attended with ſuch immenſe Difficulty; and to what Purpoſe and what Trade is carried on there, we are at preſent entire Strangers to. It is by Accident only that we have this Account; and if the *Spaniſh* Nation have uſed this Precaution, with reſpect to the Knowledge of their Coaſts, undoubtedly they would uſe the ſame Caution with reſpect to giving us any Inſight as to how we might find a more ready Acceſs to ſuch Coaſts by a *North-weſt* Paſſage.

The Point of *Sueſte del Eſtrech d'Anian*, inſerted in ſuch Tables, ſhews the Opinion of the Streights is far from being exploded; but it is acknowledged by the Geographers of *Peru* and *New Spain*, at the preſent Time, that there are ſuch Streights. The naming the *South Point* of the *Streight* implies there is Land to the Northward, as to which it doth not ſeem to be conſiſtent with the Purpoſe of the Perſon who compoſed this Table to take any Notice, but that there is ſuch Land is confirmed by the *Ruſſian* Diſcoveries.

The Extent of *America* to Northward and Weſtward, that *America* and *Aſia* were contiguous and only ſeparated by a Streight, that *California* was an Iſland, that a *Paſſage* by the *North-eaſt* was practicable, have been by later *Geographers* treated as *Chimeras*, contrary to the earlieſt Accounts, and the Reports of the firſt Diſcoverers, and which, by later Accounts, the Conſequence of actual Obſervations are found to be true. There was a Simplicity and Honour in the People of that Age; there was no Motive for telling the Lie, that they faithfully reported the Diſcoveries they made, and if a Falſhood was diſcovered it might be dangerous in the Conſequences; their Voyages were not lucrative Jobs, in Hopes of a Repetition of which they formed their Accounts accordingly. There was no particular Syſtem to ſupport, for the Parts they went to were entirely unknown, that a Reward and Reputation ſhould be procured through a prevailing Intereſt to ſuch as ſpoke in Favour of the Syſtem. While thoſe to whoſe Fidelity and Aſſiduity alone it would be owing that such Discoveries were made, though repeated Endeavours were used to render the Undertaking ineffectual; and through whose Means alone the Truth would be made known to the Publick; should be ill spoken of, accused of Bribery, discountenanced, and the whole Merit ascribed to, where it would be least deserved, and, in Truth, where there could not be the least Pretension. Nevertheless the Reward given would be an Instance of a generous Regard in those who had Power to bestow of rewarding Merit, though they were inevitably deceived as to the proper Persons to whom such Reward should have been given.

No Authorities have been produced from Tradition or History which oppose the Probability of there being a North-west Passage, or the Reality of this Account of *de Fonte*, which the more we examine the less there appears to be of a Falsity, the Circumstances of it so consistent and united, and there are so many extra Circumstances which concur with that Account, that we cannot but admit to be an inconteftable Truth. We have not had a full Account of the Voyages and Expeditions of the *Spaniards* in *New Spain*, as some of them have not been permitted to be published. *Venegas* particularly mentions, Vol. i. P. 14, and in other Parts, There are also Accounts of Voyages made to other Parts of the World, which are only preserved in the Collections of the Curious, and it is known but to few Persons that such Voyages were ever made. There are some Voyages which are mentioned to have been made, but cannot, after the most diligent Inquiries, be procured; yet it is no just Objection to the Authenticity of such Voyages, or as to their not having been made. What the first Discoverers represented as to the Extent of *America*, its being contiguous to *Asia*, as to *California*, and as to a North-east Passage, being in all Respects found to be true, there is the greatest Reason to believe that there is a North-west Passage; and it is consistent with that Precaution which the *Spanish* Nation have made Use of, that we should not have any authentick Accounts relating to such Passage, which they were desirous of discovering as a shorter Way to the *Spice* Islands and the *Indies*. But when the King of *Portugal* and *Spain* came to an Agreement as to the *Moluccas*, the principal Reason for making such Discovery was determined, and it became their mutual Interest that it should not be known that there was such a Passage. Their continued Silence with respect to such Passage, implies they are

acquainted

acquainted with there being such a Passage, though not to an Exactness. It cannot imply they are dubious, when we consider the Number of Circumstances there are already mentioned, which express the contrary.

There are Circumstances in *de Fonte*'s Account which shew the Inference of there being no *Northwest Passage* is not just, though just as far as it appeared to *de Fonte*, as the River *Parmentiers* was not navigable for Shipping. One Circumstance is, that in the River *Haro*, and Lake *Velasco*, there were Salmon Trouts and large white Perch; also in *Los Reyes* and *Lake Belle*, but in Lake *de Fonte* excellent Cod and Ling; which are Fish that always abide in the Salt Water, the others come out of the Salt Water into the fresh Waters to spawn. Which *de Fonte* would account for that they came into the Lake *de Fonte* from the *North Sea*, and when he passed the Streight of *Ronquillo*, supposed himself to be in that Sea, or from the Intelligence that he obtained from *Shapley* that he was in a Gulph or Branch of it. Another Circumstance, as it flowed in the River *Los Reyes* twenty-two Feet, and in *Haro* twenty-four, and but a small Tide went into Lake *Belle*, *de Fonte* concluded that the Western Tide terminated there, and that as the Waters rose to such a Heighth at the Entrance of those Rivers, that it was a Gulph he was in which confined these Waters and occasioned their rise at such Entrances of the Rivers. That the Tides in *Parmentiers*, Lake *de Fonte*, and the Streights of *Ronquillo*, were from the *North Sea*. But by later Observations of the Rise of the Tides, a Tide cannot proceed from *Hudson*'s Bay to that Sea where *Shapley* was met by *de Fonte*, than through the Streights of *Ronquillo* into the great Lake of *de Fonte*, and afterwards to rise so high in the River *Parmentiers*. Neither can such a Tide proceed through the broken Land to Northwards of *Hudson*'s Streights, named *Cumberland* Isles (formerly *Estotland*) and which extend as far as Latitude 70; for it is evident the Strength of such Tides is spent in *Hudson*'s Bay and *Baffin*'s Bay: For at the Bottom of *Hudson*'s Bay it flowed but two Feet, at the Bottom of *Fretum Davis* or *Baffin*'s Bay, but one Foot. Which is agreeable to the Opinion of all the Discoverers of that Time, as to the Eastern Tide from the Proportion that the great Spaces or Seas which were to receive it bore to the Inlets by which it came in, that the Force of such Tide must be consumed in such Seas, and therefore expected to meet with a Tide from Westward, which counterchecked the Eastern Tide. On the other Hand, if we consider this Tide to be

from

from the Weſtern Ocean, ſuch Tide forced through various Entrances up a Streight as that of *de Fuca*, muſt enter the Sea where *Shapley* was met, with great Impetuoſity; riſe in Heighth proportionable to the Width in all Openings that there are to receive it. As it is the Tide round *Greenland*, and that which comes from the Southward along the Coaſt of *Labrador*, being both received in thoſe Indraughts of *Hudſon*'s Streights, and the broken Lands of *Cumberland* Iſles, which cauſes the Riſe of the Tides there. It may be ſuppoſed that the *North-eaſt* Part of the *South Sea*, and the Streight of *de Fuca*, received the Tides which ſet to Eaſtward along the Weſtern Main from *Beering*'s Streights, and the Tide which comes from the Southward along the Coaſt of *California*. That the Tide is not from the *Tartarian Sea*, in Lake *de Fonte*, &c. is evident from *Bernarda*'s Account, who ſhews there is no Communication with that Sea and the Sea that *Shapley* was met in.

As to the Cod and Ling in Lake *de Fonte*, or as to Salmon, it is not known that there are either Cod, Ling or Salmon in *Hudſon*'s Bay: Neither have there been found Shoals or Banks to which the Cod could repair; nor is it known that any Cod have been catched beyond Latitude 57; an Article to which *Davis* was particularly attentive: Therefore it is not probable that they ſhould come from the *North Sea* through *Hudſon*'s Bay to Lake *de Fonte*. *De Fonte* mentions Shoals in the North-eaſt Part of the *South Sea*, which he paſſed up. And in *Vizcaino*'s Voyage there is an Account that, off the Iſland *Geronymo* on the Coaſt of *California*, the Ships Companies ſupplied themſelves with Cod and Ling; which ſhews there are Cod and Ling in thoſe Seas. It was reaſonable for *de Fonte* to ſuppoſe that the Cod and Ling came from the Eaſtward from the *Baccaloos*, neither could he otherwiſe ſuppoſe, as the contrary is only known from Obſervations made much later than that Time.

Fox had advanced in 1635, when he publiſhed the Account of his Voyage, that there was a free and open Communication of the Weſtern Ocean with *Hudſon*'s Bay: Which was looked on as an inconteſtable Fact until the Voyage of Captain *Middleton*. What *Fox* ſaid was conſiſtent with the Opinion which all the Diſcoverers had of the Proximity of the Weſtern Ocean; who therefore judged of the Probability of their Succeſs in the Parts they went into, from the Courſe of the Tides, which if there was no Western Tide there was no Passage. This probably prevented that Success, as to a Discovery of a Passage, which through their Assiduity might otherwise have been obtained, had they not paid such a Regard to the Tides, but made a due Survey of the Inlets and Openings of the Coast, which on their not finding that a Western Tide came from thence they deserted, which was also the Case as to Captain *Meer* in the Search of *Pistol Bay* as called, to Southward of Lord *Southwell*'s Isles, there was no Western Tide; therefore a compleat Discovery of that Part was not made.

It is to be considered that the Northern and Eastern Parts of *America*, are more intermixed with Waters than the Parts to Southward are, being a high mountainous Country. The Mountains chiefly consisting of a brown rocky Substance, not penetrable by the melting Snows or Spring Rains, which therefore run off into the Levels and Valleys, and form inland Seas, great Lakes, and Inlets, which vent their Waters into the Ocean, necessary for carrying off that great Quantity and vast Bodies of Ice which are formed in the Winter in those Parts, not to be dissolved, as the greater Part is which is formed to the Southward, by the Influence of the Sun. The Northern and Westward Part of *America* is also mountainous; and high Ridges of Mountains were seen from the Head of *Wager* Bay on the opposite Shore of what appeared to be a Lake; therefore there must be Lakes and Seas to Westward, Reservoirs for the melting Snows and Rains, also some Outlet or Channel to carry off the great Quantities of Ice also formed in those Parts; and with which *Barnarda*'s Account is consistent, and the greatest Reservoir and Discharge seems to be to the Northward by that North-east Part of the *Tartarian Sea*. The Lake *Velasco*, Lake *Belle*, Lake *de Fonte*, may be all supposed to proceed from the same Cause, the melting Snows and Rains, receive the Ice from the Waters which run into them, which, from the Strength of the Currents and Tides, is soon shot from the Shores of such Lakes, broken to Pieces and carried off into some Passage or Inlet into the *South Sea*; and such a Vent or Channel to carry off such Bodies of Ice must necessarily be, agreeable to what is known by Observation in other Parts. The Objection of the great Distance it is between the Sea at the Back of *Hudson*'s Bay, and where *Shapley* was met, will appear of no Validity when we consider the Distance between the Streights of *Gibralter* and the Northern Part of the *Black Sea*. Between the Entrance of the *Sound* to the Entrance of the *White Sea*, between which there is Communication of Waters, or very nearly so. And from Point *Comfort* in *Hudson*'s Bay to Alderman *Smith*'s Sound in *Baffin*'s Bay, between which there is a Communication of Waters without entering into the *Ocean* or *Davis* Streights. From Lake *Superior* to the Streights of *Belle Isle* at the Back of *Newfoundland*, or to *Cape Breton*, is near forty Degrees of Longitude, or equal to 390 Leagues. And Lake *Superior* hath a Communication with *Hudson*'s Bay.

This great Afflux of Waters form such Meanders and Labyrinths, as it is impossible to say whether there is a Communication of Waters, or whether the Waters are divided by smaller or larger Tracts or Slips of Land, without an absolute Survey. The Lands so double or fold one within the other, that unless you get a proper Sight of such Lands so as to distinguish this, to discover the Opening that is between them, there is an Appearance of a Continuance of the Land, and consequently of a Termination of the Waters. So long as the Tide Argument prevailed it was not thought necessary to be so accurate in the Searches. A Sight of the Land trending a Course contrary to that Course which the Discoverers were to pursue to make a Passage, and the Tide coming from the Eastward, rendered a Search any further in those Parts unnecessary: and it may be owing to the great Impropriety of adopting a particular System, more than to any other Cause, that the Discovery of a North-west Passage was not made by those brave industrious Discoverers, who in a Series succeeded each other from *Frobrisher* to *James* and *Fox*.

This seems to be certain, that there must be one great Channel, as *Hudson*'s Streights are to Eastward, also to Westward though intricate by which the Waters to Westward pass into the *South Sea*, and as that to Northward, the North-east Part of the *Tartarian Sea*. We already know there is not a Communication by *Hudson*'s Bay, thro' any Inlet by which the Waters do come in there or sufficient for that Purpose; neither round the Head of *Repulse* Bay, for then the Current would have been met coming from Westward. Therefore this Channel must be to Southward and Westward, consistent with *de Luca*'s Account of a Streight, in some

such

such Manner as is represented in the Map annexed. Which Account also agreeable to that of *Peche*.

De Fuca says, he failed twenty-six Days up such Streight before he entered the Sea; that the Streight grew wider before he entered the Sea. If we allow him fifteen Leagues a Day, from the Entrance of such Streights out of the *South Sea* to where he entered the Sea, by him supposed the *North Sea*, the Distance is 390 Leagues. As he mentions that he found it wide enough every where, this Expression shews that he did not suppose himself in the Ocean, but in a Gulph of the Ocean. And *Martin Chacke* expresses himself, that after he overshot the *Gulph*, he set no more Sight on any other Land. Therefore the Distance is agreeable to that Distance which *de Fuca* must have gone to come into that Sea where *de Fonte* met *Shapley*; the Description that he saw both Shores, makes a Consistency also in those Accounts. Before *de Fonte*'s Expedition, *Hudson*'s Bay had been discovered, yet that Discovery made no Alteration as to the Accounts of *de Fuca* and *Chacke*, as *Fox* said beyond Lat. 64, round that Land there was incontestably a Communication with the Western Ocean. Here is an Agreement in three Accounts, by separate Persons at a Distance of Time, who had no Intelligence of what had been done by each other; for *Chacke* was a *Portugueze*; and as *de Fuca* had made his Report to the Viceroy of *New Spain* of what he had done, and what he had done seems to be mostly accounted of by himself, therefore no Regard might be had to it in drawing *de Fonte*'s Instructions: All which three Accounts agree in there being a Sea to Westward of *Hudson*'s Bay.

De Fuca mentions he was ashore; saw Marks of Gold and Silver; Marquisates the same which was made such an Account of after *Frobisher*'s return from his first Voyage, and from which it may be inferred it was a barren mountainous Country which *de Fuca* passed through. He was afraid of the Natives, who were clad in Beast Skins; and from whose Behaviour he must have had some Apprehension that they would cut him off, as he mentions that he was not armed against them. *De Fonte* is very express as to the civil Behaviour of those *Indians* he met with, so contrary to the Character of those whom *de Fuca* saw. Therefore those whom *de Fuca* saw were the *Eskemaux*, who frequent the mountainous and desolate Parts, and near to the Salt Waters where they can catch

Fish, also the Seal and the Whale, from which they get many Conveniencies besides what is necessary for their Subsistance; who are mentioned to be also on other Parts of the Coast of *California*; are represented as a fierce and barbarous People, who hold no Treaty or Amity with their Neighbours, who are always in Fear of them.

That *de Fonte* should not pass up the North-east Part of the *South Sea*, but go through Land, must have been, that the North-east Part of the *South Sea* was represented as a Gulph, not a Streight, from some Observations made prior to that Expedition, as to which the Observers might be deceived, by its taking a Southerly Course through some Inlet or Opening obscured by Islands, or the Entrance narrow, that they concluded it only to be some small Branch which soon terminated; having, at the same Time, a large open Channel before them, which they finding afterwards surrounded with Land, concluded there was no Communication with any other Waters, but that they had seen the Extremity of these Waters to Eastward. That these Waters took a Course through that desert mountainous Country, until they joined with the Waters of the Streights that *de Fuca* came up, the People of *Conosset* might not be able to give a just Account of, as they lived so far to Northward and Eastward. Though they, as the Natives of *Conibasset* also came occasionally into the North-east Part of the *South Sea*; the one mostly frequented to Northward and Eastward, the other to Northward and Westward, as is apparent from *de Fonte*'s Account; where they had level and fruitful Tracts, as they produced so much Maiz; a hunting Country, as there were three Sorts of Deer; also Fish in their Waters. Whereas the Country on the opposite Shore of the North-east Part of the *South Sea*, as is apparent from being the Resort of the *Eskemaux*, would be rugged, rocky, and remarkably barren, with little Intermixtures of level and fruitful Spots. Therefore the People of *Conosset*, or *Conibasset*, would have no Inducements to go into those Parts. May be supposed the opposite Coast was the Limits of their Enemy's Country, with whom if they went to War, and knew that the Waters of the North-east Part of the *South Sea* did communicate to Southward with other Waters; yet it cannot be imagined that they went up those Waters so far in their Enemy's Country of so wild a Disposition, where they were always in Danger of being surprized, as to know whether those Waters joined with the Sea

in

in which *Shapley* was met. Might also be jealous if the Jesuits, or *Parmentiers*, or others who came there, were very particular in their Enquiries, that they intended to go and reside amongst their Enemies, which, as the Nature of *Indians* is, would cause them to be on the Reserve, and slack in their Informations, as to those Parts.

That those Persons who were in those Parts before this Expedition of *de Fonte*, got no Information of this Streight, or of the Waters, as to the Course of them to Southward, there must be a considerable main Land to Southward of Lake *Belle* and Lake *de Fonte*, as is expressed in the Map, and as to the Sea to Eastward, that Part of it which was to Southward of *Ronquillo*, no more would be apprehended of it, being unacquainted as to the Streight, than that it was a Part of that Sea contiguous to *Hudson*'s Bay; and it not being known at that Time but the Tides came from the Eastward, would have no Reason to infer, from the Sea running to Southward, that it communicated with a Streight there.

To take away the Improbability of what is here advanced, we should reflect what Assurances former Discoverers gave, that had but the Season permitted to proceed, they should certainly have made a Passage; though when an Attempt was again made they found their Mistake; and from Observations then made, they saw good Reason to have a different Opinion as to the Nature of the Passage from what they had before, and very reasonable, as their Searches were made in Parts entirely unknown; and as to the Appearance of the Land, the Course of the Waters, and the Set of the Tides, the most judicious might be deceived.

The *Spanish* Nation had not been able to make out a Passage by their various Attempts, agreeable to the Accounts of private Persons, which probably might give an Opportunity for the Representations of the Jesuits to be attended to, who would urge every Argument in Behalf of their Discovery, and endeavour to invalidate the former Accounts as to a Passage; which by that Time, from the ill Success as to discovering a Passage, might not be at that Time so much thought of; and as Difference in Time produces a Change in Opinions, whatever makes for the reigning Opinion is adopted, as every Thing that is contradictory is depreciated.

depreciated. The Arguments for the Opinion which prevailed before for a navigable Paſſage might be treated as fallacious and inſignificant, and the Inſtructions for the Expedition of *de Fonte* might be drawn agreeable to the Jeſuits Plan, whom it is evident knew nothing of a Streight, but conſidered the Land of *America* as one continued Continent to Latitude 66. And whatever Weight this Conjecture may have, it is apparent from the Conſideration of *de Fonte*'s Letter, that the Inſtructions were drawn from the Information of ſome who had been before in thoſe Parts: And by whom can it be ſuppoſed more properly that the Court received the Information which they had than from the Jeſuits, whoſe Underſtanding and Character would admit them to a free Converſe with the Miniſter on a leſs Occaſion than they would now have, to give an Account of thoſe Parts they had been in.

The *Court* of *Spain* does not ſeem, from the Proceedings, to be of the ſame Opinion with the *Jeſuits*, or *de Fonte* after his return. As the Governor of *Cinoloa* is immediately ordered to take a Survey of the Coaſts and Harbours of *California*. And the next Year Admiral *Caſſanate* is ſent from *Old Spain*; and it is probable the Court was not of the Opinion of the *Jeſuits* when they gave this Information, but formed the Inſtructions for *de Fonte* agreeable thereto. As the moſt expedient Method, at that Time, for intercepting the People from *Boſton*, was to go the Way they gave an Account of with the Boats through Land, as the Ships might meet with Difficulties and Delays in paſſing up the Streights, alſo ran great Hazard; the *Boſton* Ship might paſs them unperceived. Whereas, on the Plan which was purſued, if they heard by the Natives that the *Boſton* Ship had paſſed, and taken her Courſe further to Southward or Weſtward, *de Fonte* would have repaired aboard his Ship, proceeded down *Los Reyes*, and with the Diligence which he would have made Uſe of, fell in with the *Boſton* Ship either in ſuch *North-eaſt* Part of the *South Sea*, or on the Coaſt of *California*, leaving Orders for *Barnardo* how to act in this Reſpect on his return. From which Conduct, and the Lookout that was kept on the Coaſt of *Mexico* and *Peru*, it would have been alſo impoſſible for the *Boſton* People, unacquainted with theſe Parts, and not expecting ſuch a Diligence was uſed to intercept them, to have made a ſucceſsful Voyage.

That there is a Sea to the Westward of *Hudson*'s Bay is reported by the *Indians*, and is represented to have Ice in it like *Hudson*'s Bay.

Governor *Dobbs*, in his Account of the Countries adjoining to *Hudson*'s Bay (P. 19.) mentions from *Joseph le France*, that their Savages reported that in the Bottom of the Northern Bay there is a Streight, they can easily discover Land on the other Side: They had never gone to the End of that Streight. They say there is Ice there all the Year, which is drove by the Wind, sometimes one Way sometimes another.

The *Indians*, who are called *Northern Indians*, having their Habitations to North-west of *Churchill*, mention a Sea to the Westward of them, and which is from *Churchill* Factory in *Hudson*'s Bay twenty-five Days Journey, not a direct Course, but from the round they are obliged to take. They speak of the *Eskemaux Indians* to Eastward of them, but never give an Account of any other Nations to Northward or Westward of them. Mr. *Scroggs*, who was sent out by the *Hudson*'s Bay Company in 1722, had two Northern *Indians*, whom he carried with him, when he was in about Lat. 62. knew the Country very well, and had a great Desire to go home, saying they were but two or three Days Journey from their Family. And the Northern *Indians* who were with Captain *Middleton*, were desirous of his going near the Shore, between Lat. 62 Deg. and 64. In Lat. 63° and 14′, Captain *Middleton* put two of the *Indians* ashore, who were desirous of returning to their own Country. And the Author saw an *Indian*, whose Daughter had married a Northern *Indian* and been home with her, direct his own Son to sketch out on a Board with a burnt Stick, the Coast of that Sea, which his Son did, and the Father afterwards took and corrected it where he said the Son had mistook.

Governor *Dobbs*, in the Account mentioned P. 45, mentions, ' that ' *Joseph le France* was acquainted with an *Indian*, who lived at some ' Distance from *Nelson* River in *Hudson*'s Bay, who, about 15 Years be-
' fore that Time, went to War against a Nation living Northward on
' the Western Ocean of *America*. When they went they carried their
' Families with them, and hunted and fished from Place to Place for
' two Winters and one Summer, having left their Country in Autumn,
' and in *April* following came to the Sea Side, on the Western Coast,
' where

' where they immediately made their Canoes. At some little Distance
' they saw an Island, which was about a League and a Half long when
' the Tide was out, or Water fell, they had no Water betwixt them and
' the Island, but when it rose it covered all the Passage betwixt them and
' the Island, as high up as the Woods upon the Shore. There they
' left their Wives and Children, and old Men, to conduct them home
' and provide them with Provisions, by hunting and shooting for them
' on the Road; and he, with thirty Warriors, went in Quest of their
' Enemies the *Tete Plat*. After they parted with their Families they
' came to a Streight, which they passed in their Canoes. The Sea
' Coast lay almost East and West; for he said the Sun rose upon his
' Right Hand, and at Noon it was almost behind him as he passed the
' Streight, and always set in the Sea. After passing the Streight they
' coasted along the Shore three Months, going into the Country or
' Woods as they went along to hunt for Provisions. He said they saw
' a great many large black Fish spouting up Water in the Sea. After
' they had coasted for near three Months, they saw the Footsteps of some
' Men on the Sand; then judged they were near their Enemies, quitted
' their Canoes, went five Days through the Woods to the Banks of a
' River, found their Enemy's Town, made an Attack, the Enemy ral-
' lied and put them to flight.' Then proceeds, ' upon which they fled
' to the Woods, and from thence made their Escape to their Canoes be-
' fore their Enemies overtook them, and after a great deal of Fatigue
' got to the Streight; and, after getting over, they all died one after
' the other, except this old Man, of Fatigue and Famine, leaving him
' alone to travel to his own Country, which took him up about a Year's
' Time.' When he reached the River *Sakie* he met his Friends again,
who relieved him.

The *Indians* that this antient *Indian* went to War against, (and this
Indian was living at *York Fort* in *Hudson*'s Bay in 1746) are mentioned
to be the *Tete Plat*, or *Plascotez de Chicus*. The Part which they inhabit
is variously laid down by the Geographers; by some in Lat. 67, Long.
265 East from *Ferro*, which is the extremest Longitude that their Country
is laid down in. Monf. *de Lisle* and others place them in Lat. 63, and Long.
280 East from *Ferro*, so their true Situation is uncertain. Yet it is apparent
that they do not live near to or on the Coast of the *South Sea*, or Western
Ocean. For what *Joseph le France* in this Account, and so of all *Indians*,

meant

meant by the Word Sea is any Mass or Collection of Salt Waters which have a Tide. P. 38, in the same Work, giving an Account of the *Indians* passing down to *York Fort*. ' The River *de Terre Rouge*, and from that ' Place they descend gradually to the Sea.' By which *Joseph le France* means *Hudson*'s Bay. Governor *Dobbs* mentioning the Western Ocean of *America* is a Mistake, which he was led into as having a Consistency with the System which he had adopted. These Warriors left their own Country in Autumn, are said to have lived near *Port Nelson* or *York Fort*, and were at the Sea Side in *April*. Their not being sooner is not to be attributed to the Length of the Journey but to the Season of the Year. The old *Indian* was a Year returning to his own Country; but he was fatigued and almost famished, so labouring under a great Debility, and had his Food to seek in whatever Manner he could procure it. The Winter also came on soon after his return from the Enemy. They were on the Western Side of the Land, which separates *Hudson*'s Bay from that Sea, where they saw so great a Tide. Afterwards passed a Streight, which Streight lay North and South. The Sea they came from and the Sea they passed into after such Streight, laid East and West. They continually kept the Western Shore, as that was the Side on which their Enemy lived; and though they were so long as three Months in their Passage, they were obliged to go every Day ashore to hunt, being thirty in Company, required a pretty considerable Subsistance. Their Canoes can bear no Serge or Wave when the Wind blows, therefore are obliged to keep close to the Shore, and must go to the Bottom of each Bay.

This Account agrees both with that of *de Fonte* and *de Fuca*. The Sea they imbarked on was that at the Back of *Hudson*'s Bay, and the Streight might be formed by some Island, or both the Shores approach each other, tho' the Account is not sufficiently intelligible to make any Description of it in the Map. *De Fuca* says the Streight grew wider when he entered such Sea, which seems to imply it had been narrow. And the *Indians*, as before-mentioned, said there was a Streight, and they can perceive the Land on the other Side. *De Fuca* also mentions he went ashore, and found the Land fruitful, and rich of Gold and Silver and Pearls, and other Things, like *Nova Hispania*. Which shews it was a mixed Country; for a fruitful Country and a Produce of Gold and Silver is not a

Description compatible with one and the same Part. The one we may suppose the Description of the Parts nearer the Ocean, the other of the Parts where the *Tete Plat* live: But the old *Indian* seems also to make a Distinction; for he says they went to hunt in the Country and the Woods. When they had passed the Streight, they came into the broader Part of the Streight of *Anian*, which appeared to them to be a Sea. As to the Place of their Imbarkation, they would be directed by where they could procure Birch to make their Canoes.

The true Situation of the Part they went to, nor where they imbarked is not to be determined with any Certainty; but it doth not carry the least Probability that the went to War with a People more than a thousand Miles distant. It is scarce probable they had ever heard the Name of the Inhabitants of those Parts, much more so acquainted with their Situation as to be able to form a Plan of going to conquer them. There must have been some particular Cause for their going to War with a People so far off; what that was it would be difficult to imagine, if it was only to shew their Prowess, they must have had Enemies nearer home, against whom there was a greater Probability of succeeding. Neither could it be at that Distance, as they had one continued Scene of Fatigue until they reached the Streights; their Hearts broken by Reason of the Disappointment, the Heat of Summer, no venturing ashore but for a very short Time, either for Food or Refreshment, as they expected the Conquerors to follow them with Canoes, it would have been impossible for them to have reached the Streight. If they had a hundred Leagues a direct Course until they attained the Place of their Imbarkation, and by going round the Bays, might be near twice that Distance, the Current also against them, it would be sufficient, stout young Fellows, and full of Blood as they were, for what they underwent to be fatal to them. It is evident the Streight was not far from where they imbarked, and the Relation seems to express it so, as they had such a Fatigue in attaining to it. Allowing the *Tete Plat* to be in Long. 108 Degrees from *London*, and the true Course was W. S. W. or E. N. E. on their return, with a Distance of a hundred Leagues, they would alter their Latitude 114 Miles, and make 277 Miles Departure, which, with 27 Miles to a Degree, would make the Place of their Imbarkation to be in Longitude 98 from *London*, about the Longitude of *Ronquillo*. As to the

Latitude where the *Tete Plat Indians* live, and as to the Longitude it is but conjecture; there is such a Discordancy and Contradiction in the Maps, there is such Uncertainty, that the North-west and West Parts beyond *Hudson*'s Bay in the Latitude of *Churchill*, seem to be entirely unknown. But this is to be observed, and which has been my Direction in these Observations, the *Northern Indians* and the *Home Indians* about the Factory of *York* Fort, mention these *Tete Plat Indians*, and speak of them as their Enemies, therefore they cannot be at so great a Distance as the Western Ocean, neither further than where I have supposed their Country to be. For as the Time the *Indians* were going there three Months, that is not to be considered so much with respect to the Distance, as they would choose a proper Season, when there were the fewest *Indians* in the Towns, and were mostly engaged abroad in their Summer hunting. Perhaps there are no People who plan better in the Partizan Way, and execute with more Success. They fix the Time they intend to make their Attack before they set out, then proceed easily and gradually towards their Enemy's Country, allowing a Sufficiency of Time in which they may recover any Accident by which they might be delayed, as unseasonable Weather, Difficulty and Disappointments as to procuring Subsistance, or any Indisposition, that they go to Action in their full Strength and Vigour; as an *Indian* who conducts an Expedition would be as much contemned for Want of Prudence, on his Return to the Towns, as he would for his Want of Conduct in leading his People to an Attack, and when the Enemy was too powerful not bringing them off without the Loss of a Scalp. In either of which Cases the young People, who observe freely the most exact Discipline, and implicitly obey what he orders, would not go any more to War with him.

Which Way the *Boston* Ship made this Passage is uncertain. *Gibbons* was acquainted with *Bylot*, was Shipmate with him in Sir *Thomas Button*'s Voyage. *Bylot* was also with *Gibbons* the Time he lost his Season, by being detained in the Ice. *Bylot* made an Expedition for Discovery of a Passage in the Year 1615, on Sir *Thomas Button* having at a Trial of a Tide off the Island of *Nottingham*, in *Hudson*'s Streights, found it came from the North-west, and to be from an Opening at the Back of *Cary*'s *Swans-nest*, this Tide he went in Pursuit of; and was as far up as Lat. 65 Deg. 26 Min. then supposed where he was was nothing but a Bay, but could not (he had gone up the East) return down the West Shore. Whether *Gibbons* took his Information from *Bylot*, and pursued his Plan, is uncertain, and found his Way round the Head of *Repulse* Bay. He was also acquainted with what *Fox* had done, who went into Lat. 66 Deg. 5 Min. so further than *Bylot*, who did not return down the Western Shore; but his People being indisposed, and not finding a North-west Tide, he hastened home. These Parts, therefore, were not properly searched, the Conclusion drawn for there not being a Passage there, being that the Tide came from the Eastward.

Or whether *Gibbens* went through *Hudson*'s Bay is equally uncertain. The undiscovered Parts of which Bay, or the Openings that were not determined in the Expedition in the Year 1747, are in a Map hereto annexed. But the Termination of *Chesterfield*'s or *Bowden*'s Inlet hath been since searched by the Direction of the *Hudson*'s Bay Company, and a Plan made of it, which I have not seen. Their Design was to go as far up such Inlet until it terminated, or there was a Passage into another Water. But as it is terminated by Land, and if there is no Inlet or Opening left on the North or South Shore unsearched, or a Survey taken from the Heights, by which they could be satisfied there was no Communication with any other Waters by which there could be a Passage, it is to be concluded that *Chesterfield* Inlet is no Streight or Passage as was expected, and it appeared to be as far as the *Californias* Boat went up, according to the Report made at that Time. The People who had been in the Boat belonging to the *California*, when the Ship was going up *Wager* Bay, where, from the Depth of the Water, the Breadth between both Shores, the high mountainous Land, there was great Reason to believe there was a Streight or Passage: Those People declared, if there was a Streight they were assured that *Chesterfield* Inlet was a Streight also.

There remains then to be searched for the Discovery of a Passage, the Opening called *Pistol Bay*, in *Hudson*'s Bay. That Part which *Bylot* and *Fox* left undetermined, along the Coast to Southward of *Baffins* Bay called *Cumberland* Isles, which entirely consists of large Inlets and broken Lands. We may be too premature in our Conclusions as to the Impracticability of such a Passage from the high Latitude and the Short-

ness

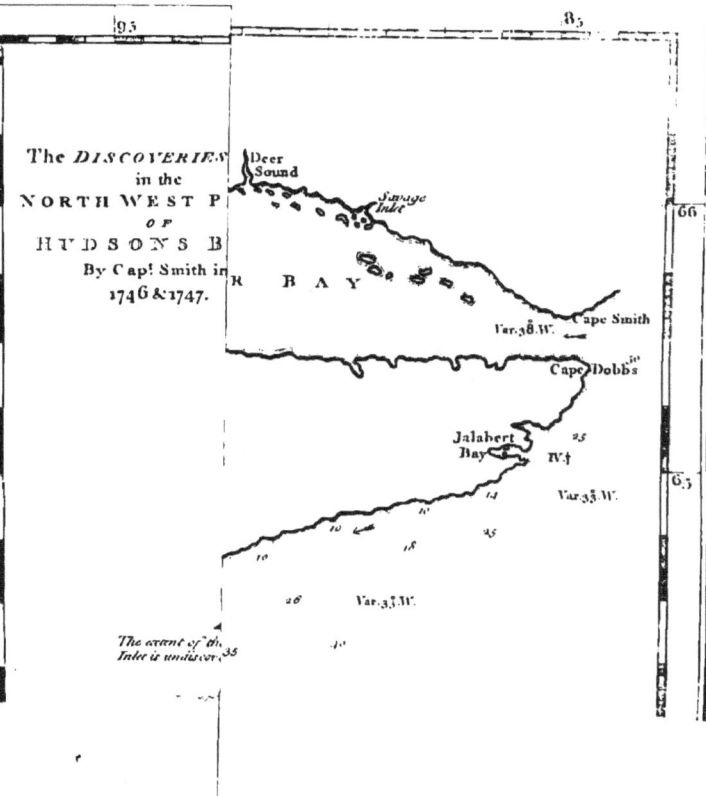

but could not (he had gone up the East) return down the West Shore. Whether *Gibbons* took his Information from *Bylot*, and pursued his Plan, is uncertain, and found his Way round the Head of *Repulse* Bay. He was also acquainted with what *Fox* had done, who went into Lat. 66 Deg. 5 Min. so further than *Bylot*, who did not return down the Western Shore; but his People being indisposed, and not finding a North-west Tide, he hastened home. These Parts, therefore, were not properly searched, the Conclusion drawn for there not being a Passage there, being that the Tide came from the Eastward.

Or whether *Gibbons* went through *Hudson*'s Bay is equally uncertain. The undiscovered Parts of which Bay, or the Openings that were not determined in the Expedition in the Year 1747, are in a Map hereto annexed. But the Termination of *Chesterfield*'s or *Bowden*'s Inlet hath been since searched by the Direction of the *Hudson*'s Bay Company, and a Plan made of it, which I have not seen. Their Design was to go as far up such Inlet until it terminated, or there was a Passage into another Water. But as it is terminated by Land, and if there is no Inlet or Opening left on the North or South Shore unsearched, or a Survey taken from the Heights, by which they could be satisfied there was no Communication with any other Waters by which there could be a Passage, it is to be concluded that *Chesterfield* Inlet is no Streight or Passage as was expected, and it appeared to be as far as the *Californias* Boat went up, according to the Report made at that Time. The People who had been in the Boat belonging to the *California*, when the Ship was going up *Wager* Bay, where, from the Depth of the Water, the Breadth between both Shores, the high mountainous Land, there was great Reason to believe there was a Streight or Passage: Those People declared, if there was a Streight they were assured that *Chesterfield* Inlet was a Streight also.

There remains then to be searched for the Discovery of a Passage, the Opening called *Pistol Bay*, in *Hudson*'s Bay. That Part which *Bylot* and *Fox* left undetermined, along the Coast to Southward of *Baffins* Bay called *Cumberland* Isles, which entirely consists of large Inlets and broken Lands. We may be too premature in our Conclusions as to the Impracticability of such a Passage from the high Latitude and the Short-

ness

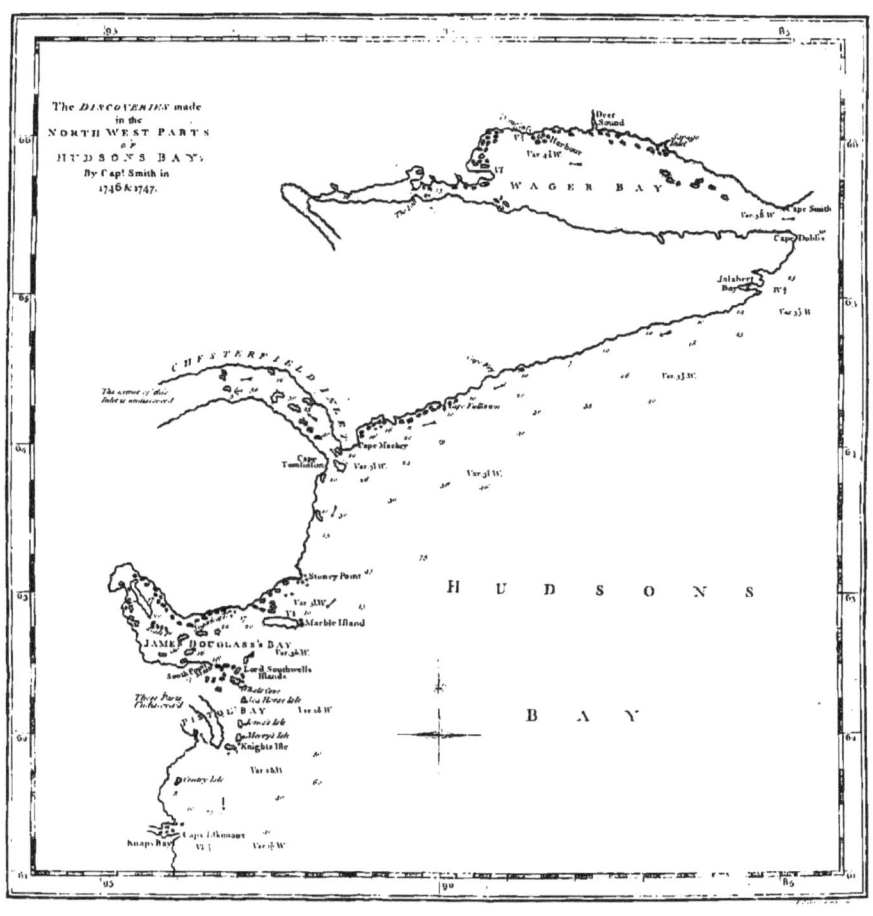

practicability of such a Passage from the high Latitude and the shortness

ness of the Season, as we have the Instance of the *Boston* Ship, which was so far advanced in the Sea to Westward of *Hudson*'s Bay in the Month of *August*; and some Time would be taken up in finding out the Way. The strong Tides that set in, and the Current when to Westward, which there is apparently in the other Sea, may give an Expedition that may compensate against the Shortness of the Season. It is but a short Time that would be required to pass that Part of the Passage which lies in those high Latitudes, as the Course would be soon altered to the Southward.

Seyxas y Lovera, in his *Theatro Naval Hydrographico*, in the seventh Chapter, P. 426, says, ' North-east of *America* there is the Coast of
' *Greenland*, from sixty to sixty-eight Degrees, where there is to the East
' the Entrance of the Streight of *Frobisher*. North-west in the different
' Islands which compose the Northern Parts of *America*, there is the
' Entrance of the Streight of *Hudson*, where the *North Sea* communi-
' cates with the *South Sea*, passing out of the Entrance of the Streight
' of *Anian*, which runs North-east and South-west to the Northward of
' the Island of *California*, which Streight is hid by great Gulphs on
' the Part that is North of *America*, which contain such great Islands,
' as *Cumberland* (or *Estotiland*) that are more than one hundred Leagues
' in Length from North-east to South-west, and their Extremity from
' East to West more than seventy Leagues.'—Page 44. ' Some hold it
' for certain that you can sail from *Spain* to *China* through those Streights,
' or to *Japan*, or to the Lands of *Eso*, in three Months. As says also
' Doctor *Pedro de Syria*; but it is the Opinion of *D. T. V. T.* Author of
' the History of the *Imperial* States of the World, that he holds it for
' uncertain whether there is such Streight by which you can pass from
' the *North* to the *South Sea.*—P. 45. There were some of the Subjects
' of the King of *France*, who offered themselves, if they could get his
' Majesty's Licence, to perform that Voyage in four Months; entering
' the *Canal de Hudson* from out of the Ocean, with a Course North-west
' or West North-west, taking always a Sight of the Coast at Noon, they
' should attain to the Height of the *Arctic* Circle, or one Degree more,
' as in making that Voyage they will be favoured in that Part by the
' Currents and Winds from the East and South-east, and afterwards in

' their

' their Paſſage by the Streight of *Anian*, the Winds and Currents would
' be from the North.—It is ſaid that ſome Strangers (on what Occa-
' ſion is not ſaid) have gone that Rout; and that there is in the Ar-
' chieves of the Admiralty of *Liſbon*, and of the *Contratacion* at *Seville*, a
' Copy of ſuch Rout; what I here obſerve is the ſame with what *Don
' Francisco de San Millan* obſerves, from which or from the Copy of
' which Rout to be ſeen in various Languages, or the Diſpoſition of the
' ſaid Streights, he holds it for certain that there is ſuch a Courſe, and
' relates, That a *Hollander*, on the Evidence of a *Spaniard* who was
' aboard his Ship, from the North of *California*, forced by the Winds
' from South-weſt, attained to ſixty-ſix Degrees North-eaſt, after-
' wards took a Courſe Eaſt, and Eaſt South-eaſt, came into fifty-eight
' Degrees, when he entered the *North Sea* to Northward of *Terra Nova*,
' from thence to *Scotland*, and from *Scotland* to *Liſbon*, in leſs than three
' Months from the Port of *Nativadad* to *Liſbon*, of which Voyage he
' makes no Doubt.' And *Seyxas* obſerves, he hath ſeen many other
Accounts of Voyages made from *Holland*, alſo from *England*, to the
South Sea in three or four Months, which he much doubts, from the
Shortneſs of the Time; alſo as in the *Spaniſh* Hiſtorians they have an
Account of what paſſes in the ſeveral Parts of the *South Sea*, in *Cathay*,
and *China*, and no ſuch Thing is to be found in the *Bibliotheca* of the
Licentiate *Antonio de Leon*, which ſets forth all the Diſcoveries and
Voyages which have been made from any Region from the Year 1200
in *America*.

It is plain from the Account of *Seyxas*, he doth not determine abſolutely for a Paſſage, but that there is a Paſſage is his Opinion. His chief
Objection is to the Accounts from the Brevity of the Time in which the
Voyages were ſaid to be performed, and there being no Account in a
careful Writer of the Diſcoveries made in thoſe Parts. He doth not
confine the Paſſage to *Hudſon*'s Bay, as I underſtand him, but to the
Streight and the other Openings to Northward through *Cumberland* Iſles,
and that they go up into as high a Latitude as the *Arctic* Circle. Which
is agreeable to *Acoſta*'s Account, and gives a further Explanation to his
Meaning than I have already done. As to which Iſles, and to the Northward and Eaſtward of *Cary*'s *Swans-neſt*, it is apparent, from the Peru-

ſal

fal of the Voyages, there hath been no certain Account on a compleat Difcovery as to thofe Parts. What he fays as to the Voyage of the *Hollander*, it muft be obferved it was while *Holland* was under the *Spanifh* Government in the Reign of *Philip* the Second, and feems to be the fame Voyage, of which Mention hath been made that an Account was found amongft the Papers of that Prince.

It hath been fhewn to have been the conftant Opinion of there being a North-weft Paffage, from the Time foon after which the *South Sea* was difcovered near the Weftern Part of *America*, and that this Opinion was adopted by the greateft Men not only in the Time they lived, but whofe Eminence and great Abilities are revered by the prefent Age. That there is a Sea to Weftward of *Hudfon*'s Bay, there hath been given the concurrent Teftimony of *Indians*; and of Navigators and *Indians* that there is a Streight which unites fuch Sea with the Weftern Ocean. The Voyage which lead us into thefe Confiderations, hath fo many Circumftances relating to it, which, now they have been confidered, fhew the greateft Probability of its being authentick; which carry with them as much the Evidence of a Fact, afford as great a Degree of Credibility as we have for any Tranfaction done a long Time fince, which hath not been of a publick Nature and tranfacted in the Face of the World, fo as to fall under the Notice of every one, though under the Difadvantage that the Intent on one Part muft have been to have it concealed and buried in Oblivion. Tranfacted alfo by Perfons in a private Part of the World, who only fpoke of it amongft their Friends at home, being themfelves Strangers to what they had effected, and made little Account of their Voyage. Befides the Chagrin of their Difappointment, and the illnatured Reflections it might fubject them to, they might think it alfo beft not to communicate it to the Publick, as it might encourage others to the like Undertaking, and fo they fall into the Hands of the *Spaniards*, not only at the Hazard of their Ship, but their Lives, or at leaft fubject them to many Hardfhips fuch as they had fuftained to no Purpofe. Therefore they thought proper to fay little about their Difcovery, as it might only be a Means of entrapping fome brave Adventurers, who might be animated by their Example to a like Undertaking. Thefe would be and were, by its being fo little publifhed on their Parts,

and

(and no Accounts of it in *England*, which shews their Friends were under an Injunction not to make it publick) the Resolutions of such sensible and sagacious Men as *Gibbons* and *Shapley* were agreeable to which they acted. All which Circumstances considered, what Degree of Evidence can be required more than hath been given to authenticate this Account of *de Fonte?*

Those who argue against a North-west Passage have no better Foundation for their Arguments, Than that there is no Tide from Westward. Which is arguing only for the Truth of a System, and hath nothing to do with the Reality of a Passage, and in all Probability hath been the principal Occasion that a Passage hath not been compleated: For a different Course of the Land, and no Tide from Westward, concluded any further Searches in such Part, but on a due Survey made of the Map, as the Tide will enter up the Streight of *de Fuca*, and probably other contiguous Entrances which are not yet known, besides the North-east Branch of the *South Sea*, which we suppose to join with such Streight; the Tide would fill that Sea on the Back of *Hudson*'s Bay, and the Openings but be checked to the Northward by the Current; and may be hindered from coming into *Hudson*'s Bay through the Inlet from Causes not known, or there being great Indraughts on the opposite Shore, which may take off the Force of the Tide, and cause it to come but a small Way up such Inlet. There is Reason to believe the proper Passage is up the Streight of *de Fuca*, therefore that is the proper Streight of *Anian*, as *de Fonte* proceeded no further than *Los Reyes*, and declared there was no North-west Passage; but the North-east Part of the *South Sea* hath a Communication, as is expressed in the Map, in describing which a Certainty cannot be expected, or an Exactness but what may be contradicted if a Discovery be made. The Design of the Map, besides what relates to the Expedition of *de Fonte*, is to shew there is a Streight, called the Streight of *de Fuca*. A Sea at the Head of that Streight, at the Back of *Hudson*'s Bay, from which Sea there is a Passage either by an Inlet into *Hudson*'s Bay, or by a Streight at the Head of *Repulse* Bay, and so to Northward of *Hudson*'s Bay; from which Streight there is a Passage into the *North Sea*, either to Eastward of the Land of *Cary*'s *Swans-nest* into *Hudson*'s Streight, or by *Cumberland* Isles, and ex-

pressed

pressed in the Map in the Manner that the respective Accounts represent, according to our Understanding of them, with a Submission to Correction and superior Judgment. But an absolute Contradiction without invalidating the Accounts on which such Map is constructed, or to say there is no North-west Passage, which it is impossible should be determined until a Search is made in the Parts which remain to be searched, are no Objections, are only Opinions, without any Authority to support them, which Time must rectify.

To make an Expedition to discover whether there is a Passage by those Parts which remain unsearched, purposely from *England*, is what I think an honest, disinterested, or impartial Person cannot recommend, as such Expeditions might be repeated with great Expence, and the Event uncertain. The Government gave their Assistance, and the Generosity of the Merchants hath been sufficiently experienced, both in *England* and *America*: Therefore it becomes every one whose Intention it is solely that such a beneficial Service should be done to avoid proposing what might, in the Consequence, be an unnecessary Expence to Government, and abuse the Generosity of the Merchants.

The Ships which went on these Expeditions, after they left the *Orkneys*, had no Place to put into, neither could they there Wood or Water, or conveniently repair a Damage. If they met with a Delay in passing *Hudson*'s Streights, they were obliged, from the small Part of the Season that was remaining, to go to the *Hudson*'s Bay Factories to winter; that they might have the more Time the next Year; were obliged to go to the Factories earlier than they were necessitated on Account of the Weather, in order to get their Ships laid up, and every other Convenience for wintering prepared before that the Winter set in. The *Hudson*'s Bay Company, jealous of a Design to interfere with their Trade, probably their Fears not ill grounded, the Consequence was, there was no Cordiality between the Factors and the Captains. The Ships People, by wintering, suffered in their Health, great Wages going on, a Consumption of Provisions, a Spirit of Discontent and Opposition amongst the inferior Officers, which obstructed the Success of the next Summer. To obviate all which in any future Proceedings, a Discovery was undertaken on the Coast of *Labrador*, to find Harbours on that Coast which Ships could repair to if necessary on their Voyage out, or to repair to on their return,

return, which they could be at fooner than at the Factories, ftay longer on Difcovery, and return the fame Year to *England*. How well this Attempt anfwered the Defign, may be collected from the Extract from a Journal of a Voyage hereunto annexed, performed in the Year 1753, giving an Account of the Coaft of *Labrador*. As what is now to be done in the Difcovery of a Paffage in *Hudfon*'s Bay may be effected in a Summer, and if there is the defired Succefs, an Inlet found by which there is a Paffage into the Sea adjacent out of that Bay, the Veffel which makes fuch Difcovery, and all Ships at their return by fuch Inlet, will have no Occafion to go to the Southern Part of the Bay, it will be out of their Courfe, but proceed through the Streights to *Labrador*, there Wood and Water, get frefh Fifh, and other Refreshments; can repair any Damage either as to their Mafts, or their Hull, and return the fame Year to *England* by the common Tract of the *Newfoundland* Ships, and not to go to the *Orkneys*.

That there was a good fifhing Bank, a Coaft convenient for carrying on a Fifhery, a Fur Trade, alfo for Whalebone and Oil with the *Efkemaux Indians*, was a Difcovery the Confequence of that Attempt from *America*. To take the Benefit of which Difcovery feems now to be the Intention of the Publick. And a Survey of fuch Coaft being ordered to be made by the Government, if fuch Survey is extended fo far as to thofe Parts, in which as already mentioned fuch Paffage muft be, and without it is fo far extended, the Defign of attaining a true Geographical Account of the Northern Coafts of *America* would be incompleat. By this Means it muft be known whether there is fuch a Paffage, the Probability of which is unqueftionable. Alfo by fuch Survey a better Account will be got which Way the Whales take their Courfes, and confequently where it is beft to go in Purfuit of them. Alfo as to thofe *Efkemaux* who frequent to Northward of *Hudfon*'s Streights, where they retire to, and a proper Place be found to keep a Fair with them. As thefe *Efkemaux* as well as thofe on *Greenland* Side, who have not come into thofe Parts any long Duration of Time, being the fame Kind of *Indians* with thofe in the *South Sea*, and as they tranfport themfelves and Families from one Part to another by Water, it feems highly probable that it is by fuch a Paffage or Streight that they have got fo far to Eaftward. This Difcovery of a

Paffage

Passage can be made without any additional Expence, wove in with other Services, as was in the Discoveries which were ordered to be made by the King of *Spain* on the Coasts of *California*. The Propriety of a Vessel to make such a Survey, and the Abilities and Fidelity of the Persons will be undoubtedly taken Care for. The Run from *Labrador*, let it be from any Harbour, will be but small to any where, where it is necessary to make the Survey. The Persons sent will go fresh out of Harbour, whereas, with a Run from the *Orkneys*, the People are fatigued; will now be refreshed as if they had not come from *Europe*. Will be out from such Harbour but a few Weeks, in a fine Season of the Year, no Way debilitated by the Scurvy, and in a few Summers will be enabled to compleat their Survey of that Coast; using such an Assiduity as they proceed as not to leave any Part on Supposition or Trust, but being assured where any Inlet or Opening determines. A Person who understands *Eskemaux*, and one or more *Eskemaux* to be procured, would be of Service as Pilots, and to give an Account of the adjacent Country. And there is no Vessel (it is mentioned as perhaps it is not so very well known) so proper and serviceable for this long-shore Work as a Marble-head Schooner, about sixty Tons, fortified as to the Ice, and would be at all Times a useful Tender, and a proper Boat if necessary to be left at the *Labrador*. What would give due Force to such Expeditions, would be the Commodore of the Man of War being so near, under whose Eye the Whole would be done, who would direct their fitting out, receive their Report on their return, order a Review if necessary, and be the Occasion of that due Subordination and Obedience both of Officers and Men, which it is often very difficult to effect on such Voyages. Merit will then be distinguished, and the Credulity of the Persons at home will not be imposed on, and no Discouragement of those who distinguish themselves in the Execution of such laudable Attempts. Such a Passage being discovered, and the Sea entered to Westward of *Hudson*'s Bay, the Manner of proceeding afterwards must be left to superior Judgment.

APPENDIX.

AN ACCOUNT

Of Part of the Coast and Inland Part of

THE LABRADOR:

BEING

An EXTRACT from a Journal of a Voyage made from *Philadelphia* in 1753.

THE Coast of *Labrador* to Northward of the Latitude of 57 Deg. 30 Min. is represented by Captain *Benjamin Gillam* (an Extract of whose Journal the Author had) as a perilous Coast, and without any Inlets; therefore the Design was to fall in with the Land to Southward of that Latitude, which was attempted *August* the 2d; a thick Fog, but expected when more in with the Land to have clear Weather. They saw Ice at times the whole Day, and in the Evening found themselves imbayed in a Body of Ice, and plainly perceiving Points of Rocks amongst the Ice, stood out again during the whole Night for a clear Sea, which they fortunately obtained the next Morning.

It was then proposed to stand yet more Southward, to make the Land in Latitude 56°, and search the Inlet of *Davis*. From the 3d to the 9th had various Weather, the Air temperate, Calms and light Winds, thick Fogs for some Days, the latter Part of the Time haizey, with Rain, which was succeeded the 10th of *August* with a hard Gale of Wind that moderated

moderated on the 11th, and clear Weather: Saw Rockweed, some Kelp, Land Birds, a Number of large Islands of Ice, but no flat Ice; concluded in the Afternoon that they saw the Looming of the Land in Lat. 56 Deg. 2 Min. Long. 56 Deg. 42 Min. at Eight at Night had Soundings 95 Fathom, at Ten at Night 80 Fathom. .

August the 12th, fine pleasant Weather; at Eight o'Clock had 40 Fathom Soundings, and at Ten made the Land, bearing W. by S. ten Leagues. Many Islands of Ice, but the Wind contrary for *Davis*'s Inlet, stood towards another Opening which promised a good Harbour; but not being able to attain it before Night, stood on and off until the next Morning, fine pleasant Weather; and *August* the 13th, by Four in the Morning, were in with the Land. A Whale-boat, with proper Hands, was sent to sound a-head, and find a Harbour. Soon after a Cry was heard from an Island to Northward; there appeared to be five Persons. Some Rings, Knives, Scissors, and Iron Hoop, being taken by the People into the Boat, after rowing about a League they entered into a small Harbour, near the Place where the five Persons were first seen, but who had retired. Entering the Harbour they saw Shallops built after the *Newfoundland* Manner, at Anchor, with Buoys and Cables, a Mast, a square Yard athwart, with a Sail bent, a Tilt made of Seal Skins abaft. These Boats were tarred, that Summer's Work. Upon the Sight of these Boats a Doubt arose whether they were *Indians* whom they had seen, or some unfortunate Shipwrecked People.

When the Boat got further into the Harbour two *Eskemaux Indians* came off, the one a Man in Years, the other a young Man. The elder Man had a small black Beard. The elder Man being presented with a Ring, immediately put it on his Finger; the young Man did the same when one was presented him. Both declined accepting Pieces of Iron Hoop, a very agreable Present to the *Eskemaux* on the Western Side *Hudson*'s Bay. They knew what Fire-arms were, which they saw in the Boat: Also asked for some Pork, which they saw, and had been taken into the Boat for Fear the Schooner and the Boat should be separated; and, on the Boatsmen not having a Knife immediately ready, they produced a Knife apiece; and the elder Man used the Word *Capitaine* in his Address; had a Complaisance in his Behaviour. From these Circumstances

cumſtances it was plain they carried on a Trade with the *French*; tho' the lateſt *French* Authors repreſented them as a ſavage People, who would never have any Commerce with them. And a Motive for this Undertaking was from an Opinion, that no Trade had been carried on in theſe Parts, either by *Europeans* or *Americans*, the printed Accounts and common Report both agreed in this. It was apparent to whom theſe Boats belonged; and there were more than twenty *Eſkemaux* aſhore, of various Sexes and Ages, who kept ſhaking of old Cloaths for Sale; and the elder Man preſſed the People in the Boat very much to come aſhore, alſo to bring the Schooner to an Anchor, which was ſtanding on and off; but as the Day advanced, the Situation the Schooner was in, being many ſmall Iſlands about, and a fine Opening which promiſed a good Harbour in the main Land, they declined the Invitation; and there was an *Eſkemaux* ready with a large Coil of Whalebone, ſeemingly for the Boat to warp in to a ſmall Cove and make faſt with. Theſe Civilities were acknowledged by a Preſent being ſent to thoſe aſhore, and after ſhewing where they intended for, the Boat returned aboard the Schooner.

The People on board the Schooner, as they advanced towards the Inlet where they expected a Harbour, hoiſted their Enſign, which was very large, and fired two Swivels by way of Salute; ſoon after the *Eſkemaux* diſplayed on the Rocks a large white Enſign, on a high Pole; and when there was Occaſion to lower the Schooner's Colours, the *Eſkemauxs* lowered theirs; the Schooner's Colours being again hoiſted, they hoiſted theirs; but a Squal of Sleet and Rain came on, which prevented their having a further Sight of each other. At Six in the Evening the Schooner was anchored in a convenient Harbour, a level Shore, with high rocky Land, bare in Spots, the other Parts covered with a good Herbage and large Groves of Trees, Firs, Spruce, and Pine. An Evening Gun was fired to give the Natives Notice where the Schooner was, and alſo a good Watch was ſet.

Auguſt the 14th, at Day, they fired a Swivel aboard the Schooner, and diſplayed their Colours as a Signal for Trade; and a Party went aſhore to aſcend the Heighths. The largeſt Trees did not exceed ten Inches Diameter, and fifty Feet in Heighth; many Runs of excellent Water, Ponds in level Spots; the Country had an agreeable Aſpect, a plentiful

plentiful Herbage, the Flowers were now blown, the Berries not ripened, and the *Angelica*, of which there was great Quantity, not seeded. They had a very laborious Walk before they attained the desired Summit; the Musquetoes very troublesome. Being on an extraordinary Eminence they saw the North and South Point of the main Land, or two Capes which form a Bay, the Northermost was computed to be something to the Northward of Latitude 56, and the Southermost in Latitude 55. The Shore high and bold, to Northward a Number of Reefs of Rocks lying out a great Way into the Sea, in the Southern Part of the Bay many Islands and two Inlets. Sixty Islands of Ice of large Dimensions in Sight. In the ascending this Heighth, saw many Moose Deer Paths, Tracts of other Animals; and in the Ponds Trouts of about ten Inches in Length. On the Shores few Fowl but Ducks, and a Plenty of Muscles. The Weather very warm and pleasant. The Schooner's People found a Barrel, a Hogshead Stave, and a Piece of hewed Wood, on which it was conjectured that this was no unfrequented Harbour.

The next Morning, the 15th of *August*, the Boat was sent to carry two Persons to the Head of the Harbour, that they might travel to a Mountain about ten Miles off, to take a View of the inland Part of the Country. When the Boat returned, the People brought Word they had seen the Ruins of a Timber House. The Boat was again manned to go and take a Survey of it; and it appeared to have been a House built for some Persons to winter in, of Logs joined together, part standing, with a Chimney of Brick and Stone entire. The House consisted of three Rooms, a Log Tent near, and a Pit dug in which they seemed to have buried their Beer. The Ground cleared at a Distance round: The Woods burnt, several Hogsheads and Barrels, and seemingly a great Waste of Biscuit, Pork, Salt Fish, and other Provisions, which seemed as if those who had been here had retired with great Precipitation; neither had been long gone, as there were fresh Feet Marks on the Strand, and some Trees lately hewn. The Marks on the Cask shewed that the People were from *London*; and it was supposed that as the *Eskemaux* had not come to trade, there had been a Fray between the *Eskemaux* and these People; and when they considered the compleat Manner in which the Boats were equipped and rigged, doubted whether the *Eskemaux* had not overpowered them, and had some of the People with them.

them. The great Earneſtneſs with which the elder of the *Eſkemaux* made Signs for the People in the Boat to go aſhore, ſeemed to be with a particular Deſign: Therefore it was thought prudent to be very careful in the Watch at Night, to ſtrike the Bell every half Hour, to keep a continual Walk on Deck, and call *All is well*, that the *Eſkemaux* might hear, if they ſhould intend a Surprize, that the People aboard were on their Guard.

The Morning of the 16th they run up to the Head of the Harbour with the Schooner, to Wood and Water, there being Plenty of Wood ready cut, and a Place conveniently dammed up to confine a fine Stream of excellent Water which came from the Heighths. There was then found ſeveral Pieces of printed Books, in *German* and *Engliſh*, the *Engliſh Moravian* Hymns. Peas, Beans, Turnips, and Radiſhes planted, which ſeemed as if they would come to no great Perfection, and judged to have been ſowed about three Weeks. The wooding and watering was finiſhed by Ten at Night, but with no ſmall Trouble on Account of the Muſquetoes, though great Smoaks made to keep them off.

The two Perſons who had been ſent to view the inland Country returned in the Morning, after having ſpent a rainy Night in the Woods; gave an Account that they had been forced to go round ſeveral ſmall Lakes, which made the Way longer than expected; and the Mountain was very ſteep and rugged: Saw ſeveral large Spots of excellent Meadow: The Timber much the ſame as that on the Shores of the Harbour: That they ſaw two Inlets to Northward, extending a great Way into the Land: That it was only the Branch of an Inlet that the Veſſel was at Anchor in; but they ſaw the Termination of the Inlet to be in large Ponds.

The 17th of *Auguſt* the Schooner was to return to her firſt Anchorage, with an Intention to ſearch the Inlets to Northward; but the Wind proved contrary, and a hard Gale, though the Weather pleaſant. The 18th the Wind moderated, and the Schooner returned to her former Anchorage; but the Wind did not ſerve to quit the Harbour until the 19th in the Afternoon; the Interval of Time had been filled up in brewing Spruce Beer, and doing other neceſſary Work with reſpect to the

Sails

Sails and Rigging. At Six in the Evening was close in with the Island, where they had seen the *Eskemaux*, but now gone. It was not until the 21st, by reason of Calms and Currents, that they attained to the Inlet to Northward. Those who had been sent out with the Boat to sound a-head, had seen on the Shore an *Eskemaux* Encampment, from which they were but very lately retired, and brought from thence a Piece of a Jawbone of a Spermaceti Whale, which was cut with a Hatchet. It was plain from that the *Eskemaux* were supplied with Iron Tools: They also found a Piece of an Earthen Jar. They judged there had been about eleven Tents.

The 22d of *August*, in the Morning, the Ship's Company catched some Cod; they were but small, but fine full Fish. The Whaleboat was sent up with some Hands, to sound and find a Harbour: And three Persons went on Shore to a nigh Summit, about four Miles off, to view the Country: Saw in their Way many Tracts of Deer, a deep Soil, good Grass, and met with several large level Spots, with Ponds of Water; thick Groves of Timber, and a plentiful Herbage. The Country, from this Summit, appeared to consist of Ridges and Mountains; and as the Weather changed from fine and pleasant, to thick and hazey, they saw the Clouds settle on several Ridges of the Mountain near them, as also on the Heighth where they were, and under them. And when they returned the People on board said they had had some smart Showers of Rain, which those who had been on the Heighth were not sensible of.

In the Afternoon they proceeded with the Schooner to a Harbour which those who had been sent out with the Whaleboat had discovered, an extraordinary fine Harbour; and it may be here observed in general, that most of the Harbours are very fine ones. There are many of them, and not far the one from the other.

There were on the Shore, in many Places, the Remainder of *Eskemaux* Encampments, but some Time since they had been there. Timbers of Boats, on the Shores, which were much decayed, had laid long in the Weather; in the Carpenter's Opinion the Boats they had belonged to must have been built fifteen or twenty Years, seemed to be the Timbers of such Boats as had been seen with the *Eskemaux*.

The

The succeeding Day there was such Weather as they could not proceed; the Day after, the 25th, run up the Inlet about eight Leagues from the Harbour, which was about eighteen Leagues from the Entrance of the Inlet. As they proceeded they found the Country more level, thick Woods, intermixed with Birch Trees, and both Shores afforded a pleasant Verdure. They could not proceed further with the Schooner, by Reason of Falls; which, being surveyed the next Day, might be passed with the Schooner, but with some Difficulty. Therefore early in the Morning of the 27th, at a proper Time of Tide, when the Falls were level, a Party went in a Whaleboat, with a small Boat in tow loaded with Provisions, Bedding, and a Sail for a Tent, to explore the Head of the Inlet. The furthest they could get with the Boat was about five Leagues, being intercepted by impassable Falls, about 300 Feet in Length, and forty Feet their perpendicular Height, though of gradual Descent. The Fall Rocks, but the Bank of the Northern Shore, which was steep, was a Kind of Marl, without any Mixture of Stone; and no frozen Earth here, or in any other Part, usual in *Hudson*'s Bay, as was proved by repeated Experiments: Therefore it may be concluded that this is a more temperate Climate in Winter than in any Part about *Hudson*'s Bay, in the same or lower Latitudes.

From the first Falls to the second there were large Levels along Shore, the Mountains at a considerable Distance within Land, especially those on the North Side. The Mountains and Shores thick cloathed with Pine, Spruce, Birch, and Alder, much larger and of better Growth than those Trees nearer the Sea Coast; some Pines measured twenty-five Inches in Diameter. In a Pond, on the North Shore, saw two Beaver Houses, and there were Plenty of Beaver Marks, as Dams, Trees barked and felled by them. The Water was fresh between the first and second Falls. Poles of *Indian* Tents in many Places along Shore, Lodgments only for single Families, tied together with Strips of Deer Skin, and no Encampments after the *Eskemaux* Manner, shewed that a different *Indians* from the *Eskemaux* resorted into this Part. The whole Country had a pleasant Appearance; but as they came near to the upper Falls, the Verdure of the Woods, barren Points of Rocks that exalted themselves, terminating the View, the Disposition of the Woods which had all the Regularity of Art, joined to the Freedom of Nature, the Gloom of the Evening, the flow steady Course of the Water, and the Echoes of the rumbling Fall, afforded such a Scene as affected even those that rowed; and they said, it was the pleasantest Place they had ever seen. On a level Point, beautifully green, situated at a small Distance from an Opening in the Woods, and in full View of and Hearing of the Falls, there were the Poles of an *Indian* Tent, which, from the Ashes scarce cold, a Breast-bone of a wild Goose, with some little Meat on it that had been broiled, Pieces of Birch Bark left, seemed to have been not long deserted, and the Situation was such as expressed the late Inhabitants to have the softest Sensations. In coming up the Inlet they had found where there had been a small Fire made, as supposed, to dress Victuals, but put out or covered with Turf, a usual Practice amongst Southern *Indians* to conceal the Smoke, when they suppose the Enemy is near. The Boats were securely harboured, a Tent erected, with a good Fire before it, and the People rested securely all Night.

The next Day, *August* the 28th, two Persons were detached to a Summit, in Appearance about twelve Miles off, others went and hung Strings of Beads, Combs, Knives, and other Peltry, on the Trees, some at a Mile, and others at a further Distance, from where they kept their Camp all Day, to invite the *Indians* to a Converse with them; but no *Indians* were seen, nor any Thing meddled with. Those who had walked to take the View from the Summit, saw the Water above the Falls extend a great Distance into the Country, but not the Termination of it, passing through Meadow Lands of large Dimensions, and by the Foot of small rising Land, they saw a large high Ridge of blue Mountains at a great Distance, running North and South, which was supposed to be the Bounds of the new discovered Sea in *Hudson*'s Bay: Saw several other Ridges of Land, but seemingly more level than those to Seaward; passed over in travelling several Spots of excellent Soil, the Timber of good Size and Growth. There was a great Plenty of Grass and Herbage; walked a great Way in an *Indian* Path, and saw several marked Trees, as is practised amongst the Southern *Indians*. They returned in the Evening, much fatigued with the Heat of the Sun, and swelled with the Bites of Musquetoes, and a small black Fly, like those in *England* called a Midge. Those that staid at the Encampment were also much plagued with these Insects.

The

The Latitude of the upper Falls was 54 Deg. 48 Min. near the imaginary Line that bounded the *English* and *French* Limits in thefe Parts; and it being fuppofed that the two Inlets, feen from the Height above the Harbour where they firft anchored, would terminate in the *French* Limits; they therefore had declined making any Search there, and proceeded to fearch the Inlet to Northward.

The next Morning they fet out to return to the Schooner, with a Defign to fearch the other Inlet to Northward, feen from the Mountain at the Back of the firft Harbour, but not feen fince by Reafon of a high Ridge of Mountains, as it was fuppofed, that covered it. In the Night there had been a fharp Froft, and early in the Morning a thick Fog. About Ten in the Morning they were returned to the Schooner. Several of the People, contrary to the written Inftructions which were left, had rambled from the Veffel, got on the Heights, rolled down the *Indian* Marks, which are Stones that they put up one on another on the Knolls and Summits of Hills, to direct them in their journeying; a Proceeding which was highly diffatisfactory to the Commander, confidering the Difpofition which it was found the Natives were in, and whom, with the greateft Induftry, they could not get a Sight of. The People had fhot fome few Fowl, which were plentier in this Inlet than any where that they had feen, but very fhy and wild. They failed that Afternoon to the Harbour which they were at when they firft entered this Inlet.

Auguft the 29th they failed out of this Inlet to go to the Northward, keeping within a Ledge of Iflands, as they might pafs no Part of the Coaft unfearched. Met with fome Difficulties amongft the Shoals and Rocks; but about Four in the Afternoon were clear of all, and plyed to Windward to enter the third or more Northern Inlet, which they had now open. Saw at the Head of a pretty deep Cove, on the South Side in that Inlet, a ftrong Smoke arife, and that immediately anfwered by a leffer Smoke on the Northern Side of the Inlet. The Smoke on the Northern Side the Inlet continued towering and frefhening; on feeing which they immediately fteered for the Cove, fuppofing the Smoke to be made by the Natives as a Signal for Trade; but were delayed entering by the Tide of Ebb. At Sunfet were furprifed with a Squall of
Wind,

Wind, which came on in a Moment, and the Schooner in extreme Danger of being afhore on the Rocks. A hard Gale fucceeded, but they fortunately attained a Harbour, which had been before difcovered by the Boat, and rode fecure.

The 31ft of *Auguft*, the Weather being moderate, two Perfons went over the Heights to the Head of the Cove, in Purfuit of the Natives; and three Perfons went in a Boat to the Head of the Cove, with fome trading Goods, and to pafs the two who walked, over the Water if it ran up into the Country, and the Natives fhould be on the oppofite Shore; but after rowing up about two Leagues they found a Termination of the Water, landed and afcended the Heights, where they found a very large Plain, without Ponds, and a fine Soil, which they paffed over and defcended into a Valley, thick Groves, good Grafs, and large Ponds. Here they met with a Bear; which one of the People firing too precipitately miffed. Several Bears had been feen before, fome Foxes, many Tracts of Wolves, both on the Shores and Inland, and in one Place Otter Paths.

Three of the People were fent to return with the Boat aboard, and two fet out to go up a Mountain which promifed a good Sight of the Country, and feemed poffible that they might attain to the Summit of it, and return to the Schooner that Night; but were deceived by the Height of the Mountain as to the Diftance they were from it. In the Afcent they found great Declivities and Hollows in the Sides of the Mountain, the Rocks rent in a moft furprifing Manner, having Rents or Fiffures in them from thirty to feventy Feet in Depth; fome tremendous to look down, and not above two or three Feet in Breadth. The Dogs that were with them would not, after looking down, jump over them, but howled and took a Sweep round. In the Levels and Hollows on the Side there lay great Heaps of fallen Rock. Some Stones or folid Pieces of ten or fifteen Tons Weight, befides innumerable leffer Pieces. And found a Patch of Snow in one of the Hollows, about forty Feet in Breadth, and fourteen Feet in perpendicular Height, frozen folid, and feemed of the fame Confiftence with the Iflands of Ice. The Perfons, though conftantly labouring, did not attain to the Top of the Mountain until about Half an Hour before Sunfet, where they found a thin

Air,

Air, and a fresh sharp cold Wind; though below, and in their Afcent, they had experienced pleafant warm Weather, and little Wind. From the Mountain they perceived a Smoke, about ten Miles off more inland, the ufual Practice of the *Indians* in the Evenings, when they form their Camps, to make a Fire to drefs their Provifions, and to be by all Night; and it was then fufpected that they were flying more inland, and that the Smokes feen the Night before were Signals from one Party to another to retire on feeing the Schooner, fuppofing us Enemies. It was too late that Night to return to the Head of the Cove, therefore encamped that Night on the Side of the Mountain in the Woods, near to a level Spot without the leaft Unevennefs of above fix Hundred Feet in Breadth, and three Hundred over, exactly refembling a Pavement without any Fiffure or Opening in it. The next Day got to the Head of the Cove, near twelve Miles from the Mountain; on a Signal made the Boat fetched them aboard, where the People expreffed in their Countenances a univerfal Joy at feeing their Commander fafe returned, which was a great Satisfaction to him, as it was an Inftance more fincerely expreffed than by formal Words addreffed to him, that they looked on their Security to depend on his Prefervation. The Wind was contrary to their getting out of the Harbour that Afternoon; but the Boats were employed in feeking the beft Channel for the Schooner to go out at.

The Morning of *September* the 2d, the Wind proved favourable, and that Evening they got a good Way up the third Inlet. When they were fome Way up the Inlet, they difcovered a Smoke upon an Ifland at the Entrance of the Inlet, and, when at Anchor, a Smoke alfo on the North Shore. Therefore by Day-light, *September* the 5d, the Time when Smokes are moft difcernable and looked out for by the *Indians*, a Perfon was fent to fire the Brufh on an Eminence afhore, to anfwer that Smoke feen on the North Shore the Night before. Then the Schooner proceeded up the Inlet, and by Ten o'Clock was come to the Extremity of it, which terminated in a Bay of very deep Water, furrounded by very fteep Mountains, with Groves of Trees on them; but they found a good Anchorage in a Cove, and an excellent Harbour. The Heights being afcended, it was perceived there was a narrow Streight out of this Inlet, which communicated with Ponds. And that there was a fourth Inlet to Northward,

Northward, and which extended further to Westward than the Inlet which the Vessel was now in, and about four Miles off, beyond the Hills there appeared a towering Smoke, upon the Sight of which the Persons who went to take the View returned aboard to get some Provisions, and a Parcel of trading Goods, and set out again with an Intention to seek the Natives, and spend the Night amongst them. The Boat put them ashore where it was thought most convenient and nearest Place to the Smoke, but it proved otherwise; for after travelling about three Miles they fell in with a Chain of Ponds, which they were forced to go round. Hot sultry Weather, the Woods thick, without the least Breath of Wind, infinite Number of Musquetoes and Midges. But by being thus to go round the Ponds, had the Satisfaction of seeing several Beavers Dams made to keep out the Tide Waters. They saw a Continuance of the Smoke, and shaped a Course for it; but when on the Heights perceived that the Smoke was on an Island about two Miles off the Shore in the fourth Inlet, therefore returned to the Vessel that Night.

The 4th of *September*, in the Morning, they towed out of the Harbour they were in, the Wind soon after sprung up, and by Night they go out of the Inlet, and anchored amongst some Islands, just at the Entrance of the fourth Inlet.

The next Morning, *September* the 5th, entered the fourth Inlet; but being becalmed a small Time catched above fifty Cod, much such as they had before taken. By Twelve o'Clock were abreast of the Island where they they had seen the Smoke on the 3d, and which was four Leagues from the Entrance: Could perceive no Natives, but several Fires, and that there had been a great burning of the Brush; soon after saw a Snow lying at an Anchor, which hoisted *English* Colours, and fired a Gun. They hoisted the Colours aboard the Schooner, fired a Swivel, and bore away for the Snow. The Wind was fresh, and, as the Schooner was entering the Harbour, two People came running over the Rocks, hailed, but it could not be well understood what they said; but it was a friendly Precaution as to some Rocks which lay off there. The Snow's People then took to their Boat, and made a Trip to view the Schooner as she was coming to an Anchor, and then returned aboard. A Whaleboat

boat was hoisted out, and a Person sent in it to go aboard the Snow, and know where she was from, and to let the Captain know they would be glad to see him aboard the Schooner.

The Person sent, and Capt. *Elijah Goff* the Commander of the Snow, returned aboard in a short Time; and the Particulars of what the Captain related were, That the Snow was fitted out by Mr. *Nesbit*, a Merchant in *London*: That he, the present Captain, had been the Year before Mate of the same Vessel on this Coast: That she was then fitted out by *Bell*, *Nesbit* and Company; the intended Voyage kept a great Secret. They had, the Year before as a Captain, a *Dane* who had used the *Greenland* Trade, and could talk the *Eskemaux* Language. That the Snow had been at *Newfoundland*, and afterwards came on the *Labrador* Coast; but being Strangers to the Coast, and the Captain very obstinate, the Vessel was several Times in Danger, which raised a Mutiny amongst the People, who had formed a Resolution of seizing the Ship, and bearing away for *Newfoundland*; which Mutiny was appeased, and the People consented to go to the *Labrador*, where they harboured *July* the 20th, in the same Harbour which the Schooner first entered this Year. They brought with them four of the *Unitas Fratrum*, or *Moravian* Brethren, who were to remain during the Winter, to attain an Acquaintance with the Natives, and lay a Foundation of Trade: That the House, the Ruins of which the Discoverer saw, was built for the Residence of these Brethren; and, being compleated by the Beginning of *September*, the Snow left them in Possession of it, and set out to make Discoveries, and pursue a Trade to Northward: That they had some Trade in *Nesbit*'s Harbour, the Name they had given to the Harbour where the House was, and also on the Coast before they arrived at the Harbour: That when they went to Northward; in about Lat. 55° 40′ off the Islands, amongst which the Schooner had harboured the preceding Night, some *Eskemaux* came aboard, and told the *Dane* Captain there were some trading Boats come from the Northward, with Plenty of Trade, and advised the Captain to come where they were. The Captain asked, Why they would not come along Side? The *Eskemaux* said, It was dangerous on Account of the Surf. The Captain and six others went in the Ship's Boat, with a Quantity of Goods to trade, but had no Fire Arms with them, though advised to take them; but the Captain said, No, they were very honest Fellows. Captain *Goff* saw the Boat go round an Island, upon which there was a Number of Natives; but the Island hindered him from having any further Sight of the Boat. After the Boat had been gone about an Hour, he saw one or two of the *Eskemaux* with his Glass peep over the Rocks; but never after saw any more of the Boat, the Snow's People, or the *Eskemaux*. That the Snow lay at a League Distance from the Island; he had no other Boat, one being left with the *Moravian* Brethren. Capt. *Goff* waited three Days, and then returned with the Snow to the Harbour where the House was. The Snow being short of Hands, he took the *Moravian* Brethren aboard, leaving a Quantity of Provisions sufficient to subsist the unhappy People who were missing should they come there, until his Return. They put the Key of the House and a Letter in a Hole of a Tree; but on his Return this Year found the House in Ruins, the Casks and Hogsheads broke to Pieces, and the Key and Letter gone. That what was sowed there was by Way of Experiment.

Capt. *Goff* judged that the *Eskemaux* traded with the *French*, as their Fishgiggs, Knives, and Boats, were *French*; and the *Eskemaux* told them there was a Settlement of twenty *Europeans* to Southward, which they supposed to be somewhere to Southward of Lat. 55, the Latitude of the Cape they had named Cape *Harrison*, which is the Southermost Cape that forms the Bay in which is *Nesbit*'s Harbour, and the high Saddleback Land within, which is first seen off at Sea they named *St. John*'s. He said that one of the *Eskemaux* offered a Quantity of Whalebone for a Cutlass, which they are very fond of; the *Danish* Captain insisted on having more, the *Eskemaux* answered, If he would not take it that Capt. *Salerco* would; alluding, as supposed, to the Captain or Factor at the *French* Settlement. The Boats the *Eskemaux* had were *French*: They spoke many *French* Words. And the Women worked the Boats, turned them to Windward, and were very expert in the Management of them.

The Account given by the Master who went in the Schooner's Boat to fish for Cod (Capt. *Goff* not having yet got any) to the People in the Boat was, That Mr. *Nesbit* was only, in this Case, an Agent or Factor for the *Moravian* Brethren, who aimed at a Settlement in these Parts, and to attain a Propriety by a prior Possession, but that no Propriety would

would be allowed of by our Government: That Petitions had been flung into the Board of Trade for Patents for the *Labrador*, but were rejected, and a free Trade would be permitted to all the Subjects of *Great Britain*; which open Trade was the original Design on which this Discovery was undertaken by the People in *America*; the Execution of which was not only interrupted by private Persons stealing the Scheme, and being before hand, but hath been a great Hindrance to the Fisheries being carried on in those Parts, a Trade established with the inland *Indians* and the *Eskemaux*, and further Advantages which will be known, on our being better acquainted with those Parts. For as to this Severity of the *Eskemaux*, inexcusably barbarous, yet there were some Provocations which might have been avoided, and which incited those *Eskemaux* to this Act, whose Hatred and Revenge, the Character of most *Indians*, are rouzed at the slightest Causes. It appears from a Journal of of the Boatswain, wherein he makes a Valuation of the Trade, that they had bought a Hundred Weight of Whalebone for Six-pence. The *Eskemaux* were also treated with great Contempt and Rudeness. A Person aboard had bought a Pair of *Eskemaux* Boots; and carrying them into his Cabbin, an *Eskemaux* followed claiming the Boots as his, saying that he who sold them had no Right to sell them; and the Buyer settled the Matter by presenting a Pistol at his Head. On which the *Eskemaux* cried out in the *French*, *Tout*, *Comerado*, and retired.

Capt. *Goff* came this Year in Hopes to recover the People who were missing with the Boat, and to make a further Essay as to the Trade, but brought no Settlers with him, intended immediately for the Coast, which he could not attain to on Account of the Ice, and went to *Trinity* Bay in *Newfoundland*, where he staid some Time. Sailed from thence the 27th of *June*; the 2d of *July* saw *French* Ships in the Streights of *Belle Isle*, retarded by the Ice; and the 9th of *July* joined Capt. *Taylor* in a Sloop of about 35 Tons, fitted out from *Rhode Island* to go in Pursuit of a *North-west Passage*; and if not successful to come down on the Coast of *Labrador*. Capt. *Goff* said he had learned by Capt. *Taylor* that the *Philadelphia* Schooner would be out, and he should have suspected this to be her, but she entered the Inlet so readily, and came up with

with that Boldness as could not but think that the Schooner was a *French* Vessel acquainted with the Coast; and he had received Orders to avoid any Harbour in which a *French* Ship should appear. Capt. *Taylor* had seen a large *French* Sloop in Latitude 53, and to the Northward three hundred *Eskemaux*, who had nothing to trade but their old Cloaths, and who were going further to Northward, but were hindered by the Ice. Capt. *Goff* and *Taylor*, who had entered into an Agreement to associate, were eight Days grappled to the Ice, and did not arrive at *Nesbit*'s Harbour until the 20th of *July*. But had traded with some of the *Eskemaux* before, though for small Matters, and had some of these *Eskemaux* aboard for three successive Days, who then left them, and came no more aboard the Vessels. Capt. *Goff* suspected, though he had altered his Dress, that they had then recollected him. The 1st of *August* they sailed from *Nesbit*'s Harbour, and attained to this Inlet where he now was; and on the 11th sailed to the Northward, when Capt. *Taylor* left him; and on the 25th returned here again. That the Smoke which the Persons saw on the Island when they travelled over Land, and which the Schooner passed that Day, was made by his Order, but that he had not made any other Smoke, and this was for a Direction for his Longboat, gone to the Northward to trade, and to signify to Capt. *Taylor* his being in the Harbour, whose Return he expected.

Capt. *Goff* said he had been in no Inlet but *Nesbit*'s Harbour, and in this where the Snow was; and that Capt. *Taylor*, in the Snow's Longboat, had searched the Head of this Inlet, shewed a Draught of the Coast, which was defective, as he knew nothing of the intermediate Inlets. Had no Account of the inland Country; of there being any Beaver or other Furs to be acquired there; or of there being any Mines, of which the Schooner's People had seen many Instances, and had collected some Ore. Capt. *Goff* had two *Dutch* Draughts of the Coast, made from late Surveys; but they were very inaccurate, the Views taken from Sea, and there the Land appeared close and continued; the Inlets, excepting that in which they now were, appearing like small Bays, their Entrance being covered by Islands. They had, this Year, found the Corpse of one of those who went in the Boat, stripped and lying on an Island.

It

It being rainy Weather, and the Wind contrary to the Schooner's going up the Inlet, they were detained, and on *September* the 8th the Snow's Longboat returned, after having been out fourteen Days, with some Whalebone, and a Quantity of *Eskemaux* Cloathing, which being examined to find out if the *Eskemaux* wore Furs, there was only seen a small Slip of Otter Skin on one of the Frocks. And Capt. *Goff*, being asked, said he never saw any Furs amongst them. It is pretty evident the *Eskemaux* only pass along this Coast, to go and trade with the *Eskemaux* in *Hudson*'s Streights, and occasionally put in as Weather or other Occasions may make it necessary, which keeps the Native or inland *Indians* from the Coast, as they are their Enemies. The *Eskemaux* go up to Latitude 58, or further North; there leave their great Boats, pass a small Neck of Land, taking their Canoes with them, and then go into another Water which communicates with *Hudson*'s Streights. Carry their Return of Trade into *Eskemaux* Bay, where they live in Winter; and the *French* made considerable Returns to *Old France*, by the Whalebone and Oil procured from these People. And this Account is agreeable to the best Information that could be procured.

While the Schooner's People were viewing the Cloaths, Word was brought that the *Eskemaux* were coming, who may be heard shouting almost before that they can be discerned, the Schooner's People repaired aboard. On the Colours aboard the Snow being hoisted, the Schooner's People displayed theirs; but the Snow being the nearest, and the Snow's People so urged the *Eskemaux* to come along-side them, that they were afraid to pass. The *Eskemaux* had no large Boats with them, only their Canoes, three of which came afterwards along-side the Schooner. It was perceived that none of the leading People were in the Canoes; they exposed no Marks or Shew of any Trade they had, which was usual for them to lay on the Outside their Canoes; nevertheless they were presented with Rings. It was some Time before they began to trade with the Snow's People, and then it was carried on in a very peremptory Manner.

The People in the Schooner, a light Wind springing up, weighed Anchor, with a Design to proceed up the Inlet, expecting to be followed by the *Eskemaux*, when they saw that they were not Associates with the Snow's People, so to have a future Opportunity of trading with them. It was also consistent with the Design they had of searching this Inlet, the first Opportunity that offered. They took their Leave of Capt. *Goff* as they passed, and when advanced further beat their Drum. The *Eskemaux* quitted the Snow and came after the Schooner. The Fire Arms were all primed and in order aboard the Schooner, but concealed; each Man had his Station; and they were ordered to treat the *Eskemaux* as Men, and to behave to them in an orderly Manner; no hallooing, jumping, or wrestling with them when they came aboard; not to refuse some of the *Eskemaux* to come aboard, and let others, as there were but nine Canoes in all.

As the *Eskemaux* came along-side the Schooner, they were presented each with a Biscuit, a Person standing in the main Chains with a Basket of Biscuit for that Purpose. Then they aboard the Schooner shewed a Kettle, a Hatchet, and some other Things, which seemed much to please the *Eskemaux*. One of them attempting to get into the Schooner, two of the People helped him in: He was received civilly on the Quarter-deck; the trading Box shewed him, a Spoon, a Knife, and a Comb with which he touched his Hair and seemed desirous of, were given him. Other *Eskemaux* were by this Time aboard. They were presented with Fish-hooks, small Knives, Combs, and a King *George*'s Shilling apiece, which they carefully put into their Sleeves. In the interim the *Eskemaux* who came first aboard was gone to the Side, and called to another yet in the Canoe under the Title of *Capitane*. The *Eskemaux* so called to immediately came aboard, saluted the Commander with three Congees, and kissed each Cheek. He was presented with a Spoon and a Knife. Being shewn the Goods, appeared very desirous of a File, offering old Cloaths for it. But the Commander signified he would not trade for old Cloaths, but *Shoceock* (which is Whalebone in their Language) or Skins; and the latter he denoted to the *Capitaine* by a Piece of white Bear Skin that the *Capitaine* had brought in his Hand. The *Capitaine* expressed by his Action that he had not either Bone or Skins: He was then presented with the File; was shewed a Matchcoat, which he surveyed very accurately; signed to the Commander if he was not come round

round from the South-west, meaning, as supposed, from *Quebeck* or the Gulph of *St. Lawrence*. Afterwards took the Commander under his Arm, and shewed a Desire of going into the Cabbin, which was complied with. He passed the Door first, and sat down in as regular a Manner as any *European*, having first accurately looked about him; but there were no Fire-Arms in Sight. Refused Wine, drank Spruce Beer; was shewed a Sample of all the Kind of Goods, with which he seemed well pleased; and it was signified to him that there was Plenty of them. While in the Cabbin the other *Eskemaux* who were on Deck, called to their *Capitaine*, they were invited down. Three of the *Eskemaux* came, but it was observable the *Capitaine* covered the Goods with a Woollen Cloth, which lay on the Table. They were presented with Beef and Pudding, which they took, and returned on Deck. The *Eskemaux Capitaine* put the Goods into the Box himself very honestly, and seeming to admire a small Brass-handled Penknife, it was presented to him. He then returned on Deck, pointed to the Sun, lowered his Hand a little, then made a Sign of sleeping by shutting his Eyes, and laying his Hand to his Cheek, and shewed with his Hand to have the Schooner to come to an Anchor just above. By which it was understood that a little after that Time the next Day he would be there with Trade. The Schooner, being by this Time opposite to a narrow Passage, or Streight formed by Islands, through which the *Eskemaux* had come into this Inlet, the *Capitaine* ordered his People into their Canoes, and retired with a Congee himself, after repeating the Commander's Name, to see if he had it right, and which he had been very industrious to learn while he was in the Cabbin. The Commander attended him to the Side; and seeing in his Canoe a War-bow and Arrows, which are of a curious Construction, pressed him to let him have them, though the same Thing as asking a Man to part with the Sword he wore. The *Capitaine*, by Signs, shewed he could not part with it, and seemed to express it with great Reluctance that he could not. This Circumstance, and their having no Women with them, caused the Schooner's People to think they looked upon themselves, when they set out, as coming amongst their Enemies. The Drum was beat until they were out of Sight; and the *Capitaine*, just before he lost Sight of the Schooner by being shut in by the Islands, pointed to the Sun, and the anchoring Place. The *Eskemaux*, while

aboard,

aboard, behaved with great Decency and Silence; though at firſt they began to jump and halloo, as they had done aboard the Snow; but finding the People of the Schooner not ſo diſpoſed, ſoon left off.

Soon after the Schooner was anchored in an excellent Harbour, the Snow's Boat came along-ſide, with the firſt Mate and Agent. They were aſked to meſs; and it being enquired of them how far they had been with the Longboat in the laſt Trip, ſaid to Latitude 57° 14′: Had ſeen no *Eſkemaux*, but within a few Days, though they had been out fourteen Days. The Mate ſaid, that he had chaſed a trading Boat, with two *Eſkemaux* in it, who had endeavoured to avoid them, and dodged amongſt the Iſlands; but he came up with them as though he had been a Privateer's Boat; run bolt aboard them, and ſo frightened the *Eſkemaux* that they fell on their Knees, cried out, *Tout Comerado*, and they would have given him all they had. He ſaid they took out the Whalebone, which he brought aboard, about a Hundred and fifty Weight, and paid them for it as much as he ſaw the Captain give. He ſaw other *Eſkemaux* at times aſhore, where they invited him, but would not venture; and fired a Blunderbuſs, charged with thirteen Bullets, over them, which cauſed ſome of them to fall down, others to bow. Some *Eſkemaux* came along-ſide, and traded their Cloaths; but with great Fear, crying out, *Tout Comerado*, as he had four Men armed ſtanding in the Bow of the Boat. Said that thoſe *Eſkemaux* had, who were juſt gone from the Schooner, the Peoples Cloaths who had been trepanned the laſt Year, particularly a brown Waiſtcoat, which had had white Buttons on it, and a white Great-coat. The Great-coat meant was a *French* Matchcoat, which the *Eſkemaux* Captain had on, made up in a Frock according to the Manner that they wear them. The ſuppoſed brown Jacket was a *French* brown Cloth, and there were two *Eſkemaux* who had them. The Mate ſaid the Schooner's People had talked of ſome Inlets; but no Anſwer was made, on which he declared there was no Inlet between *Neſbit*'s Harbour and where they then were, nor any Inlet to Northward between that and Latitude 57° 14′. After making ſome Enquiries, as to what the Schooner's People further intended, quitted, and made for the Streight the *Eſkemaux* had paſſed through.

This

This is mentioned as an Instance of what Caution should be used, as to the Choice of Persons sent on Expeditions to explore unfrequented or unknown Parts, as the Adventurers may be Sufferers, and the Reason of their being so a Secret, and thereon pronounce decisively no Advantages are to be made, thus deprived of what might be greatly to their private Emolument in Time under a proper Conduct, and to the Benefit of the Publick. And there is a further Misfortune attending an improper Choice, which every social and generous Man will consider. That according to the Impressions that *Indians* receive on the first Acquaintance, a lasting Friendship may be expected, or an Enmity and Jealousy very difficult to remove, who, in the interim, will execute their Revenge; not on those who gave the Offence, but on all indiscriminately of the same Complexion, when an Opportunity offers. Reasons would be unnecessarily urged in Support of what Experience proves, and of which there have been several melancholy Examples on this Coast. By a Privateer from *New York*, some Years since, the first Offence was given; those who have gone since have done nothing to mollify or abate this Enmity and Revenge. There could be no Expectation of a Reconciliation with these *Indians*, to the great Improvement of Commerce in various Branches, but by the Measures taken, the sending some of his Majesty's Ships into these Parts to explore and get a Knowledge of the Coast; and the Commanders to establish a Regulation, which will be a Satisfaction and Encouragement to every fair Trader; and where the Trade long since might have been brought to some Perfection, had it not been from the little dirty Avarice of those employed by private Adventurers, who hindered the original Design having a due Effect; and by interfering the one with the other, to their mutual Prejudice, they prevented those Returns on their Voyages which might have been otherwise made. The Consequence was, all future Attempts were dropt, and it was indeed rendered almost impossible that any fresh Undertakings should meet with Success, by the Difficulties flung in the Way on Account of the Natives, but which will now be effectually removed by the Government giving their Assistance.

The next Morning three People were sent from the Schooner to go on the Heights, to discover the Water the *Eskemaux* had gone into, and to see if the *Eskemaux* were coming. The Account brought back was, that there was seen an *Indian* trading Boat or Shallop under Sail, which presently tacked and stood towards four other Shallops. They all lowered Sail, and the *Eskemaux* seemed to be consulting together. Soon after the People saw the Snow's Longboat coming, the Shallops hoisted Sail, then went one Canoe, afterwards two more, to the Snow's Longboat, while the Shallops crouded away. The Schooner's People, after this Time, had no Opportunity of seeing the *Eskemaux*; and attributed their coming no more to their Fear of meeting the Longboat, or the bad Weather, it being wet and blustering for the several succeeding Days. But they learned, after the Schooner had returned to *Philadelphia*, that those in the Snow's Longboat followed the Shallops, came up with them, and took what they had. The Reason is apparent for their not coming to the Schooner as they had no Trade, and as they might have a Suspicion that the Schooner's People had a Connivance with those in the Boat, especially as they might see the three People from the Schooner standing on the Heights.

The Commander searched the Head of this Inlet, the Shores of which were the most barren of any that had yet been seen, from the Sea to the Head of it, about nine Leagues. Upon their Return they found the Snow gone; they then went through the Streight by which they saw the *Eskemaux* pass to explore that Water. From this the Discoverer passed between Islands, without going out to Sea into a second Inlet; and from that to a third from where he had met the Snow, and the seventh from *Nesbit*'s Harbour. And the seventh or last Inlet ran a North and Westerly Course, and terminated the furthest inland, or had the most Western Longitude of any of the Inlets; and its Head about fifteen Leagues from the Sea.

These last three Inlets to Seaward are separated by very large Islands, and have Islands lying off directly athwart their Entrance, so that it is difficult to discover, when within these Islands, that there is any Outlet to the Sea. The Islands have little Wood on them, and are mostly barren Rock; but the main Land much as in the other Parts, only the Inland more level. The blue Ridge of Mountains appeared plainer than from any other Part. The Latitude of the furthest Inlet about 56.

Having

Having explored thefe refpective Waters and adjacent Country, and Davis's Inlet, confequently, though it is difficult to which properly to affix the Name; and the Autumn being far advanced, as was apparent from the Birch Leaves becoming yellow, the Berries Froft-bit, the Pines and Spruce turning brown, fevere Gales, Snow and Sleet at times, and exceffive cold on the high Land; fo as nothing further could be carried on with any Spirit, but exceffive Fatigue, and the Health of the People, as well preferved as on firft fetting out, would be now impaired, with no certain Profpect of doing any Thing further that was material, fufficient Harbours having been found; on the 20th of *September* they fet out on their Return.

Leaving the Land favoured with pleafant Weather, an Opportunity waited for to make an accurate Survey of the Fifhing Bank, and to find the Diftance it lay from the Land, which from the Soundings on making the Land, the feeing the Iflands of Ice aground, and the Account of *Davis*, was known to be there, and named by him *Walfingham's* Bank, after the true Patriot and generous Patron of a Difcovery of a Northweft Paffage. Sounding about a League from Land, with one Hundred and fifty Fathom of Line, had no Ground. At about fix Leagues from Land, twenty-five Fathoms afterwards various Soundings, and catched a great many Cod, large and full fed, reckoned by the People aboard to be very extraordinary Fifh, fome of whom from *Bofton* followed the Employ of fifhing for Cod. The Bank was concluded to be about nine Leagues broad, and ninety Fathom Soundings on the going off it, on the Eaftern Side; and it was concluded, on a pretty good Affurance, that it reaches from Lat. 57 to Lat. 54, if not further; but the Weather proving boifterous, as they ran to the Southward, could not continue their Soundings.

The Schooner founded with a Hundred and fifty Fathom of Line, clofe by an Ifland of Ice, of a furprifing Magnitude, between the Bank and the Shore, which was aground, and they did not get Soundings.

F I N I S.

ERRATA.

Page 15. L. 23. de Fuentes. The, *read* de Fuentes, the.
    44. L. 11. de Fonte's, *read* de Fonte's Account.
    45. L. 36. Don Ronquillo, *read* Don Pennelossa.
    49. L. 18. from, *read* in.
    54. L. 11. to the Southward, *read* to the Northward.
    61. L. 15. it, *read* this Mission.
    67. L. 29. as that worthy, *read* that worthy.
    82. L. 6. New Spain, *read* Florida.
        L. 9. Florida, *read* Peruan Part.
    83. L. 28. is consistent, *read* is not consistent.
    90. L. 17. Rivers and Harbours, *read* River and Harbour.
  106. L. 32. in the Year 1746, *read* until the Year 1745.
  111. L. 6. between the Sea, *read* the Ocean and the Sea.
  136. L. 14. nigh Summit, *read* high Summit.

DIRECTIONS for placing the MAPS.

- Map of *de Fonte*'s Discoveries, in Front.
- Map of *New Spain*, from *Torquemada*, Page 86.
- Map of the Discoveries in *Hudson*'s Bay, Page 122.

www.ingramcontent.com/pod-product-compliance
Lightning Source LLC
Chambersburg PA
CBHW020246170426
43202CB00008B/253